"Phil Moore's new commentaries are outstanding: biblical and passionate, clear and well-illustrated, simple and profound. God's Word comes to life as you read them, and the wonder of God shines through every page."

– Andrew Wilson – Author of Incomparable *and* If God, Then What?

"Want to understand the Bible better? Don't have the time or energy to read complicated commentaries? The book you have in your hand could be the answer. Allow Phil Moore to explain and then apply God's message to your life. Think of this book as the Bible's message distilled for everyone."

– Adrian Warnock, Christian blogger

"Phil Moore presents Scripture in a dynamic, accessible and relevant way. The bite-sized chunks – set in context and grounded in contemporary life – really make the make the Word become flesh and dwell among us."

– Dr David Landrum, Evangelical Alliance

"Through a relevant, very readable, up-to-date storying approach, Phil Moore sets the big picture, relates God's Word to today and gives us fresh insights to increase our vision, deepen our worship, know our identity and fire our imagination. Highly recommended!"

– Geoff Knott, former CEO of Wycliffe Bible Translators UK

"What an exciting project Phil has embarked upon! These accessible and insightful books will ignite the hearts of believers, inspire the minds of preachers and help shape a new generation of men and women who are seeking to learn from God's Word."

– David Stroud, Leader of Christ Church London and author of Planting Churches, Changing Communities

For more information about the *Straight to the Heart* series, please go to **www.philmoorebooks.com**.

You can also receive daily messages from Phil Moore on Twitter by following **@PhilMooreLondon**.

STRAIGHT TO
THE HEART OF

1 & 2 Kings

60 BITE-SIZED INSIGHTS

Phil Moore

MONARCH
BOOKS

Published by
Lion Hudson Limited
Wilkinson House, Jordan Hill Business Park
Banbury Road, Oxford OX2 8DR, England
www.lionhudson.com

ISBN 978 0 8572 1940 4
e-ISBN 978 0 8572 1941 1

First edition 2019

Acknowledgments

Scripture quotations taken from the *Holy Bible, New International
Version* Anglicised. Copyright © 1979, 1984, 2011 Biblica, formerly
International Bible Society. Used by permission of Hodder & Stoughton
Ltd, an Hachette UK company. All rights reserved. "NIV" is a registered
trademark of Biblica. UK trademark number 1448790. Both 1984 and
2011 versions are quoted in this commentary.

Extract p. 92 from "Foreword" by A.W. Tozer in L. Ravenhill's *Why Revival
Tarries* (Bethany House Publishers, 2004). Copyright © 2004 L. Ravenhill.
Extracts reprinted with permission from Baker Publishing Group.
Extracts p. 102, p104, p110 and p113 from E. Crossman, *Mountain Rain:
a New Biography of James O. Fraser* (OMF Books, 1982) and G. Taylor,
Behind the Ranges (OMF Books, 1944). Copyrights © 1982 E. Crossman
and © 1944 G. Taylor. Extracts reprinted with permission from OMF
International UK.
Extracts p. 121 and p. 133 from MERE CHRISTIANITY by C.S. Lewis
copyright © C.S. Lewis Pte. Ltd. 1942, 1943, 1944, 1952. Extracts
reprinted by permission.

A catalogue record for this book is available from the British Library

Printed and bound in the UK, February 2019, LH26

This book is for the Church in the West,
with so many wondering why it has seen such steep decline.
May God use this book to encourage the remaining Western
believers and to show them the story behind the story.

CONTENTS

2 KINGS 9–17: NORTHERN LIGHTS

2 KINGS 18–25: SOUTHERN COMFORT

About the *"Straight to the Heart"* Series

On his eightieth birthday, Sir Winston Churchill dismissed the compliment that he was the "lion" who had defeated Nazi Germany in World War Two. He told the Houses of Parliament that *"It was a nation and race dwelling all around the globe that had the lion's heart. I had the luck to be called upon to give the roar."*

I hope that God speaks to you very powerfully through the "roar" of the books in the *Straight to the Heart* series. I hope they help you to understand the books of the Bible and the message which the Holy Spirit inspired their authors to write. I hope that they help you to hear God's voice challenging you, and that they provide you with a springboard for further journeys into each book of Scripture for yourself.

But when you hear my "roar", I want you to know that it comes from the heart of a much bigger "lion" than me. I have been shaped by a whole host of great Christian thinkers and preachers from around the world, and I want to give due credit to at least some of them here: Terry Virgo, Dave Holden, Guy Miller, John Hosier, Adrian Holloway, Greg Haslam, Lex Loizides, Malcolm Kayes and all those who lead the Newfrontiers family of churches; friends and encouragers, such as Stef Liston, Joel Virgo, Stuart Gibbs, Scott Taylor, Nick Derbridge, Phil Whittall, and Kevin and Sarah Aires; Jon Oliver and Jessica Tinker at Monarch; the pastors and congregation that serve alongside me at Everyday Church in London; my great friend Andrew Wilson. Without the friendship, encouragement and example of you all, this series would never have happened.

I would like to thank my parents, my brother Jonathan, and my in-laws, Clive and Sue Jackson. Dad – your example birthed in my heart the passion which brought this series into being. I didn't listen to all you said when I was a child, but I couldn't ignore the way you got up at five o'clock every morning to pray, read the Bible and worship, because of your radical love for God and for his Word. I'd like to thank my children – Isaac, Noah, Esther and Ethan – for keeping me sane when publishing deadlines were looming. But most of all, I'm grateful to my incredible wife, Ruth – my friend, encourager, corrector and helper.

You all have the lion's heart, and you have all developed the lion's heart in me. I count it an enormous privilege to be the one who was chosen to sound the lion's roar.

So welcome to the *Straight to the Heart* series. My prayer is that you will let this roar grip your own heart too – for the glory of the great Lion of the Tribe of Judah, the Lord Jesus Christ!

Introduction: The Story Behind The Story

All this took place because the Israelites had sinned against the Lord their God.

(2 Kings 17:7)

We know better than to take all we see and hear at face value. We are taught from a young age that, when watching an advert or listening to a politician or reading a news story, we need to take a step back in order to spot what's really going on. We are taught to look for the story behind the story.

Take, for example, this character reference given by a man's previous employer:

> *I understand from David Brown that he has applied for a job at your company. I simply cannot find enough good things to say about him. I can only commend him to you as a job candidate with no qualifications whatsoever. I have never known anybody like him. His talents were wasted at our company and I frequently felt that there was nothing I could teach him. I'm sure that you will find out quickly that his true ability is deceiving. He never seemed to care how many hours were needed to complete a task, and you will be extremely lucky if you can persuade him to work at your company. I have never known a worker fired with such great enthusiasm, and I know I speak for everybody when I say that when he left us we were all very satisfied. I would encourage you to waste no time in interviewing him.*

We need to remember this when we read 1 and 2 Kings. These books were written at a moment of great crisis and confusion for the Jewish nation, and they were written to reveal to them the story behind the story. The ten northern tribes of Israel had been defeated, destroyed and taken into exile by the Assyrians in 722 BC. The two remaining tribes in the south had held out longer, but they had suffered the same disaster at the hands of the Babylonians in 586 BC. This was more than a political and military defeat for them. It had brought into question all that they believed about their God. Where had he been when they needed him most? Why had he failed to rescue them from their enemies? Why had Israel's God abandoned Israel in its darkest hour?

The writer of 1 and 2 Kings sets out to answer those questions. It's significant that the Hebrew Old Testament lists them, not just as history books, but among the writings of the "Former Prophets". They are more than a mere record of the past. They are a God-given commentary on what had just happened to Israel and Judah.[1] Jewish tradition teaches that the prophet who wrote these books was Jeremiah.[2] All we know for sure is that, whoever the prophet was, he felt inspired by God to tell the story behind the story – from the start of King Solomon's reign in 970 BC, to the release of King Jehoiachin from a Babylonian prison in 561 BC. The writer prophesied to the Jewish exiles that these events had not befallen their nation in spite of God, but because of God. He had not been unfaithful to them. They had been unfaithful to him, and he had done all that he promised he would do to bring their nation back to him.

---

[1] The other books listed among the "Former Prophets" are Joshua, Judges, and 1 and 2 Samuel. The "Latter Prophets" are the seventeen final books of the English Old Testament, from Isaiah to Malachi.

[2] The writing style of 1 and 2 Kings is quite similar to that of the book of Jeremiah. His authorship would also explain why these books fail to mention Jeremiah – surely unthinkable for such a giant of a prophet unless a result of the author's own humility. The biggest challenge to this view is that the narrative of 1 and 2 Kings ends in Babylon, whereas Jeremiah seems to have spent his own exile in Egypt (Jeremiah 43:6–8).

The writer believed that only this prophetic commentary could revive the hopes of the despondent Jewish exiles in Babylon. If the God of Israel had been true to his promise that he would drive them into exile if they turned their backs on him, then they could also trust him to be true to his promise to restore their fortunes if they turned back to him. They could trust him to be working out his master plan in the background to bring them back to the Promised Land and to launch a glorious new chapter in Israel's story.

If all we want is a superficial history of ancient Israel, then the author says we can look elsewhere. He points us once to "the annals of King Solomon", fifteen times to "the annals of the kings of Judah" and eighteen times to "the annals of the kings of Israel". He quotes from these sources liberally, but he offers us something far more useful than a record of events as they played out on the evening news. He gives us the story behind the story.[3]

This explains why the writer is so selective in his prophetic commentary. King Omri of Israel was such a mighty ruler that many decades later the Assyrians still referred to any king of Israel as a "son of Omri", yet the writer dismisses his reign in six short verses – just enough space to explain that he missed out on his true calling by doing evil in the eyes of the Lord.[4] King Jeroboam II's reign was seen as a triumphant golden age for Israel, yet the author skirts over it in just six verses, focusing instead on what the Lord was doing, often unnoticed, behind the scenes.[5] These aren't just history books. They are a great

13

---

[3] The author makes it obvious that he is quoting from these primary sources. He even preserves intact their statements that certain things remain in place *"to this day"* despite their having been destroyed by the Babylonians (see 1 Kings 8:8; 9:20–21 and 12:19). 2 Chronicles 5:9 takes the same approach to preserving these primary sources, despite it being written more than a century after 1 and 2 Kings.

[4] The Black Obelisk of Shalmaneser III, now in the British Museum in London, refers to *"Jehu son of Omri"*. Time and time again, modern archaeology has confirmed the historical reliability of 1 and 2 Kings.

[5] By way of contrast, the author devotes thirty-eight verses to a single prayer of King Solomon – three times as much attention as he devotes to the reigns of Omri and Jeroboam II put together!

prophetic sermon that explains the story behind the story – what the Lord did to ancient Israel and Judah, why he did it, and what that means for our own lives today.

Ancient Hebrew was written down without any vowels, so the author was able to fit his whole sermon into a single book on a single scroll. When the book was translated into Ancient Greek in the third century BC, it no longer fitted on a single scroll so ever since then it has been divided into 1 and 2 Kings. Its message of hope remains unchanged.[6]

1 Kings 1–11 is all about **Father and Son**. King David hands the crown over to King Solomon. **1 Kings 12–16** is about **North and South**, as Solomon's kingdom splits into two, and civil war breaks out between the two new kingdoms. In **1 Kings 17 to 2 Kings 8**, the theatre of war shifts to a new struggle between **Rebels and Revival**. In **2 Kings 9–17** we see the **Northern Lights** of the kingdom of Israel grow dim and finally die. **2 Kings 18–25** is about **Southern Comfort**, as the Lord rescues and revives the kingdom of Judah. Even when they reject him and are destroyed too, he continues to comfort the survivors with a promise that their story isn't over. What has happened to them is all part of God's far bigger plan to bless the entire world by renewing his covenant with their nation.

So get ready for the message of 1 and 2 Kings. Get ready for the promise which breathed hope into the hearts of a bunch of Jewish down-and-outs in Babylon and which still breathes fresh hope into the hearts of its readers for the struggling Church today. Get ready for a revelation of what is really taking place in history. Get ready for the God of Israel to catch you up into the story behind the story.

---

[6] To add to the confusion, when splitting Samuel into two scrolls for the same reason, the translators of the Latin Vulgate decided to refer to 1 and 2 Samuel as 1 and 2 Kings and to 1 and 2 Kings as 3 and 4 Kings! Despite these differences in how the text is divided, the text itself remains unchanged.

1 Kings 1–11:

Father and Son

Yesterday's Man
(1 Kings 1:1–2:12)

*"Have you not heard that Adonijah, the son of
Haggith, has become king, and our lord David knows
nothing about it?"*

(1 Kings 1:11)

The book of 1 Kings begins a bit like one of the original *Star Wars* movie. It catapults us straight into the thick of the action, and it assumes that we will quickly pick up the plot along the way. It doesn't introduce King David or tell us which prophet is writing the story. It assumes that we have read 1 and 2 Samuel, and that we therefore know all about the shepherd-boy who became king of Israel and who received a command from God to bypass his older sons and hand over his throne to his young son Solomon when he died. It expects us to know that David's eldest son Absalom attempted to defy this and was killed in his failed rebellion, making Adonijah David's oldest surviving son.[1]

If you have read 1 and 2 Samuel, then you will see a lot of continuity as the plot resumes: Bathsheba is still David's favourite wife; Joab is still commander of his army; Benaiah is still the captain of his bodyguard; Nathan is still his prophet; and Zadok and Abiathar are still serving as his two priests. But what really strikes us here is the *dis*continunity. Whereas 1 and 2 Samuel celebrate the strength of King David, the giant-killer who conquered Israel's hostile neighbours, the writer of 1

---

[1] Adonijah was originally David's fourth son (2 Samuel 3:2–4). Absalom murdered Amnon, and Kileab evidently died in childhood. At the start of 1 Kings, Adonijah is aged about thirty-five and Solomon about eighteen.

Kings goes out of his way to emphasize King David's weakness in these opening verses.

In his first sentence he describes David as "very old" – a little harsh, we might think, for a man aged sixty-nine, but the rest of the chapter reveals how much it's true. The ancient world saw political power and sexual potency as intertwined (that's why rulers had large harems as a sign of their virility), so the writer begins by informing us that David is now more interested in hot-water bottles than hot women. Even when he is given a beautiful young woman to keep him warm at night, the days are long gone when he used to turn out the light and want to do anything more than sleep.[2] This detail is not incidental to the story. There was a time when the nation of Israel looked to David as its messiah, but now the writer wants us to grasp that he is yesterday's man.

One of the most famous lines in the original *Star Wars* movie comes when Obi-Wan Kenobi assures a storm trooper that the droids in question are not the ones he is looking for. The author is saying the same thing to his readers through each of these details. He tells a Jewish nation that is looking back to the reign of David as its heyday that David was never the true messiah that Israel was looking for.

Adonijah is all that David isn't. He is so handsome and virile that he rides around Jerusalem in a chariot, the path cleared before him by a muscly team of runners. David never had the courage to confront his son's sin (1:6), and even now he is oblivious to Adonijah's attempt to usurp his throne (1:18). Adonijah quickly wins over Israel's top general and its priest. His plot is only thwarted by the quick thinking of the prophet Nathan and of Solomon's mother Bathsheba. Meanwhile, the writer emphasizes David's own inactivity by using the Hebrew word *heder* in 1:15, which means *bedroom*. David is

---

[2] David died aged seventy (2 Samuel 5:4). He had many wives, so his sexual inactivity here conveys impotence rather than purity. Even Abishag's name declares his weakness, meaning *My Father Has Gone Astray*. She came from the northern town of Shunem, in the territory of Issachar, where Elisha later stayed (2 Kings 4:8).

yesterday's man, outmanoeuvred in his pyjamas. Israel needs a new messiah.

Solomon is aged only eighteen, but he looks the part. Perhaps he is the messiah that Israel is looking for. First, God has singled him out to succeed David.[3] Second, he rides on the royal mule, reserved only for the kings of Israel. Third, while Adonijah holds his furtive coronation at the spring of En Rogel, some distance from Jerusalem, Solomon is crowned king in full public view at the spring of Gihon, just to the east of its city walls, because he has the full support of the dying king.[4] Fourth, he is anointed by Zadok the priest and Nathan the prophet using the sacred anointing oil from God's Tabernacle.[5] Fifth, he is so popular that the ground shakes with such shouting that even Adonijah trembles at the news. It is laughable when Bathsheba prays in 1:31, *"May my lord King David live for ever!"*, but nobody is laughing when Benaiah prays in 1:37 that the Lord will *"be with Solomon to make his throne even greater than the throne of my lord King David!"*

In 2:1–12, the contrast between Solomon and yesterday's man grows even stronger. David confesses that he has felt like a powerless pawn amid his scheming courtiers. He has never felt strong enough to deal with men like Joab and Shimei, but Solomon is strong enough now.[6] David's dying charge to Solomon deliberately echoes the dying charge of Moses to

---

[3] The writer assumes that we know all about this in 1:13, 17 and 30, so he jumps straight into the action of the story. God's choice of Solomon to succeed David is recorded in 1 Chronicles 28:5–7 and 29:1.

[4] Zadok and Abiathar's sons had spied for David on Jerusalem from En Rogel during Absalom's rebellion (2 Samuel 15:27–28 and 17:17). It was far enough away from Jerusalem for furtive actions to go unheeded.

[5] Exodus 30:25; 31:11 and 39:38. It is significant that Nathan anointed Solomon alongside Zadok (1:45), since prophets were to proclaim the Lord's choice of kings (1 Samuel 9:16 and 16:12, and 2 Kings 9:6).

[6] We find the record of Joab's sin, Barzillai's kindness, and Shimei's sin in 2 Samuel 3:26–30; 16:5–13; 17:27–29; 19:31–39 and 20:8–10. David admitted his own weakness in dealing with Joab in 2 Samuel 3:39.

Joshua.[7] It proclaims that Solomon is the new messiah who will finish the work that Joshua started by obeying God's commands, rewarding God's friends, dealing with God's enemies, and providing true rest for God's people.[8] It also echoes the covenant that the Lord made with David in 2 Samuel 7:12–16. It declares that Solomon is the promised Son of David, who will build a magnificent Temple for the Lord and whose throne will endure forever.

Except he isn't. At least not fully. Did you notice the great clue that the author gives us in these opening verses that, in time, the new King Solomon will himself become yesterday's man? Read the verses again, slowly, and you'll spot that Bathsheba mentions God, that David mentions God, that Benaiah mentions God, and that even the royal courtiers mention God when they congratulate King David on his son's coronation – but the author himself never once refers to God. He wants us to see something man-made even in this moment. Solomon isn't going to be the Messiah that we are looking for.

The story behind the story in these opening verses is that Israel needs a better Son of David. It needs more than a change of ruler. It needs a change of regime. It needs one who will ride into Jerusalem on a better donkey to die a better death than David. It needs one who will rise from the dead and anoint his followers with a better oil than the one stored in the Tabernacle. It needs one who will deal out a better reward to God's friends and better judgment on God's enemies. It needs one who will never become yesterday's man. It needs the one who is hidden behind these verses and revealed to us in Hebrews 13:8: *"Jesus Christ is the same yesterday, today and for ever."*

---

[7] Deuteronomy 31:1–8. It also echoes Deuteronomy 4:29; 6:2; 8:6; 11:1 and 29:9.

[8] 1 Kings 2:5 makes the same clear distinction as 1 Samuel 25:31 and 2 Samuel 3:30 between murdering in peacetime and killing in war. Pacifism tends to operate on the assumption that there is no distinction.

Truth Will Out
(1 Kings 2:13–46)

*"May God deal with me, be it ever so severely, if
Adonijah does not pay with his life for this request!"*

(1 Kings 2:23)

My grandmother was a factory worker in Huddersfield. She filled my childhood with her Yorkshire expressions. I only discovered later that one of them was actually a quote from Shakespeare. Whenever she caught me fighting with my brother, she would listen to both sides of the story and then would warn us: "Truth will out. Truth will out."[1]

That's what the writer of 1 and 2 Kings wants us to understand from the very outset. These two books don't merely tell us the story behind Israel's story. They warn us that God sees the story behind our own stories too. It's easy to imagine that he will declare us innocent on Judgment Day, but the writer warns that truth will out. To illustrate this, he describes at length how the new King Solomon dealt with his father's enemies.

Adonijah had attempted to usurp his father's throne. The writer hints at who inspired him to do so, since *the Stone of Zoheleth* in 1:9 is Hebrew for *the Stone of the Slithering Snake*. Adonijah is a false messiah, an antichrist, and Bathsheba is probably right in 1:21 to suspect that the first act of his reign would have been to murder both her and Solomon. When he discovered that his plot had failed, the writer tells us in 1:50–53 that he ran six miles to Gibeon to seek sanctuary at the Tabernacle of the Lord. He confessed that his younger brother was Israel's rightful ruler and he begged him for forgiveness:

---

[1] *The Merchant of Venice* (2.2.645).

"Let King Solomon swear to me today that he will not put his servant to death with the sword."

Solomon couldn't know for sure in that moment what Adonijah was truly thinking. His older brother's name meant *"The Lord is My Master"* and he was certainly doing what the Lord had commanded sinners to do in the Jewish Law. The bronze altar in the courtyard of the Tabernacle was where God told people to offer blood sacrifices whenever they wanted to humble themselves and to ask him to forgive them for their sin.[2] Solomon therefore gave his older brother the benefit of the doubt. He sent him home with a warning that *"If he shows himself to be worthy, not a hair of his head will fall to the ground; but if evil is found in him, he will die."* Solomon warned his brother: Truth will out.

It doesn't take long in these verses for Adonijah's actions to prove that he still takes his orders from the Slithering Snake. Returning to Jerusalem, he tells Bathsheba that *"The kingdom was mine. All Israel looked to me as their king."*[3] He asks for permission to marry Abishag, the woman who had warmed his father's bed. In the ancient world, a dead king's harem passed down to his successor, so this conversation marks a second bid to claim the throne.[4] Solomon is furious when he hears the news.[5] It no longer matters that his older brother laid hold of the horns of the altar at Gibeon or that he pleaded for forgiveness through the blood of the animals sacrificed upon it. Outward professions of faith are meaningless unless they are accompanied by genuine humility and real repentance. Adonijah's actions reveal his true heart to Solomon. The usurper must die.

Next, the writer turns to the priest Abiathar, who remained loyal to King David during Absalom's rebellion but later sided

---

[2] Exodus 21:12–14. It was therefore an Old Testament picture of the cross of Jesus Christ.

[3] In reality, it was only a few dinner party friends. When we lie, the person most deceived is ourselves.

[4] See 2 Samuel 3:7; 12:8 and 16:21–22.

[5] His oath – literally *"May the Lord do thus to me and may he add to it"* – was one of the strongest oaths in the Hebrew language. It is used again in 1 Kings 19:2 and 20:10, and 2 Kings 6:31.

with Adonijah in David's old age. Solomon had pardoned his treachery, remembering his longstanding faith in the Lord and his willingness to suffer alongside David before he became king of Israel. After executing Adonijah, Solomon places Abiathar under house arrest. He may live in peace at his family farm in Anathoth but he must never leave it. His days of ministering as a priest at the Tabernacle are over. He must prove his repentance by staying at home.[6]

Truth will out, and in Abiathar's case his obedience proves that he is genuinely sorry for his sin. This is the Old Testament equivalent of Matthew 3:8 – *"Produce fruit in keeping with repentance"* – and of the apostle Paul's testimony in Acts 26:20: *"I preached that they should repent and turn to God and demonstrate their repentance by their deeds."* The writer wants to teach us that our own prayers of repentance are only effective if our actions after we pray prove our prayers to be genuine. Make no mistake, he says, truth will out.

Joab knows that he is next on the judgment list of Solomon.[7] He runs to the altar in the Tabernacle courtyard and he pleads for the same mercy to be extended to him as was initially extended to Adonijah. But Solomon isn't fooled. He tells us literally in Proverbs 16:6 that *"By steadfast love and truthfulness sin is atoned for"*, and there isn't any truthfulness in Joab's words.[8] Joab defied King David so many times that he was twice threatened with demotion as commander of the army, and he responded by murdering his rivals both times. King Solomon therefore follows through on his demotion and replaces Joab

---

[6] There were two clans of priests, each descended from one of Aaron's sons. The Lord now fulfils the curse he placed upon the sinful clan of Ithamar in 1 Samuel 2:30–36. As part of Abiathar's exile, his entire clan is excluded from the priesthood. From now on, only Zadok's clan of Eleazar will serve as priests. However, note God's lavish grace in raising up Jeremiah as a prophet from Abiathar's disgraced family (Jeremiah 1:1).

[7] Not only could Solomon hear Joab's voice behind Adonijah's request (compare 2:22 with 2 Samuel 14:19), but he also believed that justice must be done to cleanse his family from Joab's bloodshed (Numbers 35:33).

[8] Author's own translation.

with the captain of the royal bodyguard. He orders Benaiah to bolster his new position by executing Joab quickly before Joab can kill his rival for a third time.[9]

Solomon's last enemy is Shimei, the man who cursed David and pelted him with rocks during Absalom's rebellion. He places Shimei under house arrest so that the truth of his repentance can also be revealed. At first it looks as though he really means it when he says that he is sorry for his sin and that he now wants to follow Israel's messiah. But three years later, when it becomes a bit too inconvenient, Shimei takes a trip away from home. Truth will out, Solomon warns us, as he sends the royal executioner to find him.

So don't be offended at the bloodshed in this chapter. The writer wants us to be aware of the story behind the story. A day is coming when the true Messiah of Israel will come back from heaven to judge the entire world. On that day, it will not matter whether we call ourselves Christians, whether we sing loudly on a Sunday, or even whether we pray loud prayers of repentance and get baptized. What will matter is whether the external tokens of our repentance are matched by genuine repentance on the inside.[10]

See the story behind the story. A greater Judgment Day is coming when truth will out.

---

[9] Benaiah was one of David's mighty men, famous as a lion hunter and giant-killer (2 Samuel 23:20–23 and 1 Chronicles 11:22–25). His father was a priest, so now he "sacrifices" Joab at the altar (1 Chronicles 27:5).

[10] This is a repeated theme in Scripture. See Isaiah 1:11–20; Malachi 2:12, and Proverbs 15:8 and 21:27.

The Currency of Kings
(1 Kings 3:1–28)

They held the king in awe, because they saw that he
had wisdom from God.

(1 Kings 3:28)

If you've done any amount of travelling, then you will know that it is vital to have some of the local currency. I once stopped off in Sofia, the capital of Bulgaria, on my way from Turkey to Romania without realizing that the people there don't take euros. Could I tempt them to take my Turkish *lira* or my Romanian *lei*? Could I win them over with my pounds and euros? Not a chance. I had to rely on the kindness of a stranger to give me enough money for the parking meter so that I could go into a bank for some local money.

At the start of his reign, Solomon felt a bit like I did in Bulgaria. He felt out of pocket when it came to wisdom, the great currency of kings.[1] Although his father had encouraged him in 2:9 that he was *"a man of wisdom"*, he had proved the emptiness of his pockets only eleven verses later by saying yes to a request from his mother before asking what it was. He therefore paid a visit to the Tabernacle of the Lord at Gibeon.[2]

As soon as Solomon arrives at the Tabernacle, it is obvious that he is different from Adonijah and Joab, who so recently laid hold of the horned corners of this same altar. The wealth and

---

[1] Solomon talks about the currency of kings in Proverbs 3:13–15; 8:10–11; 16:16; 20:15 and 25:2.

[2] Gibeon was more than just any old *"high place"*. It was home to the Tabernacle of Moses (1 Chronicles 21:29 and 2 Chronicles 1:2–6). The Chronicler says that Solomon took many of Israel's leaders up there with him.

power of ancient kings was measured by how much livestock they owned, but Solomon is happy to trade in his herds for the currency of kings. Sacrificing 1,000 animals to the Lord in a single day was a clear statement of his intent to rule by God's power and by God's power alone. When at last he fell asleep, exhausted, he dreamed that the Lord had heard his prayer. *"Ask for whatever you want me to give you,"* the Lord told him as he stood at the counter of the divine currency exchange.[3]

The kings of the ancient world dealt in many different currencies. Some of them dealt in hard cash. Others dealt in military power. Others dealt in murdering their enemies at home and marrying the daughters of their enemies abroad.[4] Given carte blanche by the Lord, Solomon refuses to invest in any of those fickle currencies. He recognizes that his father's successes all came from the Lord, as did his own surprise accession to the throne – he was a younger brother crowned king in an age of primogeniture. He therefore decides to gamble everything on God. He asks the Lord in 3:7–9 to endow him with divine wisdom.

> *"I am only a little child and do not know how to carry out my duties. Your servant is here among the people you have chosen, a great people, too numerous to count or number. So give your servant a discerning heart to govern your people and to distinguish between right and wrong. For who is able to govern this great people of yours?"*

Solomon's request is music to the Lord's ears. His prayers at the altar could not be more different from those of Adonijah and Joab. Solomon confesses three times in his short prayer that the kingdom of Israel belongs to the Lord and that he is merely

---

[3] Solomon's dream came at the end of a day spent worshipping the Lord. If we don't hear God speak to us very often, then perhaps it is because we are so seldom in a place of unhurried worship ourselves.

[4] We find in 3:1–3 that Solomon, too, had a weakness for marriage alliances. More on that in the next chapter.

called to act as the earthly regent for heaven's throne. He is aged eighteen but he confesses that he is still an ignorant *child* in desperate need of a *hearing heart* – the ability to sense what the Lord is saying to him.[5] Solomon trades in what the world values for a far better currency. He asks for the internal ability to sense God's Word to him.

The Lord therefore surprises Solomon. Not only does he promise to make him the wisest man so far in history, but he also promises to reward his request by giving him everything else he didn't ask for too – vast riches and honour and, if he responds with obedience, a long life too.[6] In Matthew 6:33, Jesus encourages us to follow the example of Solomon: *"Seek first God's kingdom and his righteousness, and all these things will be given to you as well."*[7] Solomon shows us what this means by waking up and immediately acting on what he has heard. He expresses his faith that the Lord has truly appeared to him by going back to Jerusalem and offering further sacrifices at the Tabernacle of David.[8] He then throws a lavish feast for his courtiers and celebrates his readiness to rule. He can't stop smiling to find his pockets full of the currency of kings.[9]

The writer ends the chapter with a concrete example of Solomon's God-given wisdom in action.[10] Two prostitutes share

---

[5] Most English translations paraphrase Solomon's words – but in a literal translation of the Hebrew text, he describes himself as a "child".

[6] The Lord cannot be telling Solomon to try to earn his blessing in 3:14, because David was far from perfect! David was simply quick to repent. Tragically, Solomon was much slower and therefore died aged only fifty-eight.

[7] Solomon also tells us this in Proverbs 4:7–10 and 8:18–21. If you seek wise character rather than position, you may well get both. If you seek position without character, you will have neither in the end.

[8] David had built a second Tabernacle to house the ark of the covenant on Mount Zion (1 Chronicles 16:1).

[9] Luke 11:31 clarifies that Solomon was not wiser than Jesus. In fact, the mistakes that Solomon goes on to make are a sobering reminder that even the wisest of us still need Jesus to save us through his own wisdom.

[10] This incident is not mentioned in the parallel account in 2 Chronicles, but it serves here to reveal the story behind the story. A literal translation of 3:26 says what Solomon heard from God: *"The womb yearns for its son."*

a house and become pregnant at the same time. Both give birth to baby boys but one of the boys dies in bed when his mother turns over in the night and accidentally smothers him. In the morning, a fight breaks out. Both prostitutes claim that the dead baby is the other woman's and that the live baby is their own. Solomon's solution is breathtaking. He pretends he is about to slice the live baby in two. He correctly predicts that the mother of the dead baby will accept this ruling, while the real mother would rather see her son alive in another woman's arms than dead in her own. It's a pretty brutal strategy but it leaves us in no doubt about the genius of Solomon. We believe the writer when he ends the chapter by telling us that all Israel *"held the king in awe, because they saw that he had wisdom from God."*

The language that he uses in this final verse of the chapter is meant to point us to the story behind the story. The Bible begins with Eve's failed attempt to discern right from wrong without any reference to the Lord.[11] What Solomon discovers in this chapter is that true wisdom is far more than a static currency. It is a person. The New Testament explains that Jesus *is* the wisdom of God and that the Holy Spirit *is* the Spirit of Wisdom.[12] The writer's statement that King Solomon *"had wisdom from God"* is therefore his Old Testament way of telling us that he was filled with the same Spirit of Wisdom who is still available to us today. That's one of the reasons why King Solomon wrote the book of Proverbs for us. He wants us to learn to have *a hearing heart* ourselves. He wants us to ask the Lord to endow us with this same currency of kings too.

Even now, the Lord invites you through the words of James 1:5 to pray the same prayer that King Solomon prayed at Gibeon. He promises that *"If any of you lacks wisdom, you should ask God, who gives generously to all without finding fault, and it will be given to you."*

---

[11] 1 Kings 3:9 deliberately echoes Genesis 3, since Solomon asks literally to know the difference between good and evil. Proverbs 1:7; 2:6; 9:10 and 15:33 all emphasize that all true wisdom comes from listening to God.

[12] 1 Corinthians 1:24; 1:30 and 2:16, and Colossians 2:2–3. Deuteronomy 34:9; Isaiah 11:2 and Ephesians 1:17.

THE CURRENCY OF KINGS (1 KINGS 3:1–28)

Cracks
(1 Kings 4:1–34)

Solomon had four thousand stalls for chariot horses,
and twelve thousand horses.

(1 Kings 4:26)

On Tuesday 23rd April 2013, cracks began to appear on the walls of the Rana Plaza shopping mall in Dhaka, the capital of Bangladesh. The wealthy shops on the ground floor were immediately evacuated, but the poor workers in the garment factories on the upper floors were ordered to return to their sewing machines or lose their monthly salary of £30. Their bosses insisted that they had orders to fulfil for Western retailers such as Primark, Matalan, Monsoon, Walmart and Benetton.

At 8.57 a.m. on Wednesday 24th April, the Rana Plaza building collapsed, killing 1,134 workers and injuring at least 2,000 more. Rojina Bejum was among them. She was forced to saw off her own arm to escape the rubble. She blamed the building owner of appalling negligence.

> *"After I went inside I saw the rumour was true. There was a crack in the pillar and the rods had come out. There were cracks in the ceiling too."* The owner would not listen. He told her, *"This is not a crack. It's just a bit of plaster that's come off ... Go upstairs, nothing will happen. The building will stand for 100 years."*[1]

The early days of King's Solomon's rule were euphoric. Nobody wanted to be told that cracks were appearing in his character. We

---

[1] These quotations are taken from a report in the British newspaper *The Independent* on 19th July 2014.

can catch a sense of the excitement that surrounded Solomon in his early days from the words of Psalm 45, which appears to have been written for one of his first royal weddings. *"You are the most excellent of men,"* the psalmist enthuses. *"Your throne will last for ever and ever; a sceptre of justice will be the sceptre of your kingdom. You love righteousness and hate wickedness."*

Much of what the writer of 1 Kings records in this chapter reflects that early feeling of euphoria. In 4:1–19, his long list of King Solomon's officials is far more impressive than the similar lists in 2 Samuel that describe the court of David.[2] In 4:20–28, he records an unprecedented shopping list of food that these officials sent to his palace every day: 6,600 litres of fine flour, 13,200 litres of coarse flour, 30 cows, 100 sheep and goats, choice venison and poultry, and enough barley and straw for 16,000 horses.[3]

In 4:29–34, the writer tells us that King Solomon's wealth was exceeded only by his wisdom. He left the great thinkers of Egypt, Arabia and Mesopotamia in the shade.[4] He also out-thought the wisest leaders within Israel, including Ethan and Heman, who served as David's worship leaders and wrote Psalms 88 and 89. The writer tells us that Solomon wrote down 3,000 wise sayings – in other words, the 500 in the book of Proverbs and the 30 in the book of Ecclesiastes are just his greatest hits. He also wrote 1,005 songs, of which only three have survived: Psalms 72 and 127, and his Song of Songs. As if this were not achievement enough for a single lifetime, the writer also says that Solomon was an early pioneer of botany, zoology and ornithology.

If you know your Old Testament, then you'll spot that this

---

[2] Many of the names are the same as in 2 Samuel 8:15–18 and 20:23–26. Solomon went for continuity but added many extra friends, cousins and sons-in-law to the tried-and-tested servants of his father.

[3] Solomon practised what he preaches in Proverbs 17:8, using his massive larder to win favour with a vast array of courtiers. The names of the two daughters that he married off to his governors also speak of his great wealth. Taphath means *Dripping With Perfume* and Basemath means *Spicy Fragrance*.

[4] Their surviving works include *The Babylonian Theodicy* and *The Instruction of Amenemope*.

represents more than just an impressive workload. There is a spiritual purpose behind all of this detail. When the writer tells us in 4:20 that the people of Judah and Israel *"were as numerous as the sand on the seashore"*, he wants us to see King Solomon as the fulfilment of God's promise to Abraham in Genesis 22:17.[5] When he tells us in 4:20 that *"they ate, they drank and they were happy"*, he wants us to see King Solomon as the fulfilment of God's promise to Moses in Exodus 3:8. When he tells us in 4:21 that his borders reached the River Euphrates to the east and the Mediterranean coastline of the Philistines and the land of Egypt to the west, he wants us to recognize that this makes Solomon the first Israelite to rule over all the territory God promised to Joshua.[6] When he tells us in 4:25 that Solomon's subjects dwelt in safety, *"everyone under their own vine and under their own fig-tree"*, he wants us to grasp that Solomon helped Israel to enjoy all of the blessings that the Lord had promised them in Deuteronomy 28:1–14.[7] Solomon means *Peace*, and he lived up to his name.

There is plenty to celebrate here, but don't miss the story behind the story. The writer also hints at the cracks that are beginning to appear in Solomon's character, and that Solomon is as complacent about them as the owner of the Rana Plaza shopping mall. First, the writer told us in 3:1, he took a pagan wife from Egypt in order to forge an alliance with her father, one of the final pharaohs of the 21st Dynasty.[8] Next, he told us

---

[5] Until now, this phrase has only been used to describe the enemies of God (Joshua 11:4; Judges 7:12; 1 Samuel 13:5 and 2 Samuel 17:11). Now finally Solomon turns the tables on Israel's enemies. See also 4:29.

[6] Dan, Beersheba, Gaza and Tiphsah are the northernmost, southernmost, westernmost and easternmost cities that were promised to the Israelites who followed Joshua across the River Jordan.

[7] Even Solomon's naming of animals in 4:33 is meant to mark him out as a new Adam. The same Hebrew word *rādāh* is used for Solomon *ruling* over Israel in 4:24 and for Adam *ruling* over creation in Genesis 1:26.

[8] Solomon knew that this marriage was sinful (2 Chronicles 8:11) and it appears to have been childless. It would also prove disastrous when the 21st Dynasty fell in 945 BC, since it made the pharaohs of the 22nd Dynasty regard Israel as their natural enemy (11:40 and 14:25–26).

in 3:2–3, Solomon started offering sacrifices to the Lord at the old Canaanite "high places", on altars defiled by idolatry instead of on the altar at the Tabernacle of Moses.[9]

Now the writer adds in 4:7–19 that King Solomon also abused many of his subjects. His twelve tax districts failed to follow the borders of the twelve tribes of Israel. They divided the ten northern tribes into twelve and left the two southern tribes tax-free. By treating the initial two tribes that had supported David as his homeland, and the ten tribes that received him as king seven years later as conquered territory, Solomon sowed the seeds for the eventual disintegration of his kingdom. This crack was so serious that the northern tribes complain to Rehoboam in 12:4, *"Your father put a heavy yoke on us."*

The writer also reveals in 4:26 that King Solomon is starting to rely on his own power. The Lord forbade the kings of Israel to accumulate horses in Deuteronomy 17:16, because it would make them self-reliant, but Solomon foolishly ignores the Lord's command. He turns his back on the military principle taught by his father in Psalm 20:7: *"Some trust in chariots and some in horses, but we trust in the name of the Lord our God."*

So don't miss the cracks that are starting to appear in the architecture of King Solomon's reign. They are meant to communicate the story behind the story – that, just like David, Solomon is not ultimately the messiah we are looking for. He will not fulfil the wedding-day euphoria of Psalm 45. He will not deliver the long-term peace for Israel that is anticipated in 1 Kings 4:25.[10] Solomon may be the best of men, but he is still a man at best. For all the pomp and glory of this chapter, some troubling cracks are starting to appear.

---

[9] The Lord had forbidden this sternly in Leviticus 17:1–9 and Numbers 33:52. The altars at these "high places" still stank of idolatry and burned with man-made fire instead of God-given fire (Leviticus 9:24–10:1).

[10] We are told to expect these things from Jesus alone in Micah 4:4; Zechariah 3:10 and Hebrews 2:8–9.

Second Home
(1 Kings 5:1–8:66)

"I have indeed built a magnificent temple for you, a place for you to dwell for ever."

(1 Kings 8:13)

Moses had been the first to build the Lord a second home. His Tabernacle still stood at Gibeon as a reminder that the God who lives in heaven also lived among his people in the days of Moses, Joshua and the Judges of Israel.

David had upgraded the Lord's second home. The Tabernacle of Moses had been destroyed by the Philistines in the days of Eli and, though rebuilt, it had seen better days. David therefore pitched a new Tabernacle for the Lord on Mount Zion, one without an inner sanctuary into which only priests could enter. This was a Tabernacle that offered access to God's presence for all. David had brought the ark of the covenant into Jerusalem and had made it the centrepiece of his new Tabernacle. Anyone could enter the Lord's second home to sing worship psalms around the ark with the rest of the congregation.

By the time Solomon became king in 970 BC, these two Tabernacles served two different purposes. The tent at Gibeon was Israel's *sacrifice centre*, where animals were slaughtered in order to atone for people's sin. The tent on Mount Zion was Israel's *worship centre*, where no blood was shed at all. Instead the people offered sacrifices of praise to thank God for having forgiven them and for inviting them to join him in his second home.[1]

---

[1] We see this distinction in Psalm 27:6; 61:4–8 and 141:2 – all written about the Tabernacle on Mount Zion.

King David had wished to combine these two Tabernacles into one glorious new Temple. The Lord had stopped him, informing him that his hands had shed too much blood in battle. That privilege would belong to his son Solomon instead. David therefore contented himself with buying the building site, stockpiling building materials and drawing up detailed building designs from the Lord so that his son would find it easy to build when the time came.[2] We can tell how excited the writer is about this from the fact that he devotes four chapters to the building of the Temple under Solomon.

In chapter 5, he tells us that the new King Solomon spent the first four years of his reign gathering the cedar and juniper wood that was missing from his father's great stockpile. The account of his friendship with King Hiram of Tyre represents the first time that an Israelite ruler has signed any peace treaty with a pagan nation since the ill-advised alliance with the Gibeonites in Joshua 9, but this time the coalition is a wise one.[3] King Hiram allows the labour gangs of Solomon to harvest the finest logs from his forest and float them in rafts along the Mediterranean coastline down to Joppa, the chief port of Israel.[4] Hiram also teaches Solomon's men how to quarry stones from the hills of Israel and how to cut them to the right size for the Temple walls.[5] Solomon is ready to build.

In chapter 6, the building work begins. The writer is so excited that he records the month and the year. The work finally starts in April 966 BC.[6] The mass of detail in these chapters is

[2] See 1 Chronicles 21:22–26; 22:1–19 and 28:1–29:9.

[3] Hiram of Tyre had given David ad hoc help in 2 Samuel 5:11. There is a longer account of this treaty in 2 Chronicles 2, including the loan of the top designer Huram, who isn't mentioned here until 1 Kings 7:13.

[4] We are told in 2 Chronicles 2:16 that these rafts docked at Joppa, about thirty-eight miles from Jerusalem.

[5] The stone was soft enough to cut with a saw while underground, but it became rock hard once it came into contact with sunlight. Some of the stones needed to be 4.5 metres long, so cutting them was a real skill (7:10).

[6] This verse and the parallel 2 Chronicles 3:2 are crucial in dating the early half of the Old Testament. Since we know that Solomon began building in 966 BC, these verses date the exodus to 1446 BC.

meant to echo the amount of detail that was also given when Moses built his Tabernacle in the book of Exodus. It takes Solomon seven years to finish the Temple, but in November 959 BC, the Lord is finally able to move into his new second home.

But amid the celebrations, the cracks in Solomon's character start to widen. In 5:11, he agrees to pay King Hiram an eye-watering 4.4 million litres of wheat and 440,000 litres of oil every year.[7] This places such a heavy burden on the Israelite taxpayers that, in 1 Kings 9, Solomon has to clear his debts by renouncing Israel's claim to part of the Promised Land. In 5:13–16, his abuse of the ten northern tribes of Israel worsens. In addition to taxing them and not the two southern tribes, Solomon now keeps his building project on schedule by conscripting 30,000 northerners into his labour gangs. Up until now, the rulers of Israel have only ever conscripted foreigners, so this speaks volumes to the northern tribes. Their king clearly regards them as second-class citizens.[8]

Another crack begins to appear in 7:1–12. It turns out that Solomon is also building another type of second home. In addition to the Temple, he is building a great palace for himself. King David was embarrassed by the opulence of his palace in 2 Samuel 7:2, but for his son it isn't opulent enough. Solomon spends seven years building the Temple but thirteen years building the Palace of the Forest of Lebanon. His overtaxing and his overwork of the ten northern tribes can be traced back to the overreaching greed that stirred his heart to complement the Temple by building a second home for himself too.[9]

Having showed us some of the cracks in King Solomon's character, the writer takes us back to the celebrations. In

---

[7] 2 Chronicles 2:10 adds that he also paid Hiram 4.4 million litres of barley and 440,000 litres of wine a year.

[8] Deuteronomy 29:11; Joshua 9:21; 2 Samuel 12:31 and 1 Chronicles 22:2. Israelite northerners made up a sixth of Solomon's 180,000 labourers, spelling disaster for his kingdom later on, in 1 Kings 11:28 and 12:1–19.

[9] The Temple was 27 metres long, 9 metres wide and 13.5 metres high. The Palace of the Forest of Lebanon was 46 metres long, 23 metres wide and 13.5 metres high. Its floor space was 13 times that of the Temple.

7:13–51, Solomon hires a top designer from Tyre to make all of the bronze furnishings for the Temple.[10] He gives us such a long list of Huram's designs for the Temple, that we aren't surprised in verse 47 when the writer tells us that Solomon eventually stopped weighing the bronze furnishings.[11] The writer then lists all the gold and silver furnishings. The Lord's second home is a spectacular affair.

This paves the way for the great climax to these four chapters. In 8:1–13, the Tabernacles of Moses and David are both dismantled, and all of their sacred objects are brought into the new Temple. The Lord responds by filling the Temple with his presence in the same dramatic way that he filled the Tabernacle at Mount Sinai many centuries before, in the final verses of the book of Exodus. King Solomon is so excited that he blesses the people, prays the longest prayer in 1 and 2 Kings, and then blesses the people again. He sacrifices 22,000 bulls and 120,000 sheep and goats – an unprecedented number that puts even his lavish sacrifices at Gibeon into the shade. He leads the Israelites in celebrating the Feast of Tabernacles for seven days, then he sends them off home rejoicing. God's days of living in a tent are over. He now lives in a house of stone.

The writer invites us to join in the celebrations, but he also encourages us to spot the cracks appearing in the Temple's architecture. King Solomon has built the Lord a magnificent second home, but already it is in danger of tumbling down.

---

[10] He is called *Hiram* in 1 Kings and *Huram-Abi* in 2 Chronicles, so most English translations refer to him as *Huram* in 1 Kings to avoid confusing him with the king of Tyre. He worked in "burnished bronze" (7:45) – that is, in bronze so scoured and polished that it shone more brightly than gold under the Middle Eastern sun.

[11] Archaeologists have confirmed the writer's brilliant attention to detail by finding clay casts for moulding metal objects at Sukkoth and Zarethan, on the east bank of the River Jordan, as is described in 7:46.

Bodybuilder
(1 Kings 6:1–7:51)

So Solomon built the temple and completed it.

(1 Kings 6:14)

Many modern readers skim-read the detailed description of King Solomon's Temple in these two chapters. They feel frustrated that the writer devotes so many verses to interior design, when he could have used the same space to teach us how to perform miracles like Elijah and Elisha. I want to give you two reasons to read more slowly.

First, we need to remember that the author was writing for the Jewish exiles in Babylon. Many of them had been there on 18th July 586 BC, when the Babylonians had finally broken their way into the city of Jerusalem, plundering the Temple of its treasures before burning it to the ground. They still remembered their last glimpse of the blackened rubble that had once been the Lord's second home. They dreamed about its rebuilding.

Second, we need to remember that the author was a prophet. We can't know for sure how much he understood of what he wrote, but we do know that the writers of the New Testament treat these descriptions of Solomon's Temple as prophecies about Jesus' body. The writer of Hebrews sees them as a glorious picture of our salvation, and John's gospel records an important confrontation in the Temple courtyards. *"Jesus answered them, 'Destroy this temple, and I will raise it again in three days.' They replied, 'It has taken forty-six years to build this temple, and you are going to raise it in three days?' But the temple he had spoken of was his body."*[1] Let's therefore read these two

---

[1] John 2:19–21. Compare also Matthew 27:50–51 with Hebrews 10:20.

chapters slowly and let's remember that they are prophecy. They speak about a true and better Temple.

For a start, the author uses some pretty odd Hebrew words to describe the architecture of the Temple. He says it has a *face* in 6:3 when describing its porchway. He says that it has many *ribs* in 6:5, 8, 15, 16 and 34, and in 7:3 when describing its side rooms, storeys, door panels, rafters and wall panels. He also refers to the two sides of the Temple as its *shoulders* in 7:39. You've got to admit that that's a little bit odd. It's almost as if the author is trying to point us towards a better, human Temple, in the body of Jesus.

The writer also uses a new word to describe the inner sanctuary of the Temple, where the presence of Lord dwelt above the lid of the ark of the covenant. Like Moses, the writer refers to that inner sanctuary as the *Holy of Holies*, but unlike Moses he also refers to it as the *debīr* – a Hebrew word that means *Oracle* or *the Divine Word*.[2]

The writer prophesies that this Word of God will be holy when he comes into the world. The stone interior of the Temple is completely covered with cedar wood, and that cedar wood is in turn completely covered with gold, because Jesus would be completely holy, inside and out. Underneath the gold, the cedar wood is carved with palm trees and flowers reminiscent of the Garden of Eden before sin entered the world, and with cherubim angels like those who prevented anything unholy from entering the Garden of Eden in Genesis 3:24. The Hebrews used the number seven and symmetrical shapes as symbols of the Lord's perfection, so the Temple is completed in seven years and its sanctuary is a perfect cube. All of this detail serves a purpose, prophesying about the utter righteousness of Jesus when he came into the world.

If we read a bit more deeply, then these chapters get even better. The writers of the New Testament don't simply tell us that the Temple foreshadowed the flesh-and-blood body of Jesus.

---

[2] See John 1:1. The word is translated *sanctuary* eight times in 1 Kings 6, once in 1 Kings 7 and twice in 1 Kings 8.

They also tell us that it foreshadowed the Church, the new Body of Christ, his New Covenant Temple. We are therefore meant to see King Solomon as a picture of that true and better Temple builder. We are meant to see his building work as a picture of Christ's work in us: *"Don't you know that you yourselves are God's temple and that God's Spirit lives among you?" "You also, like living stones, are being built into a temple of the Spirit to be a holy priesthood, offering spiritual sacrifices acceptable to God through Jesus Christ."*[3]

This alone should be enough to make us slow down our skim-reading. It is seriously encouraging! If Solomon could take ordinary stones and cover them with cedar wood and gold until none of their natural blemishes was visible, then how much more can the cross of Jesus and his precious blood cover over our offences before God?[4] If the Temple was over eight times as big as the Tabernacle of Moses, then how much more will Jesus reach large numbers of people in every nation through the Gospel?[5] If the Temple, unlike the Tabernacle, had a massive porch and many side rooms, then how much can we be reassured that there is room within the Body of Jesus for the likes of you and me?

In chapter 7, the writer invites us to play our own part in building up the Body of Jesus.[6] Huram's mother is an Israelite and his father is from Tyre, so he serves as a prophetic promise that Jesus has a role in the building work for people from every nation.[7] Just as Huram builds two great bronze pillars named Jakin and Boaz, meaning *stability* and *strength*, to hold up the

---

[3] See 1 Corinthians 3:16–17 and 6:19; 2 Corinthians 6:16; Ephesians 2:21–22 and 1 Peter 2:5 (author's own translation).

[4] 1 Kings 6:30 says that even the floor was covered in gold. Jesus truly makes us spotless all over.

[5] Solomon's Temple was 27 metres long, 9 metres wide and 13.5 metres high, whereas Moses' Tabernacle was only 15 metres by 5 metres by 5 metres. It was therefore almost nine times larger than its predecessor.

[6] Seen through this lens, the writer also warns in 6:7 that Christians ought to stop fighting each other.

[7] See Isaiah 56:6–7 and 60:10. This was one of the reasons why Jesus cleared the Temple courtyards.

entrance to the Temple, so must we lend our own support to the mission of Jesus that invites the world to become part of his New Covenant Temple.[8] Just as Huram fills great baths and basins with water, so must we call people to repent of their sin and to be baptized in Jesus' name.[9] The final verse of chapter 7 encourages us that our labour will not be in vain. The writer makes a play on words when he says the work was finished, since that Hebrew verb *shālam* lies at the root of the name Solomon. When he tells us literally that Solomon *solomoned* his Temple, it is meant to assure us that the true and better Solomon will complete his Church through the likes of you and me.

For the despondent Jewish exiles in Babylon, these two chapters were therefore good news. They prophesied that the Lord had a plan to build a far better Temple than the one they saw destroyed by the Babylonians. For despondent Christians today, longing to see far greater Gospel breakthrough, these two chapters offer brilliant news too. They promise us that Jesus will do all that Solomon did, minus the cracks. They give us faith to rise up and serve him in his building of his far better New Covenant Temple today.

---

[8] These two pillars are referred back to in Galatians 2:9 and Revelation 3:12.

[9] The Sea held 44,000 litres of water, and each of the 10 basins held 880 litres. Whatever the significance of those numbers, this prophecy ought to encourage us to get busy baptizing people!

The Hope Of Israel
(1 Kings 8:1–66)

> *"Will God really dwell on earth? The heavens, even*
> *the highest heaven, cannot contain you. How much*
> *less this temple I have built!"*
>
> (1 Kings 8:27)

You can tell a person's priorities from what they talk about. If your friend says he isn't interested in a girl but then proceeds to talk about her constantly, you can be pretty sure he's lying. If your neighbour says, "it isn't about the money" but then keeps mentioning how much you owe him, you can be pretty sure he's lying too. And if the longest chapter in the whole of 1 and 2 Kings records what happened on a single day in King Solomon's reign, you can be pretty sure the chapter's lengthy for a reason. The writer wants to teach his readers what is, and what definitely isn't, the true hope of Israel.[1]

It is October 958 BC. King Solomon has waited almost a year since completing the Temple so that everyone can come from all four corners of Israel to a fourteen-day party to dedicate it to the Lord.[2] He commands the priests and Levites to dismantle the two Tabernacles of Moses and David and to put them away in the storerooms of his new Temple because Israel has no further

---

[1] *"Still there today"* in 8:8 is the first of many times when the writer clearly quotes from contemporary sources.

[2] Solomon waited 11 months after finishing the Temple in November 959 BC to incorporate these 14 days of celebration with the Festival of Tabernacles (6:38; 8:2 and 8:65). They took place from 8th to 22nd Ethanaim in the Jewish calendar (2 Chronicles 7:8–10). The first day is described in 8:1–64 and the other 14 days in 8:65–66.

need for them.[3] Then he commands them to bring the ark of the covenant into the Temple's inner sanctuary.[4] As they do so, God's presence fills the Temple, looking like a cloud of glory, just as it did at the dedication of the Tabernacle in Exodus 40:34–35.[5] The priests beat a hasty retreat in fear but King Solomon is delighted.[6] God's presence has always been the true hope of Israel.

The king cannot contain his excitement that the Lord has actually come to live in his new Temple. In 8:14–21, he turns around and proclaims a blessing over the people of Israel. We are told that it's a blessing, but it sounds more like a boast.[7] We can almost picture Solomon punching the air with his fists and shouting out: "Mission accomplished!" All of his childhood he had been told by his father that the Lord had chosen him to build the Temple and now, through God's faithfulness, he has completed the task given him.

This launches Solomon into a prayer in 8:22–53. The writer devotes more space to this single prayer than he does to most of the reigns of the kings of Israel, so it is clearly vital to his message. On the face of it, the prayer compounds the feeling of despair that the Jewish exiles felt whenever they remembered their ruined Temple, but don't miss what the writer is trying to do through the words of Solomon. He intends to undermine their feeling of despair and to reassure them that the Temple was never the true hope of Israel.

As we read the prayer, the first thing that strikes us is just how many times Solomon confesses that his new Temple

---

[3] We never hear about either Tabernacle again, except when used as prophetic pictures of the Gospel.

[4] He offered countless sacrifices along the way because of what David learned the hard way in 2 Samuel 6.

[5] While God's "light" speaks of his holiness (1 John 1:5) this "cloud" speaks of the mystery of his presence.

[6] The Hebrew text of 8:11 says literally that *"they could not stand to minister"*. This probably means that they could not enter the Temple, but it may mean that they fell flat on their faces in fear.

[7] I don't mean boasting in a bad sense. Solomon shows us that, whenever we don't feel like praising God, we should look back on our lives to stir ourselves to praise him for his faithfulness to us. See Isaiah 51:1.

is only the Lord's home in a limited sense of the word.[8] His great confession in 8:27 – *"But will God really dwell on earth? The heavens, even the highest heaven, cannot contain you. How much less this temple I have built!"* – is followed by eight further confessions that God's true dwelling place is heaven, not a man-made building.[9]

Although this prayer appears at first glance to be a celebration of the Temple, in many ways the opposite is true. The ark of the covenant is mentioned for the ninth time in eight chapters in 8:21 – but then the writer never mentions it again.[10] As for the Temple itself, it is remarkable how small a role it plays in the story after the end of this chapter. Solomon has barely said "Amen" at the end of his prayer than he runs after foreign idols. Almost immediately, the Temple recedes from view. Very few of his successors come to pray there. Instead, they come to desecrate it with their idols and to plunder its treasures to buy off invading armies.[11] This emphasis is deliberate. The writer wants to encourage the Jewish exiles to see that their ruined Temple was never the true hope of Israel.

The true hope of Israel is God's faithfulness to his Word. That's the main message of this chapter. *"You have kept your promise to your servant David my father; with your mouth you have promised and with your hand you have fulfilled it."*[12] That explains why there are at least a dozen references in this chapter to God's covenant promises towards Israel as a nation.[13] It also explains why Solomon's prayer sounds like a long quotation of the blessings and the curses that are listed in Leviticus 26 and

---

[8] Isaiah 6:1 confirms this. The Temple could scarcely contain even the hem of the Lord's royal robes.

[9] 1 Kings 8:30, 32, 34, 36, 39, 43, 45 and 49. If we miss this, we miss the meaning of the prayer. It is meant to correct the foolish thinking about the Temple that we find in Jeremiah 7:4–15 and Micah 3:11–12.

[10] The ark remained in the sanctuary throughout this period (2 Chronicles 35:3), so the silence is deliberate.

[11] The two big exceptions are King Hezekiah in 2 Kings 19 and King Jehoshaphat in 2 Chronicles 20.

[12] 1 Kings 8:24.

[13] 1 Kings 8:15, 20, 23, 25, 26, 29, 36, 40, 51, 53, 56 and 57.

Deuteronomy 28. It's why he fails to tell us that fire fell from heaven onto Solomon's new altar (2 Chronicles 7:1–3), and why he ends the chapter with talk of *David* rather than of Solomon (8:66 and 2 Chronicles 7:10). The writer wants to take our eyes off Solomon's sanctuary – it proved to be a false hope for Israel – and on to God's promise to build a true and better Temple.

The true hope of Israel is not a sanctuary, but a Saviour. The writer expects Solomon's prayer to convince us that he is not the messiah we are looking for. In 8:25, it emphasizes that the Lord's promises to David's dynasty depend on its kings obeying God's Word, and we can tell from the cracks appearing in Solomon's reign that David's dynasty is about to fall at the first hurdle. When Solomon prays in 8:26 for the Lord to be faithful to his promises to David, in spite of his own sin, we are meant to grasp that this is going to require death and resurrection for David's dynasty, for Solomon's Temple and for the whole nation of Israel. That's why the apostle Paul refers to the death and resurrection of Jesus as *"the hope of Israel"* in Acts 28:20. He had seen the story behind the story here.

King Solomon confesses in his prayer that the Israelites will sin, that God will judge them, that they will be defeated by their enemies and that they will become exiles in a faraway land. On that day, the great significance of his Temple would not be that the exiles could *"pray towards this place"* (the cloud of God's presence left the Temple years before its destruction), but that it revealed the humble character of the Lord.[14] Although he lived in heaven, the Temple proved he was not too proud to come and "tabernacle" in the midst of his people. The God of heaven would one day come down to earth in flesh and blood, as the true and better Temple. *That* was the true hope of Israel.[15]

---

[14] 1 Kings 8:29, 30 and 35. Ezekiel saw the cloud of God's presence leave the Temple on 17th September 592 BC (Ezekiel 9:3; 10:4–5; 18–19 and 11:22–23).

[15] This is why the writer emphasizes in 8:65 that this 14-day dedication party in October 958 BC incorporated the Festival of Tabernacles.

Fork In The Road
(1 Kings 9:1–28)

"If you walk before me faithfully ... I will establish your royal throne over Israel for ever ... But if you or your descendants turn away from me ... I will cut off Israel from the land."

(1 Kings 9:4–7)

King David had come to a fork in the road midway through his reign. At the halfway mark of his monarchy, he had spotted his friend's wife bathing naked and allowed his life to take a disastrous turn. Faced with two paths to take, he had chosen the one that led to adultery, murder and the sudden implosion of his kingdom.[1]

King Solomon now faces a fork in the road midway through his own reign.[2] It is 950 BC. He has spent seven years building the Temple and a further thirteen years building the Palace of the Forest of Lebanon.[3] As his busy hands fall idle for the first time as a ruler, the Lord appears to him in a dream, just like the one he had at the start of his reign at the Tabernacle in Gibeon.[4] In the dream, God extends him another generous offer, only this time it is accompanied by a stark and sobering warning.

44

---

[1] 2 Samuel 11. We know that this event took place halfway through his forty-year reign because the woman was Bathsheba, and her second son Solomon was aged eighteen when King David died.

[2] It is no coincidence that Saul, David and Solomon each reigned for forty years (1 Kings 2:11 and 11:42, and Acts 13:21). The Lord asked each of them to make a clear choice at the midway mark of their reign.

[3] The *"twenty years"* in 9:10 account for four years of stockpiling wood; and for seven and thirteen overlapping years of Temple- and palace-building.

[4] 2 Chronicles 7:12 confirms that *"as he had appeared to him at Gibeon"* (9:2) means that he gave him a second dream.

The Lord tells Solomon that he has heard the prayer he prayed at the dedication of his new Temple.[5] He will indeed do all he asks. He has declared his Temple holy, and he promises to set his Name, his eyes and his heart on it forever. But whereas Solomon's first dream twenty years earlier was big on promises and light on warnings, this second dream is the other way around. The Lord points out that the king's life is at an important fork in the road. If he chooses the path of obedience, or at the very least repentance like his father David, then all of God's "forever" promises about his Temple and his dynasty will be fulfilled the easy way for him. But if Solomon takes a wrong turn at this fork in the road, then those "forever" promises will be fulfilled in a different way.

Up until now, Solomon has been busy with the goals his father set for him in God. In the second half of his reign, he needs to set his own goals for his walk with God, or else the Devil will find work for his idle hands to do. If he is enticed to worship idols, the Lord vows to respond by handing his dynasty over to its enemies and allowing them to demolish his Temple. Instead of making Solomon's pride and joy a place for pagans to come and see the blessing of the Lord, God will make it a place where the pagans can observe the type of judgment that he metes out to those who worship their vile gods. The Lord will not rest until David's disobedient dynasty and Solomon's Temple are both dead and buried. He will still fulfil his "forever" promises, but he will do so by leading Israel down the death-and-resurrection pathway in the footsteps of its true Messiah.[6]

The Lord chooses his words carefully.[7] His call for Solomon

---

[5] It is 950 BC and Solomon dedicated his Temple in 958 BC, an eight-year wait for his prayer to be answered. This should encourage us. God hears us at once but he responds with perfect timing (Daniel 9:23 and 10:12–13).

[6] The Hebrew word *shālah*, which is used for God *rejecting* Solomon's Temple in 9:7, is also used for God banishing Adam and Eve from the Garden of Eden in Genesis 3:23 and divorcing Israel in Isaiah 50:1. God is therefore threatening to cut Solomon's Temple out of his story and to raise up a better Temple instead.

[7] He even uses the Hebrew plural form of *you* in 9:6 to emphasize that this dream presents the same choice to each of Solomon's successors as king – and to each of us.

to walk before him with *integrity of heart* takes us back to the young king's request in 3:9 to receive *a hearing heart* from the Lord. It also echoes his confession in 8:39 that the Lord knows the true state of people's hearts, and it readies us for the tragic verdict in 11:4 that *"his heart was not fully devoted to the Lord his God, as the heart of David his father had been."* If the writer of 1 Kings was indeed the prophet Jeremiah, then it also echoes his own warning in Jeremiah 17:9 that *"The heart is deceitful above all things."* Even the best of men prove to be men at best.

As if to demonstrate it, Solomon awakes from his dream and immediately takes the wrong fork in the road. He has accrued large debts to King Hiram of Tyre by building such a lavish palace, so he tries to solve the problem by ceding him twenty cities in Galilee. We can tell how repugnant this was to the Lord by contrasting Solomon's attitude towards the Promised Land with that of godly Naboth in 21:3. These cities may well have included Nazareth, Capernaum, Cana and Nain, where Jesus spent the bulk of his earthly ministry, so what Solomon jeopardizes here is far more serious than he knows.[8] The Lord intervenes by making Hiram despise the twenty cities and throw them back in Solomon's face, but it is a worrying sign that a wise man is fast becoming a fool.[9]

In 9:15–24, the writer reminds us of some of the cracks that have already appeared in Solomon's character. They start to widen further. His marriage to the pagan princess of Egypt turns into a full-blown military alliance when his father-in-law conquers the Canaanites of Gezer for an Israel whose own army has failed to do so.[10] Solomon starts to imitate the pharaohs by creating store cities, like the ones in Exodus 1:11. He grows increasingly self-reliant, continuing to defy the Lord's command in Deuteronomy 17:16 not to accumulate large numbers of horses and chariots. When Solomon decides

---

[8] Isaiah 9:1 and John 1:46 both emphasize that Jesus turned these worthless cities into something worthy.

[9] 2 Chronicles 8:2 confirms that Hiram returned them to Solomon to be resettled by Israelites.

[10] Joshua 16:10 and Judges 1:29. Pharaoh seems to care more about the Promised Land than Solomon does.

to beef up his army of slave labourers, it is hard to square the statement that he *"did not make slaves of any of the Israelites"* with what we are told in 11:28; 12:4 and 12:18. The best explanation appears to be that Solomon has actually stopped recognizing many of God's people from the ten northern tribes as the bona fide Israelites they are.

In 9:25-28, the writer reveals some new cracks that are starting to appear in the king's character. He seems to think that offering sacrifices at the Temple three times a year is enough to fulfil all of his *"temple obligations"*. That's a far cry from his early days as king, when he longed to know the Lord with unhurried pleasure at his presence. Solomon also begins to ignore the Lord's command in Deuteronomy 17:17 that no king of Israel must foster a spirit of self-reliance by accumulating large quantities of silver and gold.[11] His creation of a Red Sea trading fleet to bring back precious metals from exotic lands suggests that he is now more influenced by the King of Tyre than by the Law of Moses.[12]

King Solomon was very wise, yet he took a wrong turn at a fork in the road halfway through his reign. The writer encourages us to take a good look at our own lives and at the choices we are making. He urges us to keep pursuing the path of obedience to God.

---

[11] Strictly speaking, *Ophir* was southern Arabia, famous for its fine gold (Job 22:24 and 28:16; Psalm 45:9 and Isaiah 13:12). However, it could also refer more loosely to the uncharted lands of Africa and India.

[12] 2 Chronicles 8:18 tells us that Hiram helped Solomon to build these ships as well as man them. This gives us the impression of Hiram goading Solomon into doing this, perhaps to pay off the debts he owed him.

What They Could Have Won
(1 Kings 10:1–29)

The whole world sought an audience with Solomon
to hear the wisdom God had put in his heart.

(1 Kings 10:24)

If you've ever watched the classic British TV gameshow *Bullseye*, then you will know its famous catchphrase. The host Jim Bowen shows the losing contestants the prizes they have missed and tells them, "Let's take a look at what you could have won!" That's why it feels in 1 Kings 10 as though the writer has been watching too much *Bullseye*. He shows us what the Israelites could have won had King Solomon taken the other fork in the road.

In 10:1–9, we see the *missionary breakthrough* that the Israelites could have seen had King Solomon remained faithful to the Lord. They had prayed for many nations to come to know the Lord at David's Tabernacle, and Solomon had prayed in 8:41–43 that this would carry over into his Temple.[1] The arrival of the Queen of Sheba and her retinue therefore grants us a glimpse of what might have happened to the pagan nations of the world had King Solomon called them to swap their worthless idols for the Lord instead of joining them in running after their worthless idols.[2]

The Queen of Sheba comes to Jerusalem because she has heard about the new palace and Temple. This dates her visit

[1] See also 8:60. We can see this in 1 Chronicles 16:7–36, and in the way that the apostles hail the sudden salvation of first-century pagans as the renewal of David's Tabernacle in their own day (Acts 15:16–18).

[2] The Hebrew word translated "merchants" in 10:15 can also be translated "tourists". If Solomon had remained obedient, people from all over the world would have come to surrender their lives to the God of Israel.

to shortly after Solomon's second dream – late enough for the building work to have finished, but early enough for Solomon to still appear wise. She arrives with many questions, but the main motive for her visit is to find out about *"his relationship to the Lord"*. Jewish tradition and the words of Jesus in Matthew 12:42 and Luke 11:31 suggest that she may well have been converted.[3] Before she returns home, she hints at the missionary breakthrough that Israel might have now seen. Her confession of faith in 10:9 could have been repeated by many other foreigners: *"Praise be to the Lord your God, who has delighted in you and placed you on the throne of Israel. Because of the Lord's eternal love for Israel, he has made you king to maintain justice and righteousness."*[4]

In 10:10–15, we see the *riches* that the Israelites could have enjoyed had King Solomon remained faithful to the Lord. Sheba was the land of the Sabeans in southern Arabia, in modern-day Yemen. That's why Jesus refers to her as the *Queen of the South*. She ruled over part of Ophir, the faraway land which was so famous for its gold that Solomon built a trading fleet to visit Ophir at the end of chapter 9. The writer wants us to spot this tragic irony. He tells us in 10:10 that the Queen of Sheba presented Solomon with four tons of gold, the exact amount that he told us in 9:14 was owed to King Hiram of Tyre. Had Solomon taken the road of obedience, the Lord would have helped him with his money problems. No contestant on *Bullseye* ever missed out on more riches than him.

The Red Sea fleet returns with further gold for Solomon. He adds it to the gold that is pouring in from his taxation of busy trade routes and of his vassal territories. Yet even as the writer tells us about the precious jewels and the exotic wood that the Red Sea fleet brings back to adorn Solomon's palace

---

[3] The Hebrew word *rūach* in 10:5 either means that she was *breathless* with astonishment or that there was *no spirit left* within her. Either way, what she saw made room for the Spirit of God to move within her.

[4] This remains an enduring principle for nations and for churches. When God wants to bless us, he gives us good leaders. Whenever he wants to curse us, he takes them away (Isaiah 3:1–7 and Ephesians 4:7–13).

and Temple, he drops a hint at how far it falls short of the riches of obedience. In Hebrew thought, the number seven represented God's perfection, so the number *777* spoke of total perfection. When the writer says that Solomon's annual income of gold amounted to *666* talents, he is therefore hinting that his treasures fell short of God's desire to entrust Israel with the true riches of heaven.[5]

In 10:16–22, we see the *power* that the Israelites could have wielded had King Solomon remained faithful to the Lord. For the rest of 1 and 2 Kings, they will feel like pawns in the power games of their much stronger neighbours, so the detail here is meant to convey to us that Israel was once more powerful than Egypt, Aram, Babylon and Assyria combined. None of the rulers of those nations ever armed their palace bodyguard with gold shields, requiring almost two tons of gold. None of them ever sat on a colossal throne of gold and ivory, its six large steps enabling them to tower over anybody fortunate enough to be granted an audience with them. None of those rulers ever owned so much golden crockery and cutlery that silver plates were only used by their servants below stairs. None of them ever commanded a Red Sea fleet like Israel's, bringing back exotic animals and treasures from uncharted Africa and India.[6] This is the power that the Israelites could have enjoyed had Solomon chosen a different fork in the road. Instead, within a few years this would all be plundered by their enemies.[7]

In 10:23–29, we see the *influence* that the Israelites could have enjoyed had King Solomon remained faithful to the Lord. Not only did the rulers of every other nation confess that he was richer than they were, but they also confessed that he was far

---

[5] Six hundred and sixty-six talents was almost twenty-five tons of gold, but Revelation 13:18 refers back to this verse with disapproval.

[6] A *ship of Tarshish* in 10:22 refers to any ship made to the design of the great Phoenician shipbuilders. It may also indicate that Solomon had a Mediterranean fleet that reached Spain in addition to his Red Sea fleet.

[7] 14:25–26. Ivory was very costly, yet Solomon was so rich that he covered much of his ivory over with gold!

wiser too. They queued up to receive wise advice from him.[8] When the writer says that *"The whole world sought audience with Solomon to hear the wisdom God had put in his heart"*, he is telling us that this was the greatest opportunity Israel had ever had to influence the nations for the Lord. Tragically, instead of using his influence to promote the Gospel, Solomon squanders it on promoting his trade interests.[9] He becomes a big shot wheeler-dealer in the international horse and chariot trade. We are told about his prices and his customers, but we are not told that the Israelites ever shared God's message of salvation with any of his foreign customers. Israel blew the best chance they ever had to influence the nations.

If you find the message of this chapter a bit depressing, that's because it's meant to be. It's never nice to be told by someone: "Look at what you could have won!" But the writer tells us all this for a reason. As he draws his account of the reign of Solomon to an end, he wants to redirect our gaze onto a better King. Solomon isn't the Messiah we're looking for.

Jesus makes us more than conquerors. He won the blessing of God for us when he died on the cross, and he rose again to declare in triumph: Look at what I have won for you! He declares in triumph in Matthew 12:42: *"The Queen of the South ... came from the ends of the earth to listen to Solomon's wisdom, and now something greater than Solomon is here."*

---

[8] The writer hints at Solomon's downfall in 10:23 by telling us that he was great in *"riches and wisdom"*, rather than in *"wisdom and riches"*. Israel's wisest ruler was starting to have more money than sense.

[9] *Kue* was part of modern-day Turkey. Solomon dominated the Mediterranean as well as the Red Sea trade.

So Solomon did evil in the eyes of the Lord; he did
not follow the Lord completely, as David his father
had done.

(1 Kings 11:6)

I love playing games with my children. One of our favourites is
the old family classic *Kerplunk*. If you've never played it, let me
explain. Thirty coloured straws are poked through holes in the
middle of a transparent tube. They form a lattice that supports
a pile of thirty marbles, then the players take turns to pull out
each of the straws. At first, it's easy. None of the marbles falls
through the lattice, but the game is called *Kerplunk* for a reason.
It's the noise the marbles make when a player pulls out one too
many straws.

Solomon has been playing *Kerplunk* with his kingdom for
far too long. We have already noted several ways in which he
pulled out some of its straws. He taxed the ten northern tribes
but not the two southern ones. He press-ganged some of those
northerners into forced labour. He overspent on his palace and
ended up in such debt to King Hiram that he tried to buy him
off with some of the Promised Land. He neglected the altar
at his own Temple by sacrificing to the Lord at the Canaanite
"high places" on altars that had been defiled by their idolatry.
Given how many straws Solomon had already pulled out of his
Kerplunk tube, it was a marvel that his reign had lasted this long.

The first marbles start falling at the end of chapter 10.
Solomon defies the Lord's decree in Deuteronomy 17:17 that
the kings of Israel must not stockpile gold and silver, since it will
teach them self-reliance. He stockpiles so much gold and silver

that we are told he wipes the value off the global precious metals market.[1] Solomon also defies the Lord's decree in Deuteronomy 17:16 that the kings of Israel must not accumulate stables full of horses, since that will only add to their self-reliance, and that they must definitely not conduct any kind of horse trade with the Egyptians, whose charioteers had tried to wipe out Israel at the Red Sea. Solomon thinks he knows better. He buys so many horses and chariots from Egypt that he has to create chariot cities in which to store them. He creates a standing army of 1,400 chariots pulled by 12,000 horses, then sells the rest to the bitter enemies of Israel.[2] It's utterly foolish and it sounds just like *Kerplunk*.

In 11:1–8, more marbles start falling fast. It was bad enough when Solomon sinfully married an Egyptian princess in 3:1, figuring that it was worth overlooking her idolatry for the sake of becoming friends with Pharaoh, but now he goes much further and makes marrying the daughters of pagan kings his official foreign policy.[3] He marries 700 foreign princesses and admits a further 300 into his harem.[4] This doesn't just defy the Lord's decree in Deuteronomy 17:17 that the kings of Israel must not take multiple wives, but it also leads him to worship the foreign gods of the 1,000 women with whom he shares his bed.[5] Solomon's *heart* is mentioned twice in the Hebrew text of

---

[1] 1 Kings 10:27 says he flooded the silver market. 2 Chronicles 1:15 adds that he flooded the gold market too. Wise though he was, Solomon ignored the warning in Proverbs 30:8–9.

[2] Compare 9:20 and 10:29. The Aramean army would cause misery for Israel in 1 Kings 11:23–25; 20:1, 26 and 22:31, and in 2 Kings 5:2; 6:8, 24; 8:11–13, 28; 12:17 and 13:3–4.

[3] This foreign policy ignored Solomon's own teaching about marriage in Proverbs 5:18; 12:4, 26; 18:22; 19:14; 21:9 and 27:15–16, in Song of Songs 8:6–7, and in Ecclesiastes 4:11–12 and 7:26.

[4] A *concubine* was a long-term sexual partner who had not been granted the dignity of marriage.

[5] The writer focuses less on Deuteronomy 17:17 than on Deuteronomy 7:1–6 and Joshua 23:12–13. Solomon thought that he could use these women for political gain, but 11:2 says that he *"held fast to them in love"*. Like many men before and after him, he underestimated the power of love to weaken spiritual resolve.

11:3-4 to inform us that the man with a *hearing heart* from God now prefers to listen to his wives.

Note the progression in King Solomon's drift away from God. First, he pursues a policy of *religious tolerance*, deciding that it's only fair to let his foreign wives continue to worship their own gods. Soon this develops into a policy of *religious pluralism*. He builds shrines for their gods at the old Canaanite "high places" because it isn't easy to keep 1,000 women happy and a few foreign altars feel like a small price to pay for a happy life at home. Finally, this compromise morphs into full-blown *religious syncretism*. Solomon continues to offer sacrifices at the Temple of the Lord, but he decides to mix things up a little by also offering sacrifices at the temples of his wives. This is how spiritual backsliding always happens. It's like the game of *Kerplunk*. We don't pull out all of the coloured straws at once, but we fail to notice how much we are neglecting the lattice of friendship with God. Backsliding happens by degrees, long before the marbles actually fall.

We live in a very different world to Solomon. Our nations are not theocracies. We share our cities with people from so many different nations and backgrounds that religious tolerance is to be encouraged. However, we mustn't let that tolerance morph into religious pluralism – the idea that each religion is just a different pathway to the same God. The writer gives us a few details about what Solomon did in the name of religious pluralism that ought to horrify us. It may even make us hear *Kerplunk* in our own lives.

The writer tells us that Solomon followed Ashtoreth, the Canaanite fertility goddess, who called her worshippers to have sex with one another as an act of worship at her hilltop shrines. Joshua had destroyed them and they had only ever been rebuilt at moments of great national backsliding for Israel under the Judges. Solomon's decision to rebuild her "high places" is therefore far from innocent. It has far-reaching consequences for his kingdom. The Israelites would still be having sex with one another at those shrines 300 years later during the reign of King Josiah.[6] *Kerplunk*.

The writer also says that Solomon worshipped Molek and Chemosh. The Ammonites and Moabites had different names for him, but he was pretty much the same god. He told his worshippers that, if they wanted his favour, they would need to sacrifice their babies to him in the fire. If this doesn't appal you enough, note that the hill east of Jerusalem on which Solomon built this centre for child sacrifice was almost certainly the Mount of Olives.[7] He promoted this on the very hill where Jesus would sweat drops of blood for us in the Garden of Gethsemane and from which he would ascend back to heaven. No wonder the Lord appears to Solomon again to call time on his sinful reign. *Kerplunk*.

Solomon's first vision of the Lord was full of hope. His second was full of warning. His third, in 11:11–13, is full of judgment. God informs him that his son will lose control of the ten northern tribes that his own reign has abused.[8] This break-up of his kingdom will not take place in his own lifetime, but it will take place soon. Solomon will not enjoy the long life that the Lord offered him at Gibeon. He will die soon, aged only fifty-eight.

So read these verses slowly, and be warned about your own life. Listen to the sound of *Kerplunk*, *Kerplunk*, *Kerplunk*. It's game over for the man whose reign started out so well.

---

[6] 2 Kings 23:10–13. See also Judges 2:13 and 10:6, and 1 Samuel 7:3–4 and 12:10.

[7] This is why the Mount of Olives is referred to as the *Hill of Corruption* in 2 Kings 23:10–13.

[8] The tribe of Simeon had become absorbed within the tribe of Judah, so the "one" remaining tribe was effectively two.

Son of David
(1 Kings 11:14–43)

He rested with his ancestors and was buried in the
city of David his father. And Rehoboam his son
succeeded him as king.

(1 Kings 11:43)

The author of 1 and 2 Kings writes about the reigns of forty monarchs. He doesn't allocate space to them fairly. He devotes the first eleven chapters – roughly a quarter of his entire scroll – to the reign of the first king alone. This isn't just because he is fascinated with Solomon, as the promised son of David. It is also because he sees his reign as a chance to get all of his big themes on the table. He uses these first eleven chapters of Israel's history as an introduction to the overarching story behind the story.

He wants to reassure the Jewish exiles in Babylon that *the Lord is in complete control of history*. Adonijah may attempt to thwart his choice of king, but he will fail. Many obstacles may stand in the way of building his Temple, but it will be finished on time. The rulers of pagan nations may make big plans for their kingdoms, but they will all be forced to bow down in Jerusalem and proclaim that history belongs to the God of Israel.[1]

The writer also wants to reassure the Jewish exiles that *the Lord has a Messiah who will save them*. He foresaw their sin and exile from the very start, not just in the Law of Moses but even in the prayer that Solomon prayed at the dedication of his

---

[1] God's total sovereignty is a recurring theme in these chapters. See 1:29, 36–37, 47–48; 2:4, 15, 23–24, 27, 45; 3:5–9, 28; 5:4–7; 8:15, 20, 24–26, 56, 59, 66; 9:3–9; 10:9; 11:11, 14, 23 and 31.

Temple. In these eleven opening chapters, there are at least eight mentions of God's promise to preserve Solomon's house in order to raise up the promised "lamp of David".[2] However bleak things look in Babylon, the writer focuses our eyes on this promise of a true and better Son of David, the true Messiah, the Saviour of Israel.

The writer spends eleven chapters on the reign of Solomon to convince us that *only the Lord can provide this Messiah*. The Israelites looked for a wise man to lead them, considering it to be the currency of kings. The writer therefore tells us that Solomon is the wisest ruler that the world has ever seen – before recording how he destroyed his own kingdom through his utter folly! We can quote chapter and verse back to Solomon from his own writings as he takes each of his wrong turns in the road, but that's precisely the point. It's easier to write the book of Proverbs than to live it out, easier to write the Song of Songs than to remain faithful to one woman, and easier to write Ecclesiastes than to live for what really matters. The Hebrew words for *wise* and *wisdom* occur twenty-one times in these eleven chapters, but then never again in the rest of 1 and 2 Kings. The writer spends so long on the reign of Solomon to convince his readers that even the best man-made messiah will fail us.

In order to emphasize this, the writer ends his account of Solomon's reign by introducing us to three of his enemies, each of whom is a demonic parody of Solomon as messiah. The Hebrew word that he uses in 11:14 and 23 for adversary is *sātān*.

The first enemy is Hadad who fled to Egypt as a young prince when King David conquered the land of Edom. He looks more like the great deliverer Moses than Solomon does, living half in Pharaoh's palace until the time comes for him to say, "Let my people go!"[3] Hadad also foreshadows Jesus, who fled to Egypt as a child and about whom Hosea prophesied that *"out of Egypt I*

57

---

[2] 1 Kings 2:4; 8:20, 25; 9:5; 11:12–13, 32 and 36. See also 15:4, and 2 Kings 8:19; 19:34 and 20:6.

[3] His son's name Genubath means *Theft*. Hadad clearly bore a grudge against Israel for annexing Edom.

called my son".[4] Even the support Hadad receives from Pharaoh is meant to emphasize the stupidity of King Solomon. Solomon's sinful alliance with Egypt backfires on him spectacularly, since marrying into the 21st Dynasty made him a natural enemy for the pharaoh who had recently toppled it in order to establish the 22nd Dynasty.

Next is Rezon, the Aramean, who looks a lot more like David than Solomon does. He flees from his master, just as David did from King Saul, and he gathers a band of guerrilla fighters, just as David did at the cave of Adullam. The fact that Solomon sells horses and chariots to Rezon's Aramean army in 10:29 merely serves to emphasize his utter folly.

Jeroboam is even more dangerous than these first two enemies, and he too is the product of the king's stupidity. Solomon made him leader of his forced labour gangs, so he saw first-hand the unfair treatment of the ten northern tribes of Israel.[5] When the prophet Ahijah meets him on a country road and tells him that the Lord has chosen him to lead those ten northern tribes to break away from Judah, he needs no persuading.[6] He flees to Egypt, where the 22nd Dynasty is only too happy to help him devise plans to tear apart the twelve tribes of Israel.[7] Since the words for the prophet's *cloak* and for *Solomon* look very similar in Hebrew, the writer appears to be saying that, since Solomon's heart is divided towards the Lord, his kingdom is now about to be divided too.

The account of King Solomon's reign therefore ends with a final prophecy about the coming of the true and better Son of David. The writer wants the Jewish exiles in Babylon to

---

[4] Hosea 11:1 and Matthew 2:13–15.

[5] Jeroboam came from a city in Ephraim, one of the northern tribes, so he deeply sympathized with them. His name means *The People Will Fight Back*. As a widow's son, he had experienced hardship first-hand.

[6] Ahijah also came from a city of Ephraim. He prophesied throughout Solomon's reign (2 Chronicles 9:29) and spoke to Jeroboam on a lonely road because his message could be misinterpreted as treason.

[7] The tribe of Simeon had been absorbed into the tribe of Judah, so Solomon's "one" tribe was actually two.

stop grieving that their new masters have toppled Solomon's dynasty. It takes more than being born into the royal dynasty of Judah to make a man the true Son of David. Note the deliberate parallel between what the Lord says to Jeroboam through the prophet Ahijah and what he said to Solomon in his dream at Gibeon. The similarity is meant to emphasize that messiahs like them are two-a-penny. They can save no one. Solomon is not the true Son of David. He is not the Messiah we are looking for.[8]

The first eleven chapters of 1 Kings therefore end with the death of King Solomon. Although the Lord promised him long life if he followed him, he dies aged only fifty-eight, because the kindest thing the Lord can do for Israel is to remove him swiftly from the scene. Israel needs a better Son of David. One who doesn't just dispense wisdom, but who is wisdom personified. One who doesn't just quote from the Law of Moses, but who obeys it to the letter. One who doesn't just build a Temple, but who is the Temple and who makes us living stones within that Temple. One who doesn't have a divided heart towards the Lord that results in a divided kingdom, but who is willing to see his own body torn apart in order to reunite God's people as one nation under one Messiah.

That's the true hope of Israel, and the only way back to God for exiled sinners. That's the story behind the story in this first section of 1 Kings. It points us to a better Son of David.

---

[8] The book of Ecclesiastes strongly suggests that Solomon returned to the Lord before he died. While this is a glorious testimony to God's grace, the writer of 1 Kings doesn't mention it because he wants to keep our eyes focused on the bigger story behind the story.

1 Kings 12–16:

North and South

The Pampered Prince
(1 Kings 12:1–24)

> *"My father made your yoke heavy; I will make it even heavier. My father scourged you with whips; I will scourge you with scorpions."*
>
> (1 Kings 12:14)

To say that Prince Rehoboam had grown up pampered in the palace would be a bit like saying it gets chilly at the North Pole: a massive understatement.

He was the son of the richest man in the world. His father found it hard enough to remember the names of all his wives, let alone to discipline their sons, so his crown prince quickly learned to stroll around the palace and to ask his father's servants to give him anything he wanted. Instead of giving him the hands-on parenting that might have taught him to handle such power, Solomon wrote him a book to read instead. We still have it in our Bibles. The book of Proverbs reaches out to the pampered prince and tries to parent him from afar: *"My son, do not forget my teaching."*[1]

Sadly, the pampered prince needed more than a book to prepare him to rule over the twelve tribes of Israel. His name means *The People Have Grown Bigger*, because his subjects had prospered greatly under his father, but at the start of this second section of 1 and 2 Kings the pampered prince succeeds in making his kingdom a whole lot smaller.

In 12:1–4, Rehoboam travels to the city of Shechem in order to be crowned king. Neither David nor Solomon had been

---

[1] Proverbs 1–9 consists of twelve fatherly talks, the first eleven of which start with a passionate appeal to *"my son"*.

crowned king at Shechem (only the usurper Abimelek, in Judges 9:6) so the fact that he agrees to this is an indication of the growing power of the northern tribes. Shechem was a city in the centre of the kingdom, on the border of Ephraim and Manasseh, so Rehoboam arrives at the heartland of the ten tribes that his father has treated like second-class citizens. When he arrives at Shechem he discovers that his father's enemy Jeroboam has returned from Egypt to head up the ancient equivalent of a trade union delegation. It informs the pampered prince that he must agree to a condition before he can have his coronation. If he ends his father's unfair taxes and his labour gangs, then they will gladly be his subjects. If he refuses, then there's always Jeroboam. Rehoboam isn't the only messiah these ten tribes of Israel can choose.[2]

In 12:5–11, Rehoboam sends away the trade union delegation. He wants three days to consult the wise men who served his father. After all, didn't his father say something in that book he gave him? *"For lack of guidance a nation falls, but victory is won through many advisors."*[3] The wise men who served Solomon give him a very simple answer: become a servant-leader and these northern tribes will serve you gladly.[4] The answer that he gets from his companions as a pampered prince in the palace sounds a lot more macho: show them you're a tough guy, fight fire with fire, and stand up to the bully Jeroboam. Show these northerners which of you is the real messiah.

Did you notice that at no point does Rehoboam suggest going to the Temple to consult the Lord? Perhaps that's unsurprising, with a backslidden father and an Ammonite mother, but it's fatal for his kingdom all the same.[5] Rehoboam fails to grasp what David

---

[2] David and Solomon had always ruled the ten northern tribes on a different basis to the two southern tribes (2 Samuel 2:4 and 5:1–5, and 1 Kings 1:35 and 4:20). Their wisdom had made it work for the past seventy-three years.

[3] Proverbs 11:14. Rehoboam would have done well also to remember Proverbs 15:1 and 20:29.

[4] This is wise advice for any leader. See Mark 10:42–45 and 1 Peter 5:1–6.

[5] 1 Kings 14:21. The Ammonites were the baby-burning worshippers of Molek.

taught King Solomon at the start of his reign, that the Lord is the true King of Israel and that they were simply the earthly regents of his heavenly rule.[6] Instead of developing a hearing heart towards the Lord, Rehoboam listens to his pampered palace friends.[7]

In 12:12–15, Rehoboam gives his answer to the trade union delegation. Ignoring the advice of his father's wise men, he reads the riot act to the northern tribes. Solomon taxed their ten tribes unfairly, but now Rehoboam has a few extra taxes in mind for them. Solomon press-ganged them into his labour gangs, making them feel the sting of his whip on their shoulders, but now Rehoboam has so many plans to make them work harder that the sting of his whip on their backs will feel as painful as that of a scorpion.

In 12:16–17, this answer results in the instant disintegration of Solomon's kingdom. Spurred on by the words of Ahijah's prophecy to Jeroboam, the ten northern tribes renounce all loyalty to the kings of Judah. *"'What share do we have in David, what part in Jesse's son? To your tents, Israel! Look after your own house, David!'"*[8] The writer informs us in 12:15 that the Lord's hand of judgment is behind this, but it is nevertheless tragic.[9] One minute, a united Israel is conquering the world with its God-given wisdom. The next, it self-destructs as a result of its idolatry. Its slow descent into exile begins.

In 12:18–20, the pampered prince is still in denial about this. He sends out Adoniram, who is listed in 4:6 as the chief

---

[6] David was happy to be called *melek*, or *king*, but he also used that Hebrew word to hail the Lord as the true King of Israel (Psalm 5:2 and 145:1). He preferred to call himself the *nāgīd*, or *ruler*, of Israel (1 Kings 1:35).

[7] The Lord gave instruction to his regents in Deuteronomy 17:14–20 and 1 Samuel 10:25. Rehoboam was aged forty-one when he became king (14:21), but three times the Hebrew text of 12:8–14 refers to his immature friends as *boys*.

[8] This is a deliberate quote from the war cry of Sheba's rebellion about fifty years earlier (2 Samuel 20:1–2). The ten northern tribes are determined to succeed this time where their grandparents failed.

[9] This is the great story behind the story. Even though this looks like normal politics, all of these events have been ordained by the Sovereign Lord. The same is true of every event that we see on the daily news today.

project manager for all of King Solomon's forced labour gangs. If Jeroboam won't roll over and admit defeat, then Rehoboam reckons that this old-guard official who served his father will know how to enforce his royal decree. When a lynch mob of irate northerners stone Adoniram to death, Rehoboam suddenly grasps the seriousness of the situation. He flees by chariot to Jerusalem and has himself at least crowned king of Judah. Then he musters 180,000 soldiers and marches out to force the northern tribes to accept that he is now their new king as well.[10]

In 12:22–24, a prophet named Shemaiah intervenes. His name means either *Hears The Lord* or *Heard By The Lord*, so he brings words from heaven that the pampered prince was too foolish to seek before he gave his answer. Shemaiah declares that this northern rebellion is the Lord's doing. Since Solomon developed a divided heart towards him, the Lord has now left Solomon's son with the rump of a divided kingdom. The twelve tribes of Israel will never be reunited by force through one of the sinful messiahs who sit on David's throne, but only though their death and resurrection with the true Messiah.[11]

The first section of 1 and 2 Kings was all about *Father and Son*. As the pampered prince returns to his palace, it's pretty clear that this second section is going to be all about *North and South* instead.

---

[10] Benjamin was one of the ten northern tribes, but some of its towns on the border with Judah chose to remain loyal to Rehoboam. They were even willing to fight for him against their northern brothers.

[11] This is a major theme throughout 1 and 2 Kings. The writer wants his readers to view their exile in Babylon as a national "death" and to cry out to the Lord for "resurrection".

Antichrist
(1 Kings 12:25–33)

After seeking advice, the king made two golden calves.
(1 Kings 12:28)

The writer of 1 and 2 Kings was a prophet. It isn't too hard to spot that as he constantly points us to Jesus during the reign of Solomon. The Israelites hailed their early kings as their *messiah*, which is translated *christ* in Greek or *anointed one* in English, so prophetic pictures really don't get much easier to interpret than this.[1] It's why Jesus was hailed by many first-century Jews as the ultimate *Messiah*, the true Son of David who had finally arrived to save God's people.

From the moment that the kingdom of Israel is torn in two, however, nobody ever refers again to any king of Israel or Judah as a *messiah*. Most of the rulers we will meet from now on are far too flawed in character for the writer to use them to reflect much of Jesus in his book of prophecy.[2] Instead, he begins to use them as pictures of the many *false messiahs*, or *antichrists*, that try to divert our attention away from Jesus.[3]

---

[1] See 1 Samuel 2:10, 35; 12:3–5; 16:6; 24:6, 10, 26:9, 11, 16 and 23; 2 Samuel 1:14, 16, 19:21; 22:51 and 23:1, and Psalm 2:2, 18:50; 20:6; 84:9; 89:38, 51; 132:10 and 17.

[2] Saul, David and Solomon were actually pretty flawed too. The whole of 1 and 2 Kings can be seen as a follow-on from the curse that Samuel placed on Israel for having demanded a man-made king (1 Samuel 12).

[3] Don't be put off by the word "antichrist". Matthew 24:24; 2 Thessalonians 2:3; 1 John 2:18, 22 and 4:3, and 2 John 7 tell us there have been many antichrists, or men of lawlessness, throughout history. Daniel 11:36 says that their key trait is lusting to be king instead of God, culminating in a great antichrist toward the end.

Jeroboam, the first king of the ten northern tribes of Israel, is perhaps the most obvious example. He has everything going for him, including God's promise through the prophet Ahijah that his own dynasty will be as secure as David's if he follows God more faithfully than Solomon. Instead of doing so, he immediately sets about establishing a northern kingdom that is a satanic parody of all that David and Solomon have established in the southern kingdom. Jeroboam becomes an antichrist, a false messiah.

Having fortified Shechem to resist invasion from Judah in the south, and Peniel to resist invasion from the Arameans and Ammonites in the north and east, Jeroboam immediately severs all spiritual ties between his subjects and King Solomon's Temple.[4] He is nervous that, if the Israelites travel south across the border to worship the Lord in Jerusalem, they will be won back over to Rehoboam and will come home to murder him and rally the ten northern tribes back to David's dynasty.[5]

This leads to the worst decision of King Jeroboam's reign, which in turn leads to national decline and to the northern kingdom's early exile to Assyria.[6] He decides to make a golden calf, like the one that Aaron made in Exodus 32, and to create a rival temple of his own at Bethel, a city on the tribal border between Ephraim and Benjamin. Bethel means *House of God*, but we mustn't let that fool us. Jeroboam is repeating the sin that almost led to Israel's destruction at the foot of Mount Sinai. He also makes a second golden calf for another new temple at Dan, the northernmost city in his kingdom.[7] Note the deliberate

---

[4] He was only able to do this because Solomon's own sin had weakened Israel's devotion to his Temple.

[5] The Lord had initiated Jeroboam's reign, but he reveals in 12:27 that he knows deep down that he is a usurper of David's dynasty. He never asks the Lord's priests to anoint him with oil and to crown him king.

[6] This sin of Jeroboam is cited over twenty times in 1 and 2 Kings as one of the major reasons for Israel's exile. It mirrors many citations of David's godliness as one of the major reasons why Judah survived.

[7] Having told the Israelites that Jerusalem was too far for worshippers to travel, he now builds a temple that is even further away for most of them! Dan already had a history of idolatry (Judges 18:27–31).

echo of Aaron's words in Exodus 32:4 when he deceives his subjects that *"It is too much for you to go up to Jerusalem. Here are your gods, Israel, who brought you up out of Egypt."*[8] His blasphemy serves as a prophetic picture of the many antichrists today, anybody who attempts to replace the real Jesus with a fake Jesus of their own.[9]

In English, the prefix *anti-* means *opposed to* (as in anti-ageing, anti-aircraft, anti-clockwise and anti-social), but in Greek *anti-* tends to mean *instead of.* One example of this is in Matthew 20:28, where Jesus says that he has come to give his life as a ransom *instead of* many. The New Testament warnings to be on our guard against antichrists are therefore not calling us to look out for spooky people, like Damien in the movie *The Omen*, but for normal people who sound very plausible in their reinterpretations of Jesus. Their slight adjustments to his message and to the meaning of his death and resurrection often make their message very attractive, but they are as dangerous as King Jeroboam of Israel. They are the false teachers that Paul warns us to be on our guard against in 2 Corinthians 11:3–4: *"I am afraid that just as Eve was deceived by the snake's cunning, your minds may somehow be led astray from your sincere and pure devotion to Christ. For if someone comes to you and preaches a Jesus other than the Jesus we preached ... you put up with it easily enough."* The writer of 1 Kings issues us a similar warning here.

The people of the northern kingdom swallow the religion of their false messiah hook, line and sinker. King Solomon was so inattentive to the Law of the Moses in his later years that they don't even notice how much these golden calves fly in the face of all that Moses said. When King Jeroboam builds additional shrines at the Canaanite "high places" of Israel, they simply

---

[8] *'Elōhīm* is a Hebrew plural noun, which can either refer to false *gods* or to the real *God*. It is therefore ambiguous in 1 Kings 12:28, as in Exodus 32:1–4. Jeroboam might be claiming that his golden calves are images of the Lord.

[9] "It is too much for you" is always the cry of the compromiser – yet their compromises always end up costing their followers far more than outright obedience to the Lord.

shrug their shoulders. King Solomon did the same. When he creates a new priesthood for Israel, which doesn't have anything to do with Aaron's tribe of Levi, and when he replaces the Day of Atonement at the Lord's Temple each September with his own satanic parody one month later in October, they happily comply.[10] It doesn't matter to them that the date is *"a month of his own choosing"*. Like preachers today who explain away sections of the Bible, Solomon had fatally eroded Israel's faith in God's Word. People follow a fake Jesus whenever leaders allow them to lose sight of the real one.[11]

So don't skim over these verses, as if they were written down for somebody other than you or me. They serve as a prophetic warning that the Devil still has many a fake Jesus to foist on unsuspecting people in our own day. That's why the New Testament warns us to be on our guard against his false messiahs, his antichrists, his servants who want to keep the world away from the real Jesus by filling their gaze with phoney ones instead.

It warns us: *"Who is the liar? It is whoever denies that Jesus is the Christ. Such a person is the antichrist." "I say this because many deceivers, who do not acknowledge Jesus Christ as coming in the flesh, have gone out into the world. Any such person is the deceiver and the antichrist."*[12]

---

[10] *Yom Kippur*, the Day of Atonement, was a crucial festival because it pointed to the future death of Jesus on the cross. Jeroboam's parody festival was on the wrong date, in the wrong place, with the wrong priest and altar. Our fake Jesuses may look similar to the real one, but they are powerless to save anyone.

[11] The writer says literally in 12:31 that Jeroboam appointed priests *"from the dross of the people"*. It is small wonder that the real priests and their followers emigrated south to worship the Lord with the people of Judah (2 Chronicles 11:13–17). Devout Christians should still leave churches that preach a fake Jesus today.

[12] 1 John 2:22 and 2 John 7. Don't let *The Omen* rob you of understanding what these verses actually mean.

The Prophet
(1 Kings 13:1–34)

By the word of the Lord a man of God came from
Judah to Bethel, as Jeroboam was standing by the
altar.

(1 Kings 13:1)

OK. Let's face it. This is the weirdest chapter in the whole of 1 and 2 Kings, and that's really saying something. These are books in which people hail a bronze snake as their god, a man gets ravens to do his shopping for him, and another man makes an axe-head float on water. Weird as those things may sound, what happens in this chapter is even weirder. Let me run through it slowly, attempting to explain the story behind the story.

In 13:1–6, a prophet from Judah crosses the border to confront King Jeroboam of Israel with the seriousness of his sin. Up until this moment, prophets have already played a significant part in the story. It was Nathan who foiled Adonijah's rebellion and who anointed Solomon with oil as God's chosen messiah. It was Ahijah who incited Jeroboam to lead the ten northern tribes in rebellion against Solomon's son by putting God-given ideas into his head on a lonely country road. It was Shemaiah who prevented Rehoboam from marching out to fight him in battle. But the arrival of this fourth prophet speaks of a much bigger role that the prophets now begin to play in the story. As the kings start to slacken in their devotion to the Lord, it begins to feel quite often as though the prophets are the real rulers of Israel and Judah.[1]

---

[1] Nathan means *Gift of God*, Ahijah means *The Lord is My Brother*, and Shemaiah means *Hears The Lord* or *Heard By The Lord*. Even these men's names convey something of their divine authority to rule.

We do not know the name of the prophet who confronts King Jeroboam at Bethel. Jewish tradition suggests that he is Iddo, the prophet mentioned in 2 Chronicles 9:29. All we can say for sure is that, whoever he was, he displayed remarkable courage, given that ancient rulers could arrest and execute troublesome visitors at whim. He also possessed a staggering insight into the future, since King Josiah of Judah would not be born until 648 BC, over 250 years later, yet the prophet predicts his name and what he is going to do.[2] The prophet announces to Israel that a judgment day is coming when the Lord will overthrow its fake messiahs:

> *'Altar, altar! This is what the Lord says: "A son named Josiah will be born to the house of David. On you he will sacrifice the priests of the high places who make offerings here, and human bones will be burned on you."'*[3]

King Jeroboam has heard enough. This type of prophecy is the very reason why he stopped his subjects going south across the border to worship at the Temple of the Lord. He stretches out his arm to indicate that his bodyguards should arrest the man of God, but he is suddenly arrested himself by two miracles. First, his outstretched arm is paralysed, then the stone altar splits in two, just as the man of God said it would.[4] He pleads for the prophet to heal his arm and to come back to his palace for dinner. He gets his healing but not his house

71

---

[2] Two hundred and fifty years is a long time. God was extraordinarily patient with the sinful northern kingdom.

[3] 1 Kings 13:2. He prophesies against "the altar" rather than against Jeroboam, because this was a confrontation between the Temple of the Lord and this false temple. It would long outlast the man who built it. The splitting of the altar mirrors Moses breaking his stone tablets when he saw Aaron's golden calf in Exodus 32:19–20.

[4] The Hebrew word that is used for the altar *splitting* is *qāra'*, which means literally *to tear*. It is an odd word to use for rock, but it is the same word that was used in 11:30. Because of his idolatry, the ten tribes that were *torn* from Solomon will be torn from him too, and the hand that received the kingdom will wither.

guest. The prophet declares that the Lord has commanded him to return home without eating or drinking anything in the sinful northern kingdom.

Now things get weirder. An old has-been prophet of God lives at Bethel. He hasn't dared to confront King Jeroboam's sin himself, so it seems he hopes to gain back some of his old anointing by inviting the younger prophet back for dinner at his home. Again, the man protests that he must cross back over the border without polluting himself with any food or drink in the northern kingdom. The old prophet is desperate, so he tells a lie. He pretends that an angel has appeared to him with new instructions. Instead of checking with God for himself, the young man foolishly takes him at his word.[5]

By the time they finish dinner, the old has-been prophet has indeed received back some of his old anointing, but not quite in the way that he expected. He prophesies against himself, telling the man of God from Judah that he is as good as dead for having listened to him. Sure enough, when the young man gets on his donkey to head back over the border he is killed by a lion on the road. The lion does not attack the donkey. Both animals stand as guard over the corpse until the old has-been prophet hears the news, comes to retrieve it and then buries it in his own tomb. That's it. I warned you that the story was weird. But since the writer devotes a whole chapter to it, let me try to help you understand why.

The first clue is that he uses virtually no names in this entire chapter. Jeroboam is mentioned four times, but most of the time he is simply called "the king". The prophet from Judah and the old has-been prophet from Bethel are never named. They are simply called "the man of God" and "the prophet" to distinguish them from one another. That's a clue that this whole chapter is meant to act as a prophetic foreshadowing of what will happen to the northern and southern kingdoms over the

---

[5] We are often more in danger when we rest than when we are busy serving God, and more in danger from the flattery of our so-called friends than from the obvious hostility of our enemies.

next 350 years. Judah will at first keep itself pure, confronting Israel with its sins. Israel will refuse to listen (the king asks for his arm to be healed but not for any help to destroy his idols and to lead his nation back to God) and eventually its deception will spread to Judah and end up destroying the southern kingdom too.[6] This is symbolized by "the man of God" eating and drinking with "the prophet", and accepting a ride on his donkey.

Now for the good news. The Lord will miraculously preserve what is left of Judah after it is destroyed by the Babylonian lion. He will protect its survivors and reunite them with the remnant of Israel while they are away in exile. This is symbolized by "the man of God" and "the prophet" being buried as brothers side by side in the same grave. Then, just as the young prophet from Judah received the punishment that the old prophet from Israel deserved, a Saviour from Judah will come to atone for the sin of both kingdoms and to raise them both out of the grave as one new nation. Unlike the prophet from Judah, Jesus will resist the Devil's temptation to eat bread when hungry after forty days of fasting in the desert. He will be the truly sinless Saviour who dies and is buried in another man's grave in order to grant people resurrection from the dead.

So perhaps this chapter isn't quite so weird after all. It gives us the complete history of Israel and Judah in a single story. It warns us that the penalty for our sin is always death (Genesis 2:17) and that we therefore mustn't fool ourselves that we can save ourselves by pulling our act together. Like Israel and Judah, our only hope lies in crying out to the one who can save us from the death that we deserve – to Jesus, the God of resurrection.

---

[6] In 13:6, Jeroboam continues to refer to *"the Lord **your** God"*. He is no closer to repentance than before.

Final Warning
(1 Kings 14:1–20)

"Go, tell Jeroboam that this is what the Lord, the God of Israel, says."

(1 Kings 14:7)

At 11.40 p.m. on Sunday 14th April 1912, the RMS *Titanic* hit an iceberg. Two hours and forty minutes later, the great ship sank under the waves, killing everyone who was still on board. Most of the attention since that fateful night has asked how such a state-of-the-art vessel could have sunk on its maiden voyage, but I'm more fascinated with the fact it sank so slowly and that many of the passengers who died ignored repeated warnings.

Twenty-five minutes after hitting the iceberg, the captain of the *Titanic* sent men to knock on all the cabin doors. Most of the passengers protested loudly. When forced to stand on deck, a few of them spotted a chunk of ice and began to play a football game. By now, almost 14,000 tons of water had entered the ship, and disaster was inevitable, but many of the passengers refused to board the lifeboats. John Jacob Astor, the richest man on board, complained loudly: *"We are safer here than in that little boat!"* Some of the lifeboats were lowered less than a third full. Most of them were still half-empty when the repeated warnings stopped, and the *Titanic* disappeared under the waves.

Jeroboam's dynasty is sinking fast, but what really strikes us in these verses is how patient God is towards him. The Lord had plucked him from obscurity and had catapulted him onto Israel's throne, so we might have expected a little bit of gratitude. Instead, Jeroboam bit the hand that fed him. In view of his fake gods, his fake temples, his fake priests and his fake festivals, it really is remarkable that the Lord didn't strike him down before the prophet from Judah confronted him in chapter 13. The Lord issued him a verbal warning through the prophet, a physical warning through his paralysed arm, and a third warning when he split the altar apart right before his eyes.[1] Yet even after he was healed by the prophet, Jeroboam persisted in his sin. It was time for him to receive a final warning from the Lord.

When Jeroboam's son falls ill, the alarm bells start ringing. Jeroboam was promised that his dynasty would last forever if he obeyed the Lord, so the sight of his heir in bed with a fatal disease is meant to serve as a violent wake-up call. The king decides he has to do something. He tells his wife to disguise herself and to seek out the prophet Ahijah, who created their dynasty in the first place by tearing up his cloak and giving ten pieces to Jeroboam on a country road. Taking gifts from the royal larder, she scurries the seventeen miles south to the prophet's house at Shiloh to ask him to save their dynasty.

As soon as she arrives, the alarm bells start ringing louder. The prophet Ahijah is blind but he is able see straight through her disguise.[2] She has done all of the travelling yet he is so in control of events that he tells her, *"I have been sent to you with bad news"*! Her decision to visit him comes as the direct result of his prayers. She can keep her gifts, because Ahijah is not for hire. Nothing will induce him to dilute his message. The Lord has given him a final warning for the house of Jeroboam.

The prophet Ahijah founded Jeroboam's dynasty, and now the Lord has sent him to call time on the dynasty. Because Jeroboam has failed to recognize Yahweh as *"the Lord, the God of Israel"* – the true ruler of the northern kingdom who can refer to the ten breakaway tribes as *"my people Israel"* – Jeroboam's son is as good as dead. Since Jeroboam has been more disobedient than King Solomon, King David, or even King Saul, now he is

---

[1] We are told in 2 Chronicles 13:1–18 that the Lord also gave him another warning through defeat in battle.

[2] The prophet Ahijah's name means *The Lord Is My Brother*. Prince Abijah's means *The Lord Is My Father*.

about to join them in the grave along with every other male in his family. *"The Lord has spoken!"*[3]

As for the crown prince Abijah, he will be the first of the family to die, the very moment that his mother steps back over the threshold of the royal palace at Tirzah.[4] If his parents believe that they can manipulate Ahijah into healing him, like the prophet who had healed the king's arm, then they are very wrong. The only thing that this trip has accomplished is to ensure that the boy's mother never sees her son alive again.[5] This is not because the crown prince is more sinful than the rest of his family. Quite the contrary. He is the best of the bad bunch. His early death is intended as a blessing, because it means his corpse will receive a royal burial.[6] Those who survive him in his family will all die violently, without any loved ones left to bury them. Those who die in the city will be eaten by street dogs; those who die in the country will be eaten by wild birds.[7]

Jeroboam has received his final warning, but before his wife leaves, the prophet Ahijah also starts to sound a new warning bell over the northern kingdom as a whole.[8] He predicts that the idols at Bethel and Dan will eventually cause the destruction and exile of Israel. The ten northern tribes will lose their share

---

[3] 1 Kings 14:11.

[4] This is a deliberate inversion of the Passover. Jeroboam has rejected the blood of the Lamb, so his firstborn son will die. His nation will then be led out of the Promised Land and into a land of slavery.

[5] Since God judges us based on a mixture of our sin and our revelation of its consequences (Matthew 10:14–15 and 11:20–24), a prophet's visit also serves the cause of justice. That's why God still sends us to share the Gospel with people who refuse to listen to us. Despite their refusal to listen, justice demands that they hear.

[6] Don't blame God when bad things happen. They may be blessings in disguise. See Isaiah 57:1–2.

[7] We can sense God's anger in 14:10 by the way in which he likens Jeroboam's dynasty to a pile of manure and the men of his dynasty to street dogs – literally, *"those who urinate against a wall"*.

[8] The prophet's words at the end of 14:14 can be translated, *"This is the day. What? Yes, even now!"* It appears that the Lord had only held up his destruction for the sake of Jeroboam's slightly less sinful son.

in the Promised Land and will be taken as captives to a land east of the River Euphrates. It was pretty obvious to the Jewish exiles in Babylon that this refers to Assyria, but it is also meant to remind us of the land where God first called Abraham to follow him. Since Israel has rejected its God and its place in his story, he will take them back to the start to begin all over again.

This moment marks a turning point for Jeroboam's wife and dynasty. Will she stay at the prophet's house and implore him to help her to repent of her own sins? Will she send messengers back to the palace and call Jeroboam down to Shiloh so that they can both ask for help in leading the northern kingdom back to the Lord? In a word, no.[9] She heads straight home to Tirzah, knowing full well that her son will die the moment she steps over the threshold of the palace. She ignores her final warning.

So does Jeroboam. He bounces back after the funeral, figuring that he has another son who can take the crown prince's empty throne instead. Like a passenger on the *Titanic*, he ignores his final warning, but his ship is sinking fast. His dynasty will only outlast him by a year. The good ship *Jeroboam* is already disappearing under the waves.[10]

---

[9] She remains silent throughout. Her silent resignation is as sinful as her husband's noisy rebellion.

[10] The writer does not say how Jeroboam died, but 2 Chronicles 13:20 says that *"The Lord struck him down."*

Dumb And Dumber
(1 Kings 14:21–15:24)

Shishak king of Egypt ... took everything, including all the gold shields Solomon had made. So King Rehoboam made bronze shields to replace them.

(1 Kings 14:26–27)

Leo Tolstoy was unimpressed with the stupidity he saw in nineteenth-century Russia. The writer of *War and Peace* complained that:

The most difficult subjects can be explained to the most slow-witted man if he has not formed any idea of them already; but the simplest thing cannot be made clear to the most intelligent man if he is firmly persuaded that he knows already, without a shadow of doubt, what is laid before him.[1]

Rehoboam wasn't the most intelligent man. He was the pampered prince whose foolishness had lost him the bulk of his kingdom within days of coming to the throne. Even so, when we pick back up the account of his reign, we might have expected him to learn a little faster. Sadly, he was convinced he knew all of the answers already.

Common sense ought to have taught him to demolish the sinful shrines that his father Solomon had built at the old Canaanite "high places" throughout Judah. They were one of the reasons why the ten northern tribes had stopped worshipping at the Lord's Temple in Jerusalem, and therefore one of the reasons

---

[1] Tolstoy says this in his book *The Kingdom of God Is Within You* (1894).

they found it easy to break away from his rule. Even now, the Temple remained his best hope of winning those ten tribes back to the dynasty of David. The writer points this out for us in 14:21, referring to Jerusalem as *"the city the Lord had chosen out of all the tribes of Israel in which to put his Name"*. Nevertheless, no doubt spurred on by his Ammonite mother, Rehoboam promoted worship at the "high places" even more than his father had before him. Rather than simply encouraging worshippers to have sex with one another around the altars of their fertility goddesses, he allowed an army of male prostitutes to form so that people could choose to have gay sex at the "high places" too.

When Pharaoh Shishak finally breaks into the city, he forces Rehoboam to return to the Temple. Being forced to inspect how much gold had been plundered from the Temple and from the Palace of the Forest of Lebanon ought to have driven Rehoboam to his knees before the Lord. Instead, the writer tells us, he learned nothing from his failures. Shishak *"took everything, including all the gold shields Solomon had made. So King Rehoboam made bronze shields to replace them."*[2] Rehoboam simply picked himself up and carried on.

Rehoboam dies aged fifty-eight, the same age as his father, and he is succeeded by his son in 15:1-8. If Rehoboam is dumb, then Abijah is dumber. He does nothing to reverse his father's policy of promoting worship at the "high places", and the three years of his short reign are dominated by constant war with the ten northern tribes. King Abijah proves the truth of Julius Caesar's observation that *"men willingly believe what they wish to be true"*.[3] Instead of humbling himself under God's judgment, he treats it as a reason to keep on sinning. He blames the hardships of his reign on the Lord.[4]

That's why the writer suddenly starts talking about David in 15:3-5. He expects us to be appalled by the two reigns of the

DUMB AND DUMBER (1 KINGS 14:21-15:24)

79

---

[2] See 10:16-17.

[3] He says this in his *Gallic Wars* (3.18).

[4] Rehoboam had foolishly married a daughter of David's son Absalom (15:2). She was just like her father, leading astray her son Abijah and needing to be dealt with firmly by her grandson Asa (15:13).

southern kingdom's *Dumb and Dumber*. He expects us to start longing for a Saviour who will teach these people how to know God. He doesn't mention David as the solution. He pinpoints David's adultery with Uriah's wife to remind us that David could be pretty dumb at times too. Instead, his focus in these verses is on the Lamp of David, on the Son of David, on the true Messiah who will one day come to save God's sinful people. King Abijah dies young as a reminder of how much we need a better Son of David to step quickly onto the scene.

King Asa ruled from 910–869 BC. That's one year longer than either David or Solomon, and at first his reign looks very promising. He *"did what was right in the eyes of the Lord, as his father David had done."* He removed the idols from the "high places" of Judah and he expelled the shrine-prostitutes from the land.[5] When his grandmother Maakah, the widow of Rehoboam, attempted to defy him in this, he cut down her Asherah pole and ended her influence within the royal family.[6] As a result of this, his kingdom prospered greatly.[7] We are even told in 2 Chronicles 14 that he defeated a massive Egyptian army.[8]

Sadly, in the final years of his life, King Asa starts acting like *Dumb and Dumber* too. The writer is light on detail here, so we need to fill in some of the gaps with the longer account in 2 Chronicles, but it appears that when Asa grew older and more experienced, he began to rely on his own strength instead of on the Lord. When the king of Israel blockades his northern border, King Asa rushes to the Temple, not to pray the type of prayer

---

[5] The word for *"shrine-prostitute"* in 15:12 is the same as in 14:24, but a masculine plural in Hebrew can refer to a mixed group of men and women. King Asa probably outlawed shrine-prostitutes altogether.

[6] Asherah means *Happiness* in Hebrew, and she was another Canaanite fertility goddess. The Kidron Valley where Asa burned the Asherah pole is the valley between Jerusalem and the Mount of Olives.

[7] 2 Chronicles 15:9 says that a large number of devout Israelites emigrated south from the backslidden north in order to worship the Lord with King Asa. This may be why their king eventually blockaded the border.

[8] 2 Chronicles 14:2–16:14 devotes forty-seven verses to the reign of Asa, compared to only sixteen verses in 1 Kings. The writer of 1 Kings only includes those details that will help his readers to see the story behind the story.

suggested by Solomon for times of national crisis in chapter 8, but to plunder its silver and gold in an attempt to buy the help of the King of Aram. When the Lord strikes him down with a painful disease for the final few years of his life, instead of repenting, he refuses to humble himself and to ask the Lord to heal him.[9]

The writer's message is clear. Only the Son of David can save God's people, but that clearly isn't Rehoboam or Abijah, the southern kingdom's *Dumb and Dumber*. Nor is it Asa, whose name means *Healer* but who ultimately proves too stubborn to bring healing to his own body, let alone to his kingdom. None of these three kings is the Messiah we are looking for. The story behind the story is that we need a far better Son of David.

---

[9] We do not know what this excruciating disease was, but this Hebrew word for *"feet"* is often used as a euphemism for *"genitals"* in the Old Testament (see Isaiah 7:20).

Game Of Thrones
(1 Kings 15:25 – 16:34)

As soon as he began to reign and was seated on the throne, he killed off Baasha's whole family.

(1 Kings 16:11)

You have to stay pretty wide awake to keep up with the plot in the TV series *Game of Thrones*. The balance of power is constantly shifting between rival rulers, and no sooner do you get to know one than you see them brutally murdered. It doesn't make for nice viewing, and nor does the history of the northern kingdom of Israel. In these verses, we see Israel's history in miniature. This is the Bible's *Game of Thrones*.

The first thing we notice is the utter *instability* of the northern kingdom. After Solomon's death, the kingdom of Judah is ruled by nineteen kings from a single dynasty for almost 350 years. In contrast, the kingdom of Israel is ruled by nineteen kings from nine separate dynasties for a mere 200 years.[1] Take a look at the table below.

Can you see what I mean about *Game of Thrones*? The history of the northern kingdom is pretty shocking. In the time it takes Judah to have three kings, Israel notches up seven kings from four separate dynasties! That's what happens when leaders refuse to submit to the Lord. You can be pretty sure that those who won't defer to God won't defer to anybody else either! The northern kingdom is a bloodbath of *instability*.

The second thing we notice is the utter sinfulness of the northern kingdom. Many of the kings of Judah act very sinfully

---

[1] Godly kings rule on average for thirty-three years, sinful kings for only eleven years. Sin is therefore self-harm.

UNITED MONARCHY	David (1010–970 BC)
	Solomon (970–930 BC)

JUDAH		ISRAEL	
Rehoboam (930–913 BC)		Jeroboam I (930–909 BC)	
Abijah (913–910 BC)		Nadab (909–908 BC)	
Asa (910–869 BC)		Baasha (908–886 BC)	
		Elah (886–885 BC)	
		Zimri (885 BC)	
		Omri (885–874 BC)	
		Ahab (874–853 BC)	

but at least a few of them decide to follow the Lord. In contrast, not a single northern king ever follows him. It is wall-to-wall rebellion. We can even see this in the way the writer uses subtly different formulae when he summarizes the reigns of the kings of Judah and the kings of Israel. Spot the difference:

JUDAH	ISRAEL
Date of rule	Date of rule
Length of reign	Length of reign
Obedient or sinful?	Definitely sinful
Name of mother	Name of father
Benchmark is David	Benchmark is Jeroboam
Additional sources	Additional sources
Death and burial	Death
Son succeeds	Son or usurper?

These twin themes of instability and sinfulness loom large in the accounts of the six kings in these verses. Nadab means *Generous* in Hebrew, but 15:25–32 reveals that the only lavish thing about him is his sin. He is assassinated by one of his generals while besieging a Philistine city. This general then declares himself king, slaughtering every male in Jeroboam's dynasty, just as the prophet Ahijah predicted he would. The general's name is Baasha which means *Wicked*, and in 15:33–16:7 he lives up to his name. The Lord therefore sends the prophet Jehu to confront him and to curse him in the same way that Ahijah cursed Jeroboam, reminding Baasha that the ten northern tribes are *"my people Israel"* and that he has failed in his calling to rule them as a godly regent for the Lord.[2] The Lord swears that he will wipe out every male in Israel's second dynasty too.[3]

In 16:8–14, that bloodbath takes place during the short-lived reign of Baasha's son Elah, whose name means *Oak Tree* but who is a spiritual weakling. He is caught drunk by one of his generals and assassinated, then the general proceeds to murder his whole family. Zimri means *My Music*, but the general's seven-day reign in 16:15–20 is a cacophony of violence. He barely has time to wipe the blood off his sword before he discovers that other generals have designs on the throne of Israel too.[4] Besieged by his enemies in Tirzah, he burns the royal palace down over his own head rather than allow his rivals to enjoy it. His death in the fire serves as a metaphor for the entire history of the northern kingdom. It has been caught up in an out-of-control orgy of self-destruction.

In 16:21–28, the victorious general puts out the flames to establish the fourth dynasty of Israel. Omri spends the first five years of his reign fighting off another rival general, whose name Tibni means *Intelligent* but who doesn't have the brains to outwit Omri. We know from historical sources outside the Bible that Omri was one of the most powerful rulers of the northern kingdom, but you would hardly know it from these scant verses.[5] The writer is pretty unimpressed with a king whose name means *Pupil of the Lord* but who acts as if he knows better than Yahweh. The writer tells us that he relocated his royal palace

---

[2] Jehu means *The Lord Is the One*, and his father had been a prophet under Asa (2 Chronicles 16:7–10). He uses the Hebrew word *nāgīd* in 16:2 to remind Baasha that he is only the earthly *ruler* for the true King of Israel.

[3] We are told in 15:16–22 that Baasha lost Galilee and the north to the Arameans – in other words, the false temple at Dan was destroyed. Kinnereth means *Harp-Shaped* and was the old name for the Sea of Galilee. 2 Chronicles 15:9 says that under Baasha many devout northerners emigrated south to worship the Lord.

[4] The Israelites are still besieging the Philistine city of Gibbethon in 16:15, twenty-three years after 15:27! Let's learn from this. When the people of God quarrel, the enemies of God are always granted a reprieve.

[5] For example, the *Black Obelisk of Shalmaneser III* still refers to Jehu many decades later as *"Jehu son of Omri"*.

away from the ashes of Tirzah to a brand new capital city named Samaria, but he tells us little else about Omri.[6] Successful in the world's eyes, the writer makes it clear to us that Omri failed when it came to the story behind the story.

In 16:29–34, we are told about the last of these six northern kings. Ahab means *My Father Is My Brother* – that is, *My Close Friend* – and he is definitely a chip off the old block. Ahab takes Omri's sin to a whole new level by marrying a Canaanite princess who incites him to promote Baal and Asherah worship right across the northern kingdom. He even laughs at the curse in Joshua 6:26 that anyone who rebuilt the idolatrous Canaanite city of Jericho would do so at the cost of two of his sons. He grants a building permit to Hiel of Bethel, and sure enough, the final victims in these verses are his two sons.

But it isn't all bad in these verses. The writer of 2 Chronicles pretty much ignores the monarchs of the northern kingdom, focusing exclusively on the kings of Judah, but the writer of 1 and 2 Kings gives equal attention to events on both sides of the border because he wants this mayhem to make us cry out for a better King of Israel. The mention of Jericho at the end of these verses reminds us that the King has now arrived, healing blind men and transforming the life of a tax collector in that sinful city. Israel's *Game of Thrones* would not go on forever. A far better King of Israel would come.[7]

---

[6] Tirzah means *Delightful*, and it was a stunningly beautiful city (Song of Songs 6:4). Samaria was named after Shemer but, conveniently for a city built on a high hilltop, its name also meant *Watch Station*.

[7] See Matthew 20:29–34 and Luke 18:35–19:10.

1 Kings 17 – 2 Kings 8:

Rebels and Revival

Israel's True King
(1 Kings 17:1–6)

"As the Lord, the God of Israel, lives, whom I serve, there will be neither dew nor rain in the next few years except at my word."

(1 Kings 17:1)

The first section of 1 and 2 Kings was all about King Solomon. The second section was all about the growing rift between the north and south. In the third section, the conflict shifts from war between rulers of Israel and the rulers of Judah to war between the false kings and the true King of Israel. This third section is all about the rebel kings of Israel and the prophets who try to bring about national revival. These first six verses introduce us to the two primary combatants in this battle for the souls of the northern kingdom.

On one side, we have Ahab, the quintessential antichrist, a fake messiah, the usurping son of a usurper, the worst man who ever sat on the throne of Israel. After being told in 16:25 that Omri sinned more than any other northern king before him, we are then told in 16:30 that his son Ahab sinned even more than he did! A lot of his sinfulness flowed from his disastrous marriage to Jezebel, the daughter of a Canaanite priest who had murdered the King of Tyre and muscled his way onto the throne, spending the thirty-two years of his reign promoting his gods throughout Phoenicia. When Jezebel moved south to marry King Ahab, she imported the proselytizing mission of her pagan father.[1]

---

[1] The first-century Jewish historian Josephus expands on 16:31 to tell us this in *Against Apion* (1.18).

Baal was the Canaanite storm-god. His name means *Lord* and he had long attempted to supplant the place of Yahweh in the hearts of his people. Baal is mentioned over forty times in Joshua and Judges, but Ahab and Jezebel take things to a whole new level. Knowing that Baal is being worshipped alongside Asherah, one of the Canaanite fertility goddesses, at the "high places" of Israel, they build a splendid temple for them both right at the heart of their new capital city Samaria. They do so to proclaim that the northern throne is now as intrinsically linked to the worship of Baal and Asherah as the southern throne is to the worship of Yahweh.[2] Israel's out-of-town worship centres have now moved downtown. They even encourage the rebuilding of Jericho, which means *Moon City* and which was a famous centre for Canaanite idolatry before the days of Joshua.

Against the mighty house of Ahab stands a solitary prophet named Elijah. He is outnumbered and he also has a host of other things stacked against him. He comes from Tishbe, a town on the east side of the River Jordan, not from the devout south or from the heartland of Israel. Nor is he from any of Israel's leading families. He is such a nobody that the writer doesn't even bother to tell us his father's name. Nevertheless, it's pretty obvious in these verses that Elijah is the strongman on the battlefield. His name means *The Lord Is God* and he has burst onto the scene to call a nation back to the true King of Israel. He is a one-man revival team.

In 17:1, Elijah speaks only a single sentence to King Ahab, but it shakes the entire northern kingdom. First, he declares that Yahweh is *"the Lord, the God of Israel"*. Ahab has built a temple for Baal at the heart of his capital, but he can't change the fact that his idol isn't Israel's true God. Second, Elijah proclaims that the Lord sits on the true throne of Israel. He uses the language of a palace servant when he boasts literally that the Lord is the God *"before whom I stand"*.[3] Third, Elijah declares that Yahweh is

---

[2] An Asherah *pole* was a sacred pillar that was often erected next to an altar of Baal.

[3] Author's own translation (17:1).

the real storm-god. The main thing that the worshippers of Baal expected their idol to do for them was to send them rain, so the prophet announces that there will be no more rain throughout the land of Israel until he personally commands it in the name of the Lord. There will not even be any dew in the morning. Not until Israel turns back to the real storm-god.

After this one sentence, quick as a flash, Elijah is gone. He knows better than to linger with a king and queen who are prepared to kill their own children if that is what it takes to promote their foul religion throughout the land.[4] The Lord tells Elijah to hide in the Kerith Ravine.[5] We do not know its precise location, but the word means *Cutting* in Hebrew and it was probably a minor tributary of the River Jordan. It may have been one of Elijah's childhood haunts on the east bank, a much safer place for him than Samaria.

Israel begins to suffer terrible thirst, but meanwhile the prophet enjoys the rich blessings of the Lord. We are told in Job 38:41 and Psalm 147:9 that the Lord feeds the ravens, so the Lord now commands the ravens to act as his middlemen to feed Elijah.[6] They serve him bread and meat for breakfast every morning and bread and meat for dinner every evening, all washed down with as much water as he wants from the Kerith stream.

Elijah knows that Yahweh is Israel's true King, so he gladly falls into line with this bizarre strategy.[7] He doesn't rely on his own human logic. He doesn't embark on a preaching tour

---

[4] Child sacrifice was normally associated with Molek and Chemosh, but Jeremiah 19:5 says that some of the most devout worshippers of Baal sacrificed their children too.

[5] Elijah only heard the Lord a second time after he had obeyed his first command. God expects us to act on the revelation we already have before he gives us more. This may be why we hear God less ourselves.

[6] The Lord must have given them an abundance of food to make them feed Elijah like one of their nestlings. Ravens were seen as unclean birds (Leviticus 11:13–15), so Elijah needed to submit his prejudices to the Lord.

[7] God was judging Israel by removing his prophets from the land (Amos 8:11–12 and Isaiah 30:20). He was also marking out Elijah as a new Moses for Israel, one who feasted miraculously in the desert.

of Israel, using the drought he has unleashed on its people to call them back to God.[8] He doesn't prematurely call his nation to a showdown on Mount Carmel.[9] He accepts that the Lord is *cutting* him off from the world at Kerith so that he can pray.[10] The New Testament fills in some of the blanks in the story in James 5:16–18:

> *The prayer of a righteous person is powerful and effective. Elijah was a human being, even as we are. He prayed earnestly that it would not rain, and it did not rain on the land for three and a half years. Again he prayed, and the heavens gave rain, and the earth produced its crops.*

Section three of 1 and 2 Kings therefore marks a new phase in the story. Up until now, the Lord's prophets have been important players in the story but they have usually been on the sidelines: people like Nathan, Ahijah, Shemaiah and Jehu. Now the Lord's prophet moves centre stage to confront the false messiahs of the northern kingdom. Revival is coming. The Lord is about to prove through Elijah that he is Israel's true King.

---

[8] This must have been very tempting, particularly if he felt his disappearance was being viewed as cowardly.

[9] God often takes people into the desert before he uses them. Just look at the lives of Moses, David, Jesus and Paul. In Matthew 6:6, Jesus encourages us to embrace time in the "desert" willingly.

[10] The role of a prophet is not simply to bring God's Word to us, but also to bring God's words back to him in prayer. Elijah was able to lay hold of specific promises from God in Deuteronomy 11:16–17 and 28:15–24.

Resurrection
(1 Kings 17:7–24)

*The Lord heard Elijah's cry, and the boy's life returned
to him, and he lived.*

(1 Kings 17:22)

The classic Christian writer A.W. Tozer describes the role of
God's prophet:

> *A thousand or ten thousand ordinary priests or pastors
> or teachers could labour quietly almost unnoticed while
> the spiritual life of Israel or the church was normal. But
> let the people of God go astray from the paths of truth,
> and immediately the specialist appeared almost out of
> nowhere. His instinct for trouble brought him to the
> help of the Lord and of Israel. Such a man was likely
> to be drastic, radical, possibly at times violent, and the
> curious crowd that gathered to watch him work soon
> branded him as extreme, fanatical, negative. And in a
> sense they were right. He was single-minded, severe,
> fearless, and these were the qualities the circumstances
> demanded. He shocked some, frightened others, and
> alienated not a few, but he knew who had called him
> and what he was sent to do. His ministry was geared
> to the emergency, and that fact marked him out as
> different, a man apart. To such men as this the church
> owes a debt too heavy to pay.*[1]

---

[1] Tozer writes this in his foreword to Leonard Ravenhill's *Why Revival Tarries*
(2004).

Few people have lived up to that description as much as Elijah. He bursts onto the scene when all appears lost for Israel. They have put their hope in wisdom, in the Temple and in the unity of God's people, but each of these false hopes has failed them. They have put their hope in breaking away from the southern tribes to establish a new monarchy, but four dynasties later that hope has failed them too. They have put their hope in the Canaanite storm-god Baal, but now their crops and their cattle are dying for lack of rain.

Elijah doesn't come with easy answers. The drought is the direct result of his prayers. He makes the northern kingdom of Israel taste death so that he can preach to it a message of resurrection. We misunderstand the ministry of Elijah if we think he did nothing more than call the nation of Israel back to the Law of Moses. The drought stemmed from the curses that the Law called down on anyone who broke it! His message was that Israel needed more than resolutions to try harder. It needed resurrection from the dead.[2]

In 17:7–9, the Lord instructs Elijah to leave the Kerith Ravine and to head north. This isn't just a reminder not to rely on yesterday's guidance but to stay close to God for fresh guidance each day.[3] It is also a reminder that there are no places too dead to experience God's resurrection power. Zarephath was a Canaanite town halfway between Tyre and Sidon, on the coast of Phoenicia, so it was part of the kingdom ruled by Jezebel's fanatically pagan father. If the Lord could work miracles in the heartland of Satan, then he could also work them in Israel too. If he could resurrect the fortunes of a Canaanite widow, then he could resurrect the fortunes of the down-and-out northern kingdom too.

In 17:10–16, Elijah personally embraces the path of death and resurrection. Zarephath means *Refining of Metal*, and Elijah

---

[2] The Lord wants to teach us the same lesson today. Paul writes in 2 Corinthians 1:9 that *"we felt we had received the sentence of death ... that we might not rely on ourselves but on God, who raises the dead."*

[3] It *does* show this, however. Had the Kerith stream not dried up, Elijah would not have moved on from it and he would have missed out on all the new things God had in store for him.

has to surrender the remaining dross in his heart to the Lord there. Having eaten food from ravens that the Hebrews viewed as unclean in the Kerith Ravine, he now has to eat food from the pagan hands of a Phoenician widow. He has to humble himself by asking for help from a woman so poor that she is preparing a final dinner before starving to death with her son. As Elijah embraces the path of death and resurrection, he inspires the widow to surrender the dross in her own heart to the Lord too.[4] She agrees to share her food with Elijah *before* she sees any kind of miracle.[5] She exclaims *"As surely as the Lord your God lives"*, turning from her Canaanite idols to the God of Israel, *before* she has experienced his resurrection power.[6] Her faith isn't disappointed. Her jar of flour and her jug of oil keep on auto-replenishing from the time Elijah arrives at her home until the moment that he heads back south to confront King Ahab on Mount Carmel.[7] The miracle proclaims that if Israel turns from its sin and puts its faith in the Lord again like this widow, then its fortunes will be resurrected too.

In 17:17–24, the Lord states this even more explicitly. The widow only has one son. She has no husband and no daughters. He is her life and joy, but one day he suddenly grows ill and dies. She feels as hopeless as the people of the northern kingdom as she blurts out to Elijah, *"What do you have against me, man of God? Did you come to remind me of my sin and kill my son?"* The

---

[4] These verses state a general principle that God works both ends of the line. Even as he works in our own hearts, we can trust him to be working in the hearts of all those around us too.

[5] Elijah's request is outrageous. We mustn't shy away from calling people to obey the Lord with lavish obedience, and we must not attempt to pastor them out of it when they do (Luke 21:1–4).

[6] Jesus tells us in Luke 4:25–26 that Elijah's visit to Zarephath was as much about the widow as the prophet. The Lord would save this Gentile widow, even as many Israelite widows persisted in worshipping Baal (Deuteronomy 32:21). Note how her willingness to fetch water for a stranger reflects Rebekah's in Genesis 24.

[7] Note that the Lord does not give the widow a stockpile of flour and oil. He generally requires his people to walk closely with him to receive each day's provision on the day (Matthew 6:11).

Lord's prophet doesn't answer. He simply carries the corpse of her son upstairs to his bedroom and lays it out on his own bed. He prays that, since the boy's death is the Lord's doing, the boy's resurrection must be his doing too.[8] He stretches himself out on top of the corpse, identifying with the dead Canaanite boy in the same way that "the man of God" from Judah identified with "the prophet" from Israel when they lay together in the grave.[9] He does this three times, crying out each time, *"Lord my God, let this boy's life return to him!"* Suddenly the dead Canaanite boy is dead no more. Elijah carries him downstairs to celebrate the resurrection with the boy's mother.

The Canaanite widow lives in Jezebel's heartland, but she responds to this miracle by professing her faith in the God of Israel.[10] *"Now I know that you are a man of God and that the word of the Lord from your mouth is the truth."*[11] Elijah's faith has also been refined by these miracles at Zarephath. If God can do such things in foreign lands then he can surely resurrect dead Israel. If he has put Israel to death due to its sin, then he will surely resurrect the nation due to his mercy. If he has allowed their false hopes to fail them, then he has surely done so in order to shift their gaze back onto the true hope of Israel.

The curse of Genesis 2:17 demands that Israel die for its sin, so we mustn't mistakenly think that the message of 1 and 2 Kings is: *Israel, get your act together or you will die!* Israel has sinned and death is therefore inevitable. The only question is how it will die. Will it die kicking and screaming against the God of justice, or will it die the death of repentance, placing its hope

---

[8] This is our great hope in the midst of Church decline. Since only Jesus closes churches (Revelation 2:5), the Church decline we see is the Lord's doing. We can therefore trust him that revival will be his doing too.

[9] An Israelite who touched a corpse became ceremonially unclean (Numbers 19:14). Like the "man of God" in 1 Kings 13, Elijah identifies with the boy in his death in order to lead him into resurrection.

[10] Yahweh is not only stronger than Baal, the Canaanite storm-god. He is also stronger than Mot, the Canaanite god of death and of the grave.

[11] The Hebrew word in 17:17 for the *"mistress"* or *"owner"* of the house is ba'alāh, the feminine form of the name *Baal*. The writer is offering us a choice. Will we side with the false god or with this humble widow?

in the God who makes us a glorious promise in John 11:25? *"I am the resurrection and the life. The one who believes in me will live, even though they die."*

Showdown
(1 Kings 18:1–40)

*"How long will you waver between two opinions? If the
Lord is God, follow him; but if Baal is God, follow him."*
(1 Kings 18:21)

I have been introducing my children to some of the great cowboy
classics. *High Noon, Shane, A Fistful of Dollars, Pale Rider* – you
know the type of movie I mean. Most of them follow a pretty
simple formula. A hero and a villain clash over an injustice,
leading to a final showdown in which the hero beats the villain
and restores peace to the valley. There is a pretty similar plotline
to 1 Kings 18.

The chapter begins with the hero Elijah returning to the
land of Israel after an absence of three years.[1] Like the first
sight of Shane or of Clint Eastwood's *Man With No Name*, the
arrival of Elijah causes quite a commotion. King Ahab's palace
administrator, Obadiah, can hardly believe that it is really him.
His master has searched almost every nation to find him and to
force him to call rain down from heaven. Now that he has finally
found him, Obadiah is afraid to let the prophet out of his sight, in
case he disappears again for another three and a half years.[2] But
Elijah isn't running. He has come back to the northern kingdom

97

---

[1] Luke 4:25 and James 5:17 tell us that the drought lasted three and a half
years, so *"the third year"* in 18:1 must refer to Elijah's third year in Zarephath.
He had been at the Kerith Ravine for a year before that.

[2] Elijah wasn't hard to recognize (2 Kings 1:8) but the Lord had managed to hide
him in Ahab's own father-in-law's kingdom! What Obadiah says, coupled with
2 Kings 2:16–18, leads some readers to believe that the Holy Spirit sometimes
"teleported" him around the country, like Philip in Acts 8:39–40. They may be
right, or it may just be a rumour started by his utter elusiveness.

for a showdown. He says to Obadiah. *"As the Lord Almighty lives, whom I serve, I will surely present myself to Ahab today."*[3]

The villain in the chapter is naturally King Ahab. He is a pretty pathetic shadow of the man we met in chapter 16.[4] First, we find him foraging for fodder for his animals like a common stable boy. Second, we discover that he can't even persuade his own palace administrator to worship his false god Baal instead of the Lord.[5] Obadiah means *Servant of the Lord*, and he has lived up to his name. He has helped 100 of the Lord's prophets to survive the drought by hiding them in two caves and by feeding them from the royal larders of the very palace that wants them dead. The writer uses a Hebrew play on words in 18:4 to laugh at the king's powerlessness. When he talks about Jezebel cutting off the Lord's prophets from Israel, the word he uses is *Kerith*. The Lord is in complete control of Ahab's kingdom.

This leads to the first clash between the hero and the villain. As soon as Ahab sees the prophet, he accuses him: *"Is that you, you troubler of Israel?"* Elijah shoots back that none of the troubles of the northern kingdom was caused by him.[6] After all, we know from 2 Chronicles 17:11–19 that at this very time King Jehoshaphat of Judah was enjoying an economic boom that enabled him to put a million men on the battlefield, whereas Ahab can't even feed his chariot horses! It really didn't have to be this way for Israel. Elijah therefore sets a date for a showdown. He tells King Ahab to summon all the prophets of Baal and Asherah to Mount Carmel. Israel must choose its god, one way or the other.

[3] Elijah's resolve is meant to contrast with the compromise that lies at the root of spiritual backsliding (18:21). Churches that are radically committed to God prosper, but it only takes a little compromise to destroy them.

[4] God's judgment doesn't automatically lead to repentance. Ahab is just as sinful as he was before.

[5] Like Daniel in Babylon, Obadiah does not see his devotion to the Lord as a reason not to work for an evil king. The people of the light need to place themselves in places of darkness and to let their light shine.

[6] The Hebrew word for Troubler is *Achor*, the other name for Achan in Joshua 7:26. Israel's troubles have been caused by Ahab rebuilding Jericho (16:34) and reversing Joshua's destruction of the Canaanite gods.

Mount Carmel was a high mountain ridge in the north of Israel that jutted out into the Mediterranean Sea. Its name means *Fertile Garden* because it saw heavier rainfall than anywhere else in the country.[7] As a result, it became one of the most important "high places" for the storm-god Baal, which is why Elijah needs to build an altar there but the priests of Baal do not. Elijah therefore sets up a showdown like the ones that end a cowboy movie. It will be on Ahab and Jezebel's turf, with all of Baal and Asherah's prophets present, and with the nation of Israel as their witnesses. King Ahab agrees. After all, why wouldn't he? His prophets outnumber Elijah by 850 to 1.[8]

Elijah's idea for the showdown is very simple. He and the prophets of Baal will both put wood on their altars, sacrifice a bull and ask their god to send down fire from heaven. The Lord did that for Israel in the days of Moses, David and Solomon, so it shouldn't be hard for Baal to follow suit if he is worth following.[9] Elijah shouts to the watching crowd: *"How long will you waver between two opinions? If the Lord is God, follow him; but if Baal is God, follow him."*[10] He is staking everything on this showdown.

The prophets of Baal go first, since they have the home advantage and there are 450 of them. After they have danced around their altar all day, Elijah starts to taunt them that perhaps Baal is a bit distracted, a bit too busy or on the toilet.[11]

---

[7] Amos 1:2 says that Carmel was the last place in the country where rain would ever stop falling.

[8] Truth is never decided by majority vote. Let's take God's side, even if we have to do it alone (Romans 3:4).

[9] Leviticus 9:24; 1 Chronicles 21:26 and 2 Chronicles 7:1. We must not be content with the Christian equivalent of Baal worship – noisy and excited, but totally lacking the fire of Matthew 3:11 and Acts 2:1–3.

[10] Elijah asks them literally how long they will *"limp"* between two opinions. They need to use two legs to follow the Lord, not just one. This same Hebrew word *pāsah* is also used in 18:26 to describe the prophets of Baal *dancing* and in Exodus 12 for the Lord *passing over* the bloodstained doors of the Israelites in Egypt.

[11] The word translated *"travelling"* means literally *"withdrawing"*. It was a polite word for going to the bathroom.

The prophets are so ashamed and so desperate that they start self-harming in the hope that Baal will see their blood and take them seriously when they pray.[12] After a whole day of shouting, they finally give up. It is now Elijah's turn.

Elijah rebuilds the Lord's altar on the mountain, which evidently hasn't been used for a long time. He uses twelve large stones – not ten – in order to declare to the crowd that Israel and Judah are still really one kingdom under one true King. He digs a fifteen-litre trench around the altar and commands the crowd to douse his sacrifice with twelve large jars of water, one for each of the twelve tribes of Israel.[13] Then he calls on the Lord to prove that he is the true God of Israel. Immediately, fire falls from heaven and burns up the sacrifice, the stone altar, the soil under it and even the water in the trench![14]

Peace will be restored to Israel, but only once the violence of God's judgment has fallen. When the crowd rallies to Elijah, exclaiming, *"The Lord – he is God! The Lord – he is God!"*, the prophet seizes the moment to slaughter the 850 prophets of Baal and Asherah.[15] Ahab and Jezebel fed them from the royal table, intending to make them the chief officials in their paganized kingdom, so Elijah knows he has to deal with them fast.[16] This is a moment for radical repentance and revival. Israel must deal a voluntary death blow to all of its false idols in order to experience the Lord's resurrection power.

---

[12] Sincerity, passion and volume don't make what we believe true. The Lord forbids religious self-harming in Leviticus 19:28 and Deuteronomy 14:1, because our prayers are heard through much better blood.

[13] This looked like madness, but Elijah was so confident in God that he did this to prove that his fire hadn't come through any sleight of hand. Besides, earthly fire travels up whereas this fire travelled down.

[14] If we tone down the offence of the Gospel to "make it easier" for God to save people, we will never see the Holy Spirit fall. Only if we preach the unadulterated Gospel will we see the Lord descend with heavenly fire.

[15] Since Elijah's name means *The Lord Is God*, this showdown marks the crescendo of his life's mission.

[16] The Kishon River, or *Winding* River, flowed into the Mediterranean Sea at the foot of Mount Carmel. Elijah calls for radical repentance. Even the corpses of the prophets must be thrown out to sea.

Middleman
(1 Kings 18:41–46)

Elijah climbed to the top of Carmel, bent down to the ground and put his face between his knees.

(1 Kings 18:42)

The British missionary James Fraser saw such amazing Gospel breakthrough among the Lisu people of China that many historians trace the rapid growth of Christianity in China over the past seventy years back to him. His explanation is disarmingly simple:

> *I feel like a businessman who perceives that a certain line of goods pays better than any other in his store, and who purposes making it his chief investment; who, in fact, sees an inexhaustible supply and an almost unlimited demand for a profitable article and intends to go in for it more than anything else. The DEMAND is the lost state of these tens of thousands of Lisu and Kachin – their ignorance, their superstitions, their sinfulness; their bodies, their minds, their soul; the SUPPLY is the grace of God to meet this need – to be brought down to them by the persevering prayers of a considerable company of God's people. All I want to do is, as a kind of middleman, to bring the supply and the demand together.*[1]

101

Elijah was a middleman between God and Israel. He spoke to God for Israel and he spoke to Israel for God. If we want to see Gospel breakthrough in our own day, we are therefore urged to

---

[1] Quoted by Eileen Crossman in *Mountain Rain* (1982).

learn from him in James 5:16-18. We are to learn from what he says to Ahab and in 17:1 and 18:15 – literally, *"I stand before the Lord."* We need to learn from the year that he spent praying in the Kerith Ravine and from the two years he spent praying at Zarephath. If we don't get this, we don't get Elijah at all. He was a man of prayer.

That's how Elijah ended up at Mount Carmel. The most remarkable thing about Elijah's strategy in these chapters is that he hasn't really got one. He just spends time with God and then does whatever he says. In 17:2-4, the Lord tells him to go to the Kerith Ravine to be fed by ravens. It sounds ludicrous – not just about the ravens, but about hiding away when there is so much to be done in Israel – yet Elijah does it. In 17:8-9, the Lord tells him to leave Kerith and to go to Zarephath. Again it sounds ridiculous – if you want to hide from Jezebel then stay out of her dad's backyard – yet Elijah sets out straightaway. In 18:1, the Lord says it's time to go back to the land of Israel to confront Ahab, and again he obeys. Elijah's plan is simple: get alone with God, listen and obey.[2]

It wasn't Elijah who cooked up the idea of a showdown with the prophets of Baal on Mount Carmel. Listen to his prayer in 18:36: *"Lord, the God of Abraham, Isaac and Israel, let it be known today that you are God in Israel and that I am your servant and **have done all these things at your command**."*[3] The Lord planned all the detail, even down to the fact that Elijah would call down fire from heaven *"at the time of the sacrifice"* – at 3 p.m., the time when lambs were sacrificed at the Temple in Jerusalem and the time when Jesus would one day give up his spirit on the cross at Calvary. Prayer isn't primarily about asking God to do what we want. It is creating space for him to tell us what he wants to do. If we want the Lord to act when we speak, then we have to act when he speaks.

---

[2] Jesus never promised us a map. He promised us a relationship. He said, *"I am the way"* (John 14:6).

[3] Elijah emphasizes that the Lord is Israel's historic national God and that Baal is a mere Canaanite imposter.

A.W. Tozer reflects that *"Some people in reading the Bible say they cannot understand why Elijah and other men had such active power with the living God. It is quite simple. God heard Elijah because Elijah had heard God. God did according to the word of Elijah because Elijah had done according to the word of God. You cannot separate the two."*[4]

James 5:16–18 says that Elijah prayed *earnestly*. That doesn't mean he shouted. That's what the prophets of Baal were forced to do. It simply means that he was resolutely determined to get a specific answer. He asked three times in 17:21 for the widow's boy to be raised from the dead. Not just any boy, but *this* boy. Not just to comfort the widow, but to comfort her through resurrection. We need to be just as resolutely specific. A few weeks before he saw his breakthrough, James Fraser wrote in his diary: *"I am now setting my face like a flint: if the work seems to fail, then **pray**; if services, etc., fall flat, then **pray still more**; if months slip by with little or no result, then **pray still more and get others to help you.**"*[5]

The writer therefore takes us back up Mount Carmel with Elijah in 18:41–46. The prophet knows the Lord so well that he tells Ahab he can hear the sound of heavy rain long before there is a single cloud in the sky.[6] That's faith: to have such a close friendship with God that the answers to our prayers seem more real to us than the things that we can see. Elijah squats down on the mountaintop in the position of a Hebrew woman giving birth and he goes into "labour" in prayer. Seven times he prays to receive what he knows is his by faith. Six times he

---

[4] Tozer says this in his book, *I Talk Back to the Devil* (1972). This seems to be what James is getting at when he tells us that the prayer of a *"righteous person"* is powerful and effective. It's also why James treats the statement in 17:1 that Elijah spoke *for* God as if it were a statement that Elijah spoke *to* God.

[5] He wrote this on Saturday 5th February 1916, as quoted in Eileen Crossman's biography *Mountain Rain* (1982) and in Geraldine Taylor's biography *Behind the Ranges* (1944). Within weeks, hundreds of Lisu were saved.

[6] Ahab probably expected to be assassinated when the people lynched his 850 prophets. Elijah spared him so that he could repent, but he proved more interested in eating and drinking than in repenting.

sees nothing.[7] After the seventh prayer, his servant reports that a tiny cloud of water has just evaporated from the sea. The prophet stands up and declares that his prayers have been answered. A heavy rain is about to fall.

If you're a follower of Jesus then I know you'd love to see this. The fire, rain and wind in this chapter are all metaphors for the Holy Spirit that are meant to spur you on to ask for the same Spirit to fall again. I know you'd love to see miracles like the ones at Zarephath. I know you'd love to see your nation turn back to the Lord, like Israel on Mount Carmel. I know you'd love to receive the same power from heaven that enabled Elijah to outrun King Ahab's chariot at the end of the chapter.[8] So here's my question: Are you willing to become a middleman for the Lord?

Are you willing to put all other things aside in order to pray until you truly know the Lord as your friend, like Elijah?[9] Are you willing to keep on praying, even when it seems there is no answer, until God gives you what you are asking for? Are you willing to pay the price tag of serving God as radically as Elijah? Are you willing to listen to James Fraser when he urges you to become a middleman for the Lord in the place of prayer?

---

[7] Fire fell from heaven immediately, but it took three prayers to resurrect a boy and seven prayers to bring down rain. God doesn't just want to get the job done. He often grows our faith by keeping us praying (2 Kings 5:14).

[8] Elijah outrunning Ahab in the seventeen miles from Mount Carmel to the royal palace in Jezreel was meant to stir him to repent. Instead, he attributed the miracle to Elijah (19:1) and sought solace in the arms of Jezebel.

[9] Ahabs can eat and drink, but Elijahs need to fast and embrace the labour pains of effective prayer.

Discouragement
(1 Kings 19:1–21)

"I have had enough, Lord," he said. "Take my life; I am no better than my ancestors."

(1 Kings 19:4)

You don't have to like boxing movies to appreciate what Rocky says to his son in the movie *Rocky Balboa*. He explains that what matters is not how hard a boxer can hit the other person, but how hard they can get hit and keep on fighting. What makes the difference isn't how much punch you can pack, but how long you can keep going after you've fallen down.

Elijah was hit, and hit hard, after Mount Carmel. He assumed that his showdown with Ahab would cause the king to repent of his sin and lead Israel back to God. When that doesn't happen and Queen Jezebel sends the royal executioners to kill him, Elijah falls into deep despair. This isn't how the story was meant to end after three years of prayer! Elijah feels that the Lord has let him down.

Maybe that's one of the reasons why I really like this chapter. I get discouraged, and I'm guessing you get discouraged too. Many of the Christians that I set out with in my early days of faith have grown disillusioned and given up on their dreams. It's harder than we think to go the distance as a Christian, let alone as a Christian leader, which is why God outlines his great antidote to discouragement here.

First, God reassures us that *discouragement is normal*. Elijah was such a giant of faith that even Obadiah – a man who rescued 100 of the Lord's prophets from Jezebel – speaks in 18:10 about *"the Lord **your** God."* If someone as courageous as

Obadiah was forced to recognize that his own walk with God was a far cry from Elijah's, then these verses ought to set our expectations. If even Elijah battled with discouragement, then let's not be surprised that we get discouraged too.[1]

Next, God warns us that *discouragement robs us of victory*. Elijah panics when he receives a death threat from Jezebel, but if he had taken a step back then he might have stood his ground.[2] Nobody sends advance warning when they are actually plotting murder. If Jezebel is issuing death threats then it means she knows she cannot follow through on them. She can see that all Israel is firmly on Elijah's side. He is on the brink of victory, unless he panics and throws it all away.[3] The Israelites know that the rain that is falling on their land after three and a half years of drought is a result of their confession of faith in the Lord on Mount Carmel. Revival is therefore Elijah's for the taking unless he listens to the lying voice of discouragement.[4] It's like the moment in *Rocky IV* when Rocky warns his son that winning is more about stamina than strength. It's about going one more round when you feel as though you simply can't go on. God wants us to grasp that *discouragement isn't the unforgivable sin*. Yes, it is appalling that Elijah uses legs that have just outrun a chariot to run away from Israel's moment of revival. Yes, it is odd that he keeps on running, even after crossing the border into Judah, not stopping until he arrives at its southernmost town. Nevertheless, 100 miles south of Jezreel, he finds that the Lord is waiting for him there. An angel feeds him, lets him sleep and then feeds him

---

[1] James 5:17 tells us that Elijah *"was a human being, even as we are"*. It appears from 19:5–8 that a lot of his discouragement stemmed from a poor diet and insufficient sleep. Discouragement is often physical.

[2] Note how wrong Elijah's perspective was when he panicked. Not only had the Lord resolved to protect Elijah on this occasion, but he had actually determined that his prophet would *never* die! (2 Kings 2).

[3] Paul says three times in Ephesians 6:11–14 that all we have to do to beat the Devil is to *"stand"* in Christ's victory.

[4] It always lies. Having stood up to 850 prophets, Elijah could easily have stood up to this one woman too.

some more.[5] Even when Elijah squanders strength which was meant to help him head back north to Jezreel by running for a further forty days in the opposite direction, he still finds God waiting for him patiently when he arrives at Mount Sinai.[6] The Lord gently asks him, *"What are you doing here, Elijah?"*, but he doesn't give up on him. Nor will he give up on you and me.

God teaches us that *discouragement comes from looking at the wrong things.* The Hebrew word that says Elijah "feared" Jezebel in 19:3 can just as easily be translated that he "saw" her. Like Peter, when he looked at the storm and sank under the waves of Lake Galilee, Elijah has made the mistake of filling his gaze with the size of his enemy, rather than the size of his God. He has also fixated on his own weakness: *"I have had enough, Lord. Take my life; I am no better than my ancestors."*[7] The Lord therefore prescribes him the same medicine that he gave to Job. Discouragement lifts when we feast our eyes on the Lord.

God wants us to grasp that *discouragement comes from a sense of wounded pride.* It looks like humility, but it is actually a form of self-pity, which itself is simply pride in disguise. Just listen to the self-centredness of Elijah's complaint: *"I have been very zealous ... I am the only one left ... I am no better than my ancestors."* The Lord's antidote is therefore to agree with him. He is right, the journey really is too much for him. Before God can use him to save Israel, he needs to stop trying to be its saviour. He needs to repent of ignoring Obadiah's 100 prophets, thinking that he didn't need them, and to take God seriously when he informs him that there are 7,000 prophets dotted all

---

[5] The Hebrew word for *"angel"* in 19:5 is the same as the word for *"messenger"* in 19:2. We can tell how discouraged Elijah is from the way he sees a beautiful angel and simply rolls over and goes back to sleep!

[6] Horeb was the other name for Mount Sinai, where Moses received the Law for Israel. This cave may be the cleft in the rock where God met with Moses in Exodus 33:22. It didn't take anything like forty days to run the 200 miles from Beersheba to Sinai, so Elijah was clearly so panicked that he ran aimlessly in the desert.

[7] Our discouragement is often ridiculous. Elijah fled to save his life but now he asks God to take it!

around the northern kingdom who are ready to follow his lead.[8] As a first step towards this, he must go back to Israel and anoint a man named Elisha to be his companion in ministry. His days as a Lone Ranger are over. From now on, he will operate as part of a team.[9]

Finally, God promises that, even now, *there is a way back from our own discouragement.* Elijah doesn't need to grovel to the Lord about his missed opportunities. He doesn't need to go on a probation period as a prophet. He simply needs to pick himself up and make a beeline for Elisha's farm in the tribal territory of Manasseh, right back at the heart of the northern kingdom. He needs to look back on his discouragement as a form of loving discipline. It has helped him to shed his pride, confessing that he is no more the hope of Israel than Solomon's wisdom or his Temple.[10] It is a humbler, wiser and stronger prophet who returns to Israel to recommence his ministry. The Lord has prepared Elijah to go back and confront King Ahab and Queen Jezebel another time.

---

[8] This number may well be symbolic. Romans 11:2–5 says that God still speaks these words to us too.

[9] The Lord commands Elijah to anoint Elisha, Jehu and Hazael. As it turned out, Elisha would anoint Hazael (2 Kings 8:7–15) and one of their other teammates would anoint Jehu (2 Kings 9:1–10).

[10] The writer wants Elijah's stillborn revival on Mount Carmel to shift our eyes towards a better Saviour on Mount Calvary. There, instead of fire falling on an altar, the fire of God's judgment would fall on his Son.

What Winning Looks Like
(1 Kings 19:9–18)

The Lord was not in the fire. And after the fire came a gentle whisper.

(1 Kings 19:12)

It is striking how many great Christian leaders have suffered from fits of despair. James Fraser's daughter writes that, before seeing breakthrough among the Lisu, *"Day after day and night after night he wrestled with doubt and suicidal despair. Suicidal? Not once, but several times he stared over the dark ravine into the abyss. Why not end it all?"*[1]

The same was true for Charles Spurgeon, despite being hailed as one of the greatest preachers and church planters in Victorian Britain. *"My spirits were sunken so low that I could weep by the hour like a child, and yet I knew not what I wept for."*[2] Perhaps it shouldn't surprise us, then, that Christian leaders often struggle to stand firm for God's light in a world that prefers darkness. Even the apostle Paul confesses in 2 Corinthians 11:28 that he struggles to withstand *"the pressure of my concern for all the churches".* So let's linger with Elijah a little longer at Mount Sinai. Let's remind ourselves what winning looks like.

The Lord dealt with Elijah's discouragement *physically* by giving him plenty of water, food and sleep. He dealt with it *vocationally* by renewing his calling and sending him back home the way he came. He dealt with it *relationally* by calling time on his Lone-Ranger ministry and by giving him Elisha to

---

[1] Quoted from Eileen Crossman's *Mountain Rain* (1982).

[2] From his sermon "The Christian's Heaviness and Rejoicing" (7th November 1858).

help him find a pace to match God's grace. But the biggest way God deals with Elijah's discouragement is *spiritually*. He takes the prophet out onto Mount Sinai and he puts his finger on the heart of the issue. I think he puts his finger on the heart of our own discouragement too.

The Lord lets Elijah do most of the talking. The prophet is only too happy to oblige. He has a thing or two to tell the Lord about what winning looks like. Hasn't he seen the low spiritual state of Israel – how its people have rejected his covenant with David by breaking away from the south, and his covenant with Moses by worshipping Baal? Hasn't he noticed the way they have murdered his prophets? Elijah alone has escaped by running 300 miles south to Mount Sinai.[3] How dare the Lord ask him what he is doing there? Can't he see that he is fleeing from God's defeat in the north?

The Lord doesn't answer the prophet's angry rant with words. Instead, echoing Exodus 33:18–34:8, he simply invites Elijah to *"Go out and stand on the mountain in the presence of the Lord, for the Lord is about to pass by."*[4] Suddenly the rocks are shattered by a powerful wind that almost knocks Elijah off his feet – but the writer says God isn't in the wind. Then there is an earthquake, as violent as the thunder and lightning that shook Mount Sinai when Moses received the Law – but God isn't in the earthquake either.[5] When a raging fire breaks out on the mountain, we feel more certain. We've just seen fire fall on Mount Carmel, plus Exodus 24:16–17 says that *"the glory of the Lord settled on Mount Sinai .... To the Israelites the glory of the Lord looked like a consuming fire on top of the mountain."* But we are wrong again. God isn't in the fire. Last of all and very easy to miss, there is a gentle whisper. Now *that*, insists the writer, is the presence of the Lord.

[3] Discouragement always warps our perception. In reality, it was Elijah who just killed 850 false prophets!

[4] Israel's prophets were to call the nation back to faith in God's Law, so it is significant that this renewal of Elijah's calling takes place on the same mountain where Moses received it. See also Luke 9:28–36.

[5] See Exodus 19:12–19 and Hebrews 12:18–22.

This famous encounter on Mount Sinai is all about what winning looks like. The Lord explains that we get so discouraged in Christian ministry because we tend to judge his work based on outward appearances, while he whispers gently to Elijah that there is more going on in the northern kingdom than his despairing eyes have seen. He asks the prophet the same question a second time: *"What are you doing here, Elijah?"* The prophet still replies petulantly, but he is starting to see. He is learning to spot the story behind the story. Loud bangs aren't always powerful and gentle whispers aren't always weak.[6]

This is what sustained the apostle Paul in his ministry. He learned a different view of what winning looks like in God's Kingdom: *"having disarmed the powers and authorities, Jesus made a public spectacle of them, triumphing over them by the cross"* (Colossians 2:15).

Read that again, slowly. Paul doesn't say that Jesus triumphed through his resurrection or through his ascension. He says that Jesus triumphed *through his cross*, the very place where he looked most defeated! That's why we mustn't be discouraged if the Devil's plans appear to be succeeding all around us. This is what winning looks like in God's topsy-turvy death-and-resurrection plan to save the nations of the world. Not like wind, earthquake and fire, but like a whisper. Our God is so powerful that he loves to triumph over what the world calls strong through what it disregards as weak and irrelevant.[7]

Elijah has understood this by the time he reaches Elisha's farm. His cloak looks pretty shabby from his 100-mile dash from Jezreel to Beersheba, his forty days of wandering in the desert and his 300-mile journey back again. But now he sees it with different eyes. It is the cloak he pulled over his face to hide from the presence of the Lord in 19:13 while the Lord was whispering in his ear. The writer emphasizes this by referring

---

[6] Seven thousand is probably a symbolic number in 19:18. 7 x 1,000 = a perfectly large army of devout believers. Romans 11:2–5 says that this applies to our own day too. God is winning the battle, even if the Church looks weak.

[7] Elijah calls God *the Lord God Almighty* in 19:14, but it is one thing to say it and another to believe it.

to Elijah's dirty travel coat in 19:13 and 19 as his *'adereth*, a Hebrew word for *cloak* that can also be translated *glory* or *splendour*. Elijah has had enough of judging the Lord's plan based on what he sees and hears. He sees glory and splendour and power in anything ordinary that has received a quiet touch from Almighty God.[8]

Elisha sees it too. His family is rich enough to own a farm ploughed by twelve pairs of oxen, but he humbles himself to serve as Elijah's servant. He sees God's glory in the cloak that now hangs on his shoulders, leaving his family to become part of Elijah's team.[9]

So let's leave the last word to James Fraser, as he explains that it was grasping the victory of the cross that overcame the darkness of his despair:

> *Discouragement is to be resisted just like sin. To give way to the one is just as bad and weakens us as much as to give way to the other ... The aim of Satanic power is to cut off communication with God. To accomplish this aim he deludes the soul with a sense of defeat, covers him with a thick cloud of darkness, depresses and oppresses the spirit, which in turn hinders prayer and leads to unbelief – thus destroying all power ... I went out of the city to a hidden gully on the hill-side, one of my prayer-haunts, and there voiced my determined resistance to Satan in the matter. I claimed deliverance on the ground of my Redeemer's victory on the Cross.*[10]

Now that's what winning looks like.

---

[8] Elijah was right. He and Elisha would use this cloak to part the River Jordan in 2 Kings 2:8 and 13–14.

[9] Elisha throws away a fortune but 2 Kings 8:9 reminds us that God will never remain our debtor.

[10] Quoted from Eileen Crossman's *Mountain Rain* (1942) and Geraldine Taylor's *Behind the Ranges* (1944).

Right Here, Right Now
(1 Kings 20:1–28)

"Because the Arameans think the Lord is a god of the hills and not a god of the valleys, I will deliver this vast army into your hands."

(1 Kings 20:28)

Hitchhikers hold up a sign by the side of the road telling drivers where they want to go. I once saw a hitchhiker with the most despairing sign ever: *ANYWHERE BUT HERE*.

Sadly, that's the sign that a lot of Christians hold up over their lives and their churches. They believe that God performed great miracles through Elijah. They even believe that he might perform miracles today, somewhere else in the world, but they're pretty sure he won't perform them where they are. I think the Devil is laughing at us.

So does the writer, which is why he isn't changing the subject when he talks about King Ahab's wars with the Arameans. He wants to continue his teaching about overcoming discouragement by confronting our normal coping mechanism when discouraged. He insists that faith is only faith if it believes God for right here, right now.[1]

When King Ben-Hadad II of Aram invades the northern kingdom of Israel, there are so many reasons why God isn't

113

---

[1] King Ahab took part in the Battle of Qarqar in 853 BC, one of the most significant battles of the period because it fielded more soldiers than any previous battle in history. However, the writer ignores it in favour of these ones because they illustrate his message better. He is focused on the story behind the story.

going to perform any miracles *here*.[2] There is the natural reason: he is accompanied by thirty-two other kings and they all have chariots, whereas Israel is so devastated by drought that it can barely muster 7,000 foot-soldiers. Even King Ahab accepts that defeat is inevitable and begins negotiating terms.

Then there are all of the spiritual reasons. Ahab has not repented since witnessing the miracle on Mount Carmel. He told Jezebel in 19:1 that it was all Elijah's doing, not God's. The idea of the Arameans breaking into Samaria, plundering the temple of Baal and carrying Jezebel off into captivity is therefore, frankly, rather an attractive one. When Ahab summons the elders and leading citizens of Samaria, none of them has the courage to remind him of their pledge to serve the Lord when his fire fell from heaven. They are as sinful as their king. The northern kingdom deserves what it has coming.

Furthermore, God's anointed leader is nowhere to be seen. Maybe Elijah is still with the Lord on Mount Sinai. Maybe he and Elisha are busy with team-building exercises. Whatever the reason, he isn't there when the northern kingdom needs him, so we can feel pretty confident that there won't be any miracles in this story. Not here, not now.

Of course, that's what the writer wants us to think. When King Ahab angrily tells Ben-Hadad in verse 11 that *"One who puts on his armour should not boast like one who takes it off"* (the Hebrew equivalent of *"Don't count your chickens before they hatch"*) we are meant to see it as the final suicidal boast of a defeated man. But then, suddenly, a prophet appears. We are not even told his name, but he surprises us by prophesying good news for the first time to King Ahab. The Arameans have boasted, *"Thus says Ben-Hadad..."*, so they are about to experience what happens when the God of Israel responds, *"Thus says the Lord."*

What follows next is one of the greatest miracles in the whole of 1 and 2 Kings. Seven thousand Israelite foot-soldiers

---

[2] Ben-Hadad I annexed Galilee and the north of Israel in 15:18–20. Ben-Hadad II was his son, also known as Hadadezer, and he would be forced to hand back his father's gains in 20:34.

defeat a vast chariot army.[3] We would never have believed it, but the Lord performs one of his mightiest miracles where we least expect it.

The implications here are huge. So many of us have allowed past disappointments to make us think that God performed miracles in the past but that he doesn't perform them today, or that he performs miracles in other parts of the world but not in ours. However, believing for God to work in power "over there" isn't really faith at all. It's only faith if it believes in God for right here, right now.

I recently took my family to Belgrade, the capital of Serbia. While we were there, I learned the story of Fritz Klingenberg, who captured the city during World War Two with only six men. Marching confidently into the city, he raised the Nazi flag and pretended that a massive German army was only an hour away. It was actually nothing of the kind, but the whole of Yugoslavia surrendered to him then and there. That feels to me like the way so many Christians act towards the Devil every day. He is the defeated snake, who cannot stand before any believer who confronts him in the name of Jesus, and yet he fools us into acting as if he is the victor and we are the victims.

King Ben-Hadad of Aram can hardly believe what has happened to his army at the hands of puny Israel. Just as the prophet warned, he invades again the following year, only this time he has made the same error that the Devil has made with us. He believes that the God of Israel is only powerful in the hills. That's why he wasn't able to exploit the power of his chariots at the hilltop city of Samaria. He believes that if he can force the Israelites to engage him in battle on the plains, where his chariots fight best, their God will be powerless to save them.[4] The prophet reappears to declare him wrong: *"This is what the Lord says: 'Because the Arameans think the Lord is a god of the*

---

[3] The miracle even comes through the inexperienced junior officers so that all the glory goes to God.

[4] *Aphek* in 20:26 was where the Philistines camped in 1 Samuel 29:1 before defeating and killing King Saul, so Ahab's tiny army even had historical precedent against them.

hills and not a god of the valleys, I will deliver this vast army into your hands, and you will know that I am the Lord.'"

One of my good friends leads a church in Cape Town, South Africa. He has been instrumental in teaching me and many other church leaders in England that the Lord performs all of the miracles that he promises in the Bible right here, right now. A few years ago, he gathered a group of us together and challenged us from these very verses that the honour of Almighty God is at stake whenever Europeans declare that God works in Africa and Asia and South America, but definitely not here. He then sent us out in faith to pray for people to be healed, for demons to be cast out and for large numbers of people to be saved. Surprisingly, we actually believed him. When we came back together, we had so many testimonies of bodies healed, of people forgiven and of people set free that he confessed to me when I saw him the following year that he had caught himself praying, *"Lord, I've seen you do it in Europe, but please now do it in Africa too!"*

The writer wants us to grasp that there are no difficult places for God, no difficult people for God and no "no-go" areas for the Gospel. It isn't faith if we believe it for elsewhere. The writer encourages us to believe in God for miracles right here, right now.

One Swift Cut
(1 Kings 20:29–43)

Ahab said, "On the basis of a treaty I will set you free." So he made a treaty with him, and let him go.

(1 Kings 20:34)

The Chinese emperors practised a form of execution known as *lingchi*. In English it is better known as *death by a thousand cuts*. Instead of killing their prisoners with one swift cut, they tied them to wooden frames in the city square and amputated little sections of their body at a time. It could take two or three days before the prisoner died.

The remedy for discouragement, the writer informs us, is to commit ourselves wholeheartedly to the Lord instead of attempting a form of discipleship that feels a bit like death by a thousand cuts. Jesus tells his followers in Mark 8:34–35 that *"Whoever wants to be my disciple must deny themselves and take up their cross and follow me. For whoever wants to save their life will lose it, but whoever loses their life for me and for the gospel will save it."* King Ahab is about to find this out the hard way.

Against all odds, the Lord has performed a mighty miracle to make the tiny army of Israel defeat the Aramean chariots, even on the plains. The Israelite soldiers slaughter ten Arameans each in the carnage that follows. If that isn't enough, when the Aramean survivors take refuge in a city, its wall caves in on them, killing most of the survivors. Since Ben-Hadad boasted that he would plunder Samaria and rape some of its women, he knows that he is now as good as dead. In a last-ditch plea for mercy, he sends his courtiers to King Ahab wearing sackcloth as a sign of their repentance towards him.

King Ahab ought to have asked them to lend him their sackcloth for some repentance of his own. He had only made very small steps towards the Lord since the miracle on Mount Carmel, and death by a thousand cuts just won't do. The Lord is amazingly merciful towards Ahab in these verses, literally bringing him all the sackcloth that he needs, but Ahab still won't confess that he isn't Israel's true King.

Instead, he extends mercy towards Ben-Hadad. *"Is he still alive?"* he asks. *"He is my brother."* Ahab invites him up into his chariot, receiving him as an equal, as if they were two kings together, instead of a pagan king and a regent for the Lord. Ben-Hadad can hardly believe his luck. He offers to give back the cities in Galilee that his father stole from Israel in 15:18–20, plus the right to open stalls in the bazaars of his capital city. It's a ridiculous offer, since the whole of Damascus is Ahab's for the taking![1] Yet Ahab falls for his charms and sets him free without even consulting the Lord.

Elijah is still out of town, so the Lord sends a different prophet to confront Ahab with his sin.[2] We have the first mention in 20:35 of *"the company of prophets"* – literally, *"the sons of the prophets"* – which is significant because, as we will see later, this appears to be what Elijah and Elisha are away doing. Having learned his lesson from the Lord at Mount Sinai, Elijah has established a training school for prophets in order to disciple an army of radical servants of the Lord.[3] It is probably safe to say that the first of them wasn't top of the class, because he refuses to obey a direct command from the Lord and is killed by a lion (don't be offended – it's a solemn reminder of what happened to the disobedient prophet in

[1] Worse, we discover in 1 Kings 22 that Ben-Hadad is lying and quickly reinvades Israel.

[2] Since the prophet needs to disguise himself, it is probably the same prophet that spoke to him in 20:13.

[3] These sons of the prophets lived together in community with Elijah and Elisha. They are mentioned again nine times in 2 Kings 2:3–15; 4:1, 38; 5:22; 6:1 and 9:1.

chapter 13).[4] The second student is more obedient, enabling the prophet to approach Ahab looking like one of the battle-scarred soldiers in his victorious army.

Prophets often resorted to tricking kings into passing judgment on themselves as a clever way of bypassing their pride.[5] It was what Nathan did to King David in 2 Samuel 12:1–7. The prophet tells King Ahab that he lost an Aramean prisoner during the battle and that his life will be forfeit unless he can pay the fine of thirty-four kilograms of silver.[6] Ahab has no pity on him, retorting that any Israelite who loses an Aramean prisoner deserves to die. At this, the prophet tears off his disguise and turns the table on Ahab. He says Ben-Hadad wasn't really Ahab's prisoner because Ahab isn't really the true King of Israel. *"You have set free a man I had determined should die. Therefore it is your life for his life, your people for his people."*[7] Because he refused to wear sackcloth, it is now curtains for Ahab's dynasty.

Note the contrast between the king and the prophet here. The prophet has done what Jesus says in Mark 8. He has surrendered his life to the Lord with one swift cut. He has decided up front that he will obey him, whatever the cost, even if it means asking a friend to stab him with his spear and standing up to a bloodthirsty king. Ahab, on the other hand, wants to have his cake and eat it. He pays lip-service to the Lord, but he resists him at every turn. He will only be a disciple if he can be one by a thousand cuts.

The writer therefore turns to us at the end of the chapter, as Ahab sulks back to his palace in Samaria. He tells us that the

---

[4] Following the Lord means – well – following the Lord, even if we can't see the sense in what he says. 1 Samuel 15:9 says that Saul sinned by sparing Agag (literally, "having compassion on") and therefore disobeying the Lord.

[5] It is also a warning for us of what will happen on Judgment Day. See Luke 19:22.

[6] The writer challenges us about our own half-hearted obedience in 1 Kings 20:40. How much of our sin and compromise is caused by our being too busy to focus on what the Lord tells us to do?

[7] The Hebrew noun *hērem* in 20:42 means literally *"something devoted to God by killing it"*. It is a word used throughout the book of Joshua. Ahab's failure to deal radically with Canaanite sin becomes his downfall.

ultimate cure for our discouragement is to deal with our feelings of self-pity with one swift cut. If we accept that we have no rights and that we are God's servants, not the other way around, then we will find following him a whole lot easier. C.S. Lewis explains in his brilliant essay *Is Christianity Hard or Easy?*:

> *The Christian way is different: harder, and easier. Christ says, "Give me All. I don't want so much of your time and so much of your money and so much of your work: I want You. I have not come to torment your natural self, but to kill it. No half-measures are any good. I don't want to cut off a branch here and a branch there, I want to have the whole tree down... Hand over the whole natural self, all the desires which you think innocent as well as the ones you think wicked – the whole outfit ... The terrible thing, the almost impossible thing, is to hand over your whole self – all your wishes and precautions – to Christ. But it is far easier than what we are trying to do instead ... Cutting the grass may keep it short: but I shall still produce grass and no wheat. If I want to produce wheat, the change must go deeper than the surface. I must be ploughed up and re-sown ... It is hard; but the sort of compromise we are all hankering after is harder – in fact, it is impossible. It may be hard for an egg to turn into a bird: it would be a jolly sight harder for it to learn to fly while remaining an egg.*[8]

[8] The essay is included as a chapter in his book *Mere Christianity* (HarperCollins, 1952).

Second Chance
(1 Kings 21:1–29)

"Because he has humbled himself, I will not bring this disaster in his day, but I will bring it on his house in the days of his son."

(1 Kings 21:29)

Most of us know that the Lord is a God who gives second chances. But it's one thing to know it and another thing to love it. Let's run a little test to see if what I say is true.

Jeffrey Dahmer murdered at least seventeen young men in Milwaukee, Wisconsin, from 1978 to 1991. I say at least, because those are merely the ones we know about. There may have been more. He performed sex acts with most of the corpses before eating them. When he was finally arrested, his crimes caused such national outrage that he was murdered by a fellow prisoner, but a Christian woman who watched him interviewed on TV wrote him a letter and enclosed a Bible. As a result of reading it, he requested a visit from a local church pastor and repented of his sins eight weeks before he died. So here's my question: How do you feel about the fact that Jeffrey Dahmer is now with Jesus Christ in glory? For most people, that kind of forgiveness doesn't feel fair.

The reason I ask the question is that 1 Kings 21 is a chapter all about second chances. Most of us feel happy that the Lord gives a second chance to Elijah, because we see ourselves in him, but we haven't truly understood the glory of God's mercy unless we recognize that there is also a little bit of Ahab in each of us too. The fact that God gives a second chance to Ahab is meant to encourage us that nobody – not Jeffrey Dahmer, not King

Ahab, not the northern kingdom of Israel and not ourselves – is beyond the reach of God's mercy and of his saving promise to raise sinners from the dead.

Ahab has sulked his way back to his northern palace in the city of Jezreel. The first three Hebrew words of the chapter mean literally *"after these things"* (not *"some time later"*, as in many English translations), so the events of this chapter take place hot on the heels of the prophet's warning that Ahab has sinned and is about to die.[1]

Ahab decides to chase away such troubled thoughts by creating a *vegetable garden* outside his palace.[2] The problem is that his neighbour Naboth won't sell him the land. Unlike Solomon, who gave away some of the Promised Land to pay off his debts to Hiram, Naboth believes that the Law of Moses forbids him from parting with the patch of the Promised Land that God has allocated to his family.[3] *"The Lord forbid..."* in 21:3 indicates that the issue isn't that he really likes his vineyard, but that he really loves the Lord. Naboth means *Fruits* and he cares more about God's covenant to make Israel fruitful in the Promised Land than he does the dangers of defying King Ahab.[4]

While Ahab sulks on his bed in the palace, his wife plots how to acquire Naboth's vineyard by force.[5] While it's technically

---

[1] Ahab fought his first two battles with Ben-Hadad in 857 and 856 BC. He died in their third battle, in 853 BC.

[2] Ahab's palace in Samaria wasn't enough for him, so he built a second palace in Jezreel adorned with ivory (22:39). Now even that second palace doesn't satisfy him. See Proverbs 27:20 and 1 Timothy 6:6–10.

[3] Leviticus 25:23 and Numbers 36:7. The only other place in the Bible where this Hebrew phrase for vegetable garden is used is in Deuteronomy 11:10, referring to the land of Egypt. Ahab has become an anti-Joshua, and a precursor of the sinful Jewish leaders that Jesus rebukes in the parable of the vineyard (Matthew 21:33–46).

[4] In Naboth, we see a prophetic picture of the death of Jesus. Jesus was faithful to his Father and to the Law, yet he was also executed violently outside the city (Mark 15:20 and Hebrews 13:11–13).

[5] The words for *"sullen"* and *"angry"* are the same in 20:43 and 21:4. Whenever we harden our hearts and refuse to repent of our sin, our sin begins to master us.

true that Jezebel commands the murder, Ahab knows what she is capable of doing when he allows her to send letters in his name.[6] That's why the Lord sends the prophet Elijah to confront him in the vineyard as he starts converting it into his vegetable garden, declaring in 21:19 that Ahab is the real killer of Naboth. Elijah repeats what the prophet told the king after he released Ben-Hadad in the previous chapter. It won't be long before Ahab joins Naboth in the grave.

This is God's second chance for Elijah. The prophet blew his opportunity to call the nation of Israel back to the Lord after the miracle on Mount Carmel, so the Lord now gives him a second chance to do so. Elijah responds by making three public predictions that serve as fresh signs to Israel, like the fire that fell from heaven.[7] First, he predicts that Ahab is about to die and that his corpse will be washed in the place where Naboth died. Second, he predicts that Ahab's dynasty will then be wiped out as thoroughly as the dynasties of Jeroboam and Baasha.[8] Third, he predicts that Jezebel will die in this bloodbath and that her corpse will be torn apart and eaten by street dogs at the city wall.

Few readers object to God's mercy towards Elijah, because we see a little of Elijah in ourselves. We would like to find ourselves on the receiving end of God's second chances too. The problem is that we don't see the Ahab that lurks within us. The more we spot our own tendency to sin and rebel against the Lord, the more we will see it as good news that God extends his second chances to out-and-out sinners like Ahab too.

Ahab is a murderer. Elijah has just said so. Admittedly, he hasn't behaved like Jeffrey Dahmer with the body, but his actions

---

[6] Ahab goads on Jezebel by presenting Naboth's reply in the worst possible light in 21:6, omitting any mention of his devotion to the Lord. She then murders both Naboth and his sons so that there are no heirs to stand in the way of Ahab acquiring the vineyard (2 Kings 9:26).

[7] Jehu was present to hear these predictions and he recalls them years later, in 2 Kings 9:25–26.

[8] In 21:21, Elijah copies the shocking language of Ahijah in 14:10 when he curses, not just every *"male"* in Ahab's dynasty, but *"everyone who urinates up against the wall"*.

are pretty hideous for someone called to rule the nation of Israel for God.[9] He failed to repent during the drought. He failed to repent at Mount Carmel. He failed to repent when Elijah outran his chariot after calling down a rainstorm from heaven. He failed to repent when the Lord delivered him from the Aramean army, not just once but twice. Even now, he still blames Elijah for his troubles, greeting him with, *"So you have found me, my enemy!"*[10] Stubborn Ahab deserves nothing but death, yet when he suddenly starts listening to Elijah and repents in sackcloth, with prayer and fasting, the Lord gives him a second chance to rule well. His dynasty will still be destroyed, but no longer in Ahab's own lifetime.[11] If he proves his repentance by his deeds, he may not even have to die within the next few months after all. [12]

So let's not be offended that God extends his second chances even to an arch-villain like Ahab. Let's receive it as good news, confessing that each of us has a little Ahab inside us. Let's stand amazed at the mercy of the God who extends second chances to one and all.

[9] Elijah declares in 21:20 that Ahab has sold his own soul in exchange for Naboth's vineyard.

[10] Elijah was actually a true friend to Ahab, but true friends are willing to be hated.

[11] Ahab's dynasty was destroyed twelve years after his death, in 841 BC.

[12] This chapter links back to Adonijah, Abiathar and Shimei in 1 Kings 2. Ahab's actions will prove whether or not his sudden show of repentance marks sincere surrender to the Lord.

Sin Spreads
(1 Kings 22:1–40)

Jehoshaphat replied to the king of Israel, "I am as you are, my people as your people, my horses as your horses."

(1 Kings 22:4)

I have been reading the *Labours of Hercules* to my seven-year-old son at bedtime. Our favourite is his battle against the Hydra, a snake-like monster with many heads, each of which belches out venomous fumes. When Hercules runs into the lake to kill the monster, he discovers that each time he chops off one of the Hydra's heads, two new heads instantly appear. That's what happens in this final chapter of 1 Kings. Ahab dies but his sin spreads even wider as he dies.

125

If we're not reading carefully, we may assume that sin is dealt a setback in this chapter when King Ahab finally dies. His actions prove that his repentance was superficial. He surrounds himself with 400 prophets of the Lord, not prophets of Baal, but every single one of them is a yes-man. When Ben-Hadad reneges on the treaty he should never have been given and Ahab considers going back to war, all 400 of them care more about what Ahab wants to hear than about what God wants to say.[1] The prophet Micaiah (whose name means *Who Is Like The Lord?*) has to point this out sarcastically to Ahab. When he

---

[1] Zedekiah means *The Lord Is Righteous* and his prophecy echoes Deuteronomy 33:13–17. Nevertheless, it is utter fabrication (2 Corinthians 11:14). Note that he and the other false prophets refer to the Lord in 22:6 as *Adonai*, rather than as *Yahweh*. They are carefully ambiguous in what they tell King Ahab – literally, *"Go up and the Lord will give it into the hand of the king."* They hedge their bets for either outcome in the battle.

refuses to listen, thinking that he can disguise himself in battle to prevent the Arameans from targeting him, he fares no better than the wife of Jeroboam when she visited Ahijah. When the writer tells us that Ahab is hit by an arrow *"at random"*, he expects us to see the story behind the story. Ahab dies in his chariot and his corpse is washed in the place where Naboth died, just as Elijah predicted.[2]

This looks like a setback for sin in Israel, but the writer draws back the curtain further on the story behind the story. Micaiah's vision is pretty weird. He sees evil spirits arguing before God's throne in heaven and being granted divine permission to deceive Ahab.[3] This makes it clearer than ever that the Devil is the real cause of Israel's sin and idolatry. It's why many centuries later, in Revelation 2:20, another individual can be described as "Jezebel". Ahab is dead but the spirit that inspired him isn't. His sin continues to spread.

Ahab's wife Jezebel has been active in the story ever since we met her in 16:31. She is silent in chapter 17, she appears in the background in chapter 18, she starts stepping forward in chapter 19, then she bursts into the foreground in chapter 21. We are told in 21:25 that Ahab sinned because he was *"urged on by Jezebel his wife"*, but when he dies in battle she takes over as leader of his dynasty, and hell really starts to have a field day.

Jezebel means *No Cohabitation* in the Canaanite language. She is a power-hungry manipulator rather than a team player. After her husband dies, we start to discover with horror that he was actually holding back the worst of her sin! Instead of halving the backsliding of the northern kingdom, the death of

---

[2] It isn't clear in 22:37–38 whether Samaria refers to Jezreel, home to Naboth's vineyard, as a city ruled from Samaria, or whether Ahab's corpse was washed at pools outside both cities on its way back to the capital.

[3] Don't be offended by the weirdness. Other examples of the Lord setting the parameters within which evil spirits are permitted to act are in 1 Samuel 16:14; Judges 9:23; Job 1:6–12 and 2:1–7; Matthew 8:28–32 and John 13:27. This is all part of the story behind the story.

Ahab creates a power vacuum which Jezebel immediately fills. As a result, like an aggressive cancer, sin spreads.[4]

Now for the greatest tragedy of 1 Kings 22. Jehoshaphat of Judah is a very godly king. His name means *The Lord Judges* and it is used twice as often as the name Ahab in these verses to shift the spotlight back onto the southern kingdom. Jehoshaphat has been king of Judah for almost twenty years and his track record is as devout as Ahab's is evil.[5] He has removed the "high places" of Judah and has sent priests on a preaching tour of his kingdom to bring the people of Judah back to the Lord. But this chapter reveals his Achilles' heel. He believes in unity among God's people at any price.

Jehoshaphat foolishly agrees to go and fight the Arameans with Ahab, before he is even told where or when. He boasts to Ahab that *"I am as you are, my people as your people, my horses as your horses"*, forgetting that unity is only as godly as what we unite ourselves with. It should have been obvious to Jehoshaphat that a coalition with Israel would prove toxic for Judah. Ahab clearly despises God's Word. Jehoshaphat has to insist that the two of them seek counsel from the Lord at all, and he is forced to point out that there isn't a single true prophet of the Lord among Ahab's 400 yes-men. He rebukes Ahab mildly for disrespecting Micaiah, but he does nothing to protect him from being dragged off to prison when he is faithful to his calling from the Lord. Jehoshaphat even persists in the coalition when Micaiah prophesies that it is doomed to fail.

As a result, sin spreads. Ahab's decision to disguise himself in the battle almost results in the death of Jehoshaphat, since the vindictive Ben-Hadad commands his soldiers to target the general who is seen wearing a crown.[6] One of the Lord's

---

[4] The "Jezebel" in the church at Thyatira in Revelation 2:20 defies her church leaders in order to promote herself as a prophet and teacher. The evil spirit at work in her still divides churches by promoting the sins of Jezebel in 21:7–10: deceit, intimidation, manipulation and religious hypocrisy.

[5] We are given a lot of detail about his godly reign in 2 Chronicles 17.

[6] When faithful churches pursue unity at any price, they usually end up bearing the financial cost of it too.

prophets rebukes him for taking such a stupid risk: *"Should you help the wicked and love those who hate the Lord? Because of this, the wrath of the Lord is on you."*[7] That's a sobering warning about how much the Lord detests it when Christians pursue church unity at any price, even at the cost of faithfulness to the Lord and to his Word. Christians cannot prosper through their unity with one another alone, but only through their common unity with Christ.[8]

Worst of all, we discover later that Jehoshaphat decides to cement this coalition by marrying his son Jehoram to Ahab and Jezebel's daughter Athaliah. She is every bit her mother's daughter, murdering much of David's dynasty in her crazed pursuit of power.[9] Even as Ahab dies in his chariot, his sin therefore very much lives on. Its cancer spreads across the border into Judah and starts to infect the southern kingdom too.

It is good for us to look at other religious groups and to ask, "What can I learn from them?" rather than "What is wrong with them?", but let's not miss the lesson of this chapter. False unity always helps sin to flourish. Like a fatal cancer, sin quickly spreads.

---

[7] This prophecy is recorded in the parallel passage in 2 Chronicles 19:2. See also 2 Corinthians 6:14–18.

[8] Romans 6:5; 1 Corinthians 6:17 and Philippians 2:1–2.

[9] 2 Kings 8:26 and 11:1–20, and 2 Chronicles 18:1; 21:1–6 and 24:7.

Now-But-Not-Yet
(1 Kings 22:41–53)

In everything he followed the ways of his father.

(1 Kings 22:43)

The Old Testament prophets are a bit like Doctor Who. They are constantly jumping around in time. Whenever we read them, we feel a bit like one of the Doctor's assistants. It's never quite clear in any given verse into which time zone they are prophesying.

Much of what they say is *microscopic*. They are prophesying about events that are close at hand. They name people and places and all sorts of detail about what will take place in the short-term for Israel. At other times, what they say appears to be *macroscopic*. From the vantage point of history, we can now look back and spot that they were prophesying about the earthly ministry of Jesus. That's why the writers of the New Testament are forever quoting them, but those writers also explain that much of what they prophesied is also *telescopic*. It will not be fulfilled completely until Jesus returns from heaven. The prophets are like time lords. Their words are microscopic, macroscopic and telescopic.

The prophet who wrote 1 and 2 Kings is no exception. If we read the final verses of 1 Kings through these three lenses, we discover that there is a lot more to them than at first meets the eye. There is a much bigger story behind the story.

The writer intends these verses to be *microscopic*. He gives us a detailed account of the reigns of King Jehoshaphat of Judah (872–848 BC) and King Ahaziah of Israel (853–852 BC). He tells us the names of Jehoshaphat's mother and father, his age when he became king, the length of his reign, his domestic and foreign policy agenda, and the name of his successor.[1] When people talk about 1 and 2 Kings as history books, they are not wrong. They contain a wealth of historical data. But they also contain a lot more than history.

The writer also intends these verses to be *macroscopic*. His mention of King Jehoshaphat of Judah comes as a breath of fresh air after the spiritual squalor of King Ahab of Israel. We have spent the past seven-and-a-half chapters in the northern kingdom of Israel, watching one sinful king after another rebel against the Lord. Now we cross back over the border into Judah to find a very different type of king in Jehoshaphat. *"In everything he followed the ways of his father."* The writer wants this to excite the hearts of the Jewish exiles in Babylon to believe a day is coming when their nation's failed rulers will be eclipsed by the true Messiah. He predicts the arrival of the true King of Israel, who will be able to proclaim in John 14:31 that *"I ... do exactly what my Father has commanded me."*

Jehoshaphat is the first king of Judah to live at peace with the king of Israel. He follows in his father Asa's footsteps by expelling the last of the shrine-prostitutes from his territory and by sending a team of priests and Levites on a tour of his kingdom to call his subjects to repent and return to the Lord. As a result of this, his reign is very prosperous. He rules over Edom and he scores a stunning battlefield victory over the Ammonites and Moabites.[2] We are meant to see him as a prophetic picture of the glorious Kingdom that will come to Israel when the true Son of David at last appears.

---

[1] 1 Kings 22:42 is a good example of the challenge we have in drawing clear dates from 1 and 2 Kings. The writer says Jehoshaphat ruled for *25 years*, but then later that he ruled for *18+4 years* (2 Kings 3:1 and 8:16). While superficially confusing, it is easily explained. First, Jehoshaphat ruled as regent for his ill father Asa, then he ruled jointly with his son Jehoram for his final years to train him up as the next king (1:17 and 3:1).

[2] The writer of 1 Kings is deliberately light on detail in order to keep our eyes focused on the story behind the story. We only discover this in 2 Chronicles 17 and 20. Judah ruled over Edom from the time of David (2 Samuel 8:14) to the time of Jehoshaphat's son Jehoram (2 Chronicles 21:8–10).

The writer also intends these verses to be *telescopic*. What we see here is a picture of the now-but-not-yet Kingdom of God. Amid the glories of Jehoshaphat's reign, there is a clear indication that the First Coming of Jesus will not bring people into a full experience of God's Kingdom. That will only happen with his Second Coming at the end of time. It's helpful to compare what the writer says in these verses with the parallel passage in 2 Chronicles 17, where we are told that *"he followed the ways of his father David before him"*. The writer of 1 Kings doesn't say that. He says Jehoshaphat followed the ways of his father Asa – the king who grew self-reliant, plundered the Temple of its treasures to buy support from the Arameans, and who was struck down by a mystery illness before he died. This difference between the two accounts is crucial. The writer is predicting that the Kingdom will be now-but-not-yet between the First and Second Comings of Jesus.

Jesus declared that God's Kingdom had come to earth through his arrival on earth as a human being. He promised that God's Kingdom would break out through his death and resurrection.[3] But he also warned that God's Kingdom would be now-but-not-yet until it was inaugurated in all its fullness through his triumphant return from heaven.[4] Unless we understand this, we are bound to grow despondent whenever things don't work out quite as triumphantly as we have been led to believe. That's why the writer talks so openly about the limits of Jehoshaphat's reign. It predicts the now-but-not-yet Kingdom.

King Jehoshaphat of Judah attempted to remove all the "high places", but his sinful subjects resisted him. He succeeded in destroying their idols, but they carried on worshipping the Lord at their polluted shrines. That's why the Temple is never mentioned in this account of his reign.[5] Jehoshaphat also forged an unholy alliance with the kings of Israel which resulted in

[3] Matthew 12:28 and Luke 17:20–21.

[4] Matthew 6:10; Luke 19:11–27 and John 18:36–37.

[5] Jehoshaphat destroyed the "high places" (2 Chronicles 17:6), but he couldn't stop his people from rebuilding them. Worshipping the Lord was forbidden at these polluted hilltop shrines (Leviticus 17:1–9).

the wreck of the Red Sea fleet they built together.[6] He didn't influence King Ahaziah of Israel for good. He was influenced by Ahaziah instead. His reign is an intentionally imperfect picture of the coming of God's Kingdom.

These verses are therefore meant to give us realistic expectations for the period between the ascension of Jesus to heaven and his triumphant return in power, when the now-but-not-yet Kingdom of Heaven will finally become the Kingdom that is *now*.[7]

The apostle Paul urges us in 1 Thessalonians 4:18 to *"encourage one another with these words."* C.S. Lewis also urges us to make this hope the constant topic of our conversation:

> *If you read history you will find that the Christians who did most for the present world were precisely those who thought most of the next. It is since Christians have largely ceased to think of the other world that they have become so ineffective in this.*[8]

---

[6] Again the Chronicler fills in some extra detail for us. Jehoshaphat built Phoenician-style trading ships with King Ahaziah of Israel and was confronted by the prophet Eliezer: *"Because you have made an alliance with Ahaziah, the Lord will destroy what you have made."* The ships were wrecked in harbour (2 Chronicles 20:35–37).

[7] Revelation 11:15–17.

[8] *Mere Christianity* (HarperCollins, 1952).

Second Time Around
(2 Kings 1:1–18)

Elijah answered the captain, "If I am a man of God, may fire come down from heaven and consume you and your fifty men!"

(2 Kings 1:10)

It's easy to see why the book of Kings needed to be divided in two when it was translated into other languages. The first verse of 2 Kings is twenty-six letters long in Hebrew, but forty-three letters long in Greek and fifty-six in Latin. Hebrew is a language which writes down only the consonants of words so, once translated, those missing vowels made the book too long to fit on a single scroll. The book of Kings therefore became 1 Kings and 2 Kings, as we find them in our English Bibles today.[1]

That doesn't, however, mean that the books were split arbitrarily. There is a definite sense of recap and repetition in the story as we begin 2 Kings. There are plenty of echoes of the past in this chapter, as God confronts Ahab's family for the second time around.

King Ahab has died in battle at the hands of the Arameans. While his son Ahaziah can match him sin for sin as an idolater, he can't compete with him for skill as a ruler. Things immediately start to go wrong. Israel ruled over Moab, just as Judah ruled over Edom, but the Moabites see the death of Ahab as their golden opportunity to break free.[2] Ahaziah is too weak to resist

---

[1] This began with the Greek Septuagint translation, dating back to Jewish scholars in Alexandria in about 250 BC.

[2] We will be told more about this in 2 Kings 3, but for now it simply serves as a contrast with 1 Kings 22:47. Kings who obey the Lord flourish, while kings who disobey him flounder.

them because he has fallen out of an upstairs window or off a balcony.[3] He lies on his deathbed, just like the weak King David at the start of 1 Kings. We are witnessing the death of a dynasty.

Ahaziah means *The Lord Possesses*, yet in his moment of trouble, he cries out to Baal instead.[4] We can tell how much the writer disapproves of this from the way he calls it the Baal *of Ekron*, highlighting that it is an idol of the Philistines. We can also tell from the way that he refers to the god by its derogatory Hebrew nickname – not so much Baal-Zebul, which means *Lord of the High Place*, as Baal-Zebub, which means *Lord of the Flies*. The Jews use this name in Matthew 12:24 to refer to the prince of demons – either the Devil himself or one of his senior lieutenants – because Ahaziah has failed to learn the lesson of Mount Carmel. He is still looking to the demon-god Baal instead of to the Lord.

The Lord therefore sends an angel to command Elijah to start prophesying against the dynasty of Ahab for the second time around. When King Ahaziah's envoys return to the palace in Samaria with a message from the Lord instead of one from Baal, he is furious. He recognizes Elijah from their description of his distinctive hairy cloak, and he sends them back at once to arrest him.[5] He intends to silence the troubler of Ahab's dynasty. Don't miss how similar it all sounds to the run-up to Elijah's showdown with Ahab on Mount Carmel, or how similarly things turn out this second time around.[6]

King Ahaziah sends a squad of fifty soldiers to arrest Elijah. When they find him on a hilltop, it's an instant reminder

[3] The Hebrew verb *hālāh*, in 1:2, which is translated *he was injured*, means literally that *he was weak*.

[4] Given that Elijah had raised the dead to life, it is hard to believe that Ahaziah should choose to turn to Baal instead of to the Lord. But we do the same whenever we turn to our science books rather than to Scripture.

[5] This may well be the same cloak as in 1 Kings 19 and 2 Kings 2. Elijah was so famous for his distinctive hairy cloak that many false prophets went out and bought similar cloaks themselves (Zechariah 13:4).

[6] This chapter is also meant to echo the ministry of Moses in Numbers 16:35, just as 1 Kings 18:38 and 19:8–13 echoes Leviticus 9:24 and Exodus 19:20. This link between Moses and Elijah continues into Mark 9:4.

that Israel has failed to respond to the miracle he performed at the top of Mount Carmel. Elijah throws down a fresh gauntlet to this new king of Israel with words that echo his challenge back in 1 Kings 18:24: *"If I am a man of God, may fire come down from heaven and consume you and your fifty men!"* When fire falls, it is a rerun of the miracle at Mount Carmel. King Ahaziah is given a second chance to respond better than his father, but instead he simply sends a second squad of soldiers.[7] Elijah calls down fire from heaven to burn this second squad up too, but Ahaziah is pretty slow to learn. He sends out a third squad of soldiers. Finally, Elijah responds to a humble plea from the squad leader and accompanies them to the palace in Samaria.[8] He informs Ahaziah that, since he has chosen to worship Baal in spite of all the proof the Lord has given him, he will soon succumb to his injuries. Sure enough, Ahaziah quickly dies young and childless. His little brother Joram succeeds him as king.[9]

Centuries later, this same scene would be played out in Israel a second time around. John the Baptist would appear on the scene almost nine centuries later wearing the same distinctive hairy cloak and leather belt that marked out Elijah in 1:8. He would confront a sinful king and his bloodthirsty queen, resulting in his execution, yet his courageous stand would prepare the Jews to receive Jesus as the true King of their nation.[10] Many people would recognize John the Baptist as the "Elijah" that Malachi 4:5 predicted would arrive ahead of Israel's true Messiah to call the Jewish nation back to the Lord.[11]

---

[7] The first two captains aren't innocent victims. Both of them recognize Elijah as a *Man of God* yet they both choose to side with their sinful king against him. The third captain survives by choosing differently.

[8] This required enormous courage, since Jezebel was presumably at the palace too. Not only did God protect his prophet from death, but in the next chapter he ensured that Elijah would never die at all!

[9] Marvel again at God's patience towards Israel. We assumed from 1 Kings 21:29 that disaster would fall during the reign of *this* son of Ahab. In fact, it only falls during the reign of his *next* son.

[10] Mark 1:4–8; 6:14–29; Luke 3:7–20 and Acts 19:4.

[11] Matthew 3:4; 11:14 and 17:10–13, and Luke 1:17.

After the execution of John the Baptist, Jesus would tour the region of Samaria where Elijah called down fire from heaven. When the locals rejected him, his disciples James and John would ask him furiously, *"Lord, do you want us to call fire down from heaven to destroy them?"*[12] Jesus would then reveal that the Lord had a far better plan in store for the heartland of the former northern kingdom. After the Day of Pentecost, he would send John back to Samaria in order to call down far better fire from heaven. The people of the region would repent of their sins, receive Jesus as the true King of Israel and be filled with the Holy Spirit. Things would be quite different the second time around.

So take a moment to step back and to consider the loving grace and patient mercy of God in this chapter. Even when a second king from Ahab's dynasty rejects the Lord, God's judgment only destroys his dynasty. The Israelites survive to receive the Lord when he comes to them in person and plays out this chapter for the second time around.

---

[12] Luke 9:51–56 and Acts 8:4–25.

Double Portion (2 Kings 2:1–25)

"Let me inherit a double portion of your spirit," Elisha replied.

(2 Kings 2:9)

In the H.G. Wells novel, the Invisible Man discovers the limitations of working alone: *"I made a mistake, Kemp, a huge mistake, in carrying this thing through alone. I have wasted strength, time, opportunities. Alone – it is wonderful how little a man can do alone!"*[1]

Elijah had learned that lesson the hard way when he ran away from Jezebel and met the Lord at Mount Sinai in 1 Kings 19. The Lord had shown him how much of his discouragement and failure stemmed from his ingrained practice of ministering alone. When he returned to the land of Israel, he therefore called Elisha to become his right-hand man and then the two of them set about creating a "school of prophets" that would work with them and outlast them. We don't know how many of Obadiah's 100 prophets joined them. We don't know how many of the Lord's 7,000 devout Israelites they found. All we know is that, by the end of 1 Kings, term time had started at their school. One man's lonely ministry had become the ministry of many.[2]

At the start of 2 Kings 2, Elijah senses that his time on earth is coming to an end. He is at Gilgal, the place where Israel consecrated itself to the Lord under Joshua, and where he has evidently planted one of the classes of his school. He says

---

[1] H. G. Wells in *The Invisible Man* (1897).
[2] This *company of prophets* is mentioned ten times: 1 Kings 20:35 and 2 Kings 2:3–15; 4:1, 38; 5:22; 6:1 and 9:1.

goodbye to this class of prophets and moves on to the class that he planted at Bethel, in the shadow of Jeroboam's golden calf in the most sinful city in Israel. Elisha insists on going with him, speaking words that are meant to remind us of Ruth's devotion to Naomi, and when the prophets in the school class at Bethel prophesy that Elijah is about to go up to heaven, he tells them to hush. He has bigger things on his mind today than simply saying goodbye.[3]

Elijah again attempts to leave Elisha behind when he moves on from the class at Bethel. He wants to see how committed his right-hand man is to continuing his mission after he is gone. Elisha sticks firmly to Elijah all the way to the school class in Jericho, an idolatrous city that was destroyed by Joshua and rebuilt under sinful Ahab.[4] The prophets there prophesy the same thing to Elisha, but he silences them again. He knows that Elijah's time on earth is over, but he isn't just grieving. He believes that God has called him to become the new principal of the school.

Fifty of the students are watching from afar when Elijah hits the River Jordan with his hairy cloak and parts the waters. This is the cloak that he pulled up around his face on Mount Sinai to shelter himself from the Lord's face when he whispered in his ear. It is also the cloak that he threw around Elisha's shoulders as a sign that the Lord had called him to receive the mantle of leadership from his master once he was gone. The miraculous parting of the River Jordan proclaims how far Israel has drifted from its calling, since Elijah exits the Promised Land as the Israelites entered it under Joshua. But it also proclaims the calling of Elisha and the school of prophets after Elijah leaves. They are to take up the Law of Moses, who parted the

---

[3] Joshua 5:9 and Ruth 1:16–17. The events of 1 Kings 19 take place in about 857 BC and the events of 2 Kings 2 take place about 852 BC. Elijah has therefore discipled Elisha for about five years.

[4] Joshua 6:26 and 1 Kings 16:34. Like the sites Elijah chose for his school classes, this journey from Gilgal to Bethel to Jericho and to the Jordan was a reminder of how far Israel had strayed from its history in God.

Red Sea with his staff, and to renew the work of Joshua, parting the River Jordan to rid the land of its Canaanite idolatry.[5]

Having crossed the dry river bed together, Elijah turns to Elisha and admires his dogged determination to follow in his footsteps. When he offers to bequeath him anything he wants, Elisha requests *"a double portion of your spirit"*. This isn't a request for twice as much of the Holy Spirit's power as Elijah, since an Israelite with three sons would split his property in four and give a double portion to his eldest son and heir.[6] Since the Hebrew phrase for the "school of prophets" is literally the "sons of the prophets", it appears that Elisha is asking to be recognized as the firstborn son – the school's new principal, with an anointing sufficient to his role. Like the Lord when the young King Solomon asked for wisdom rather than money or fame, Elijah is delighted. He promises to grant Elisha's prayer if he stays with him until he is taken up into heaven.

Suddenly a chariot of fire appears pulled by a team of fiery horses. It comes in a whirlwind which blows Elijah into the chariot and then straight up to heaven. As Elisha watches his mentor disappear from sight, he shouts in grief that Elijah has been the true ruler of Israel, many times more powerful than its army. King Jehoash of Judah would one day shout the same thing in grief at Elisha's deathbed in 2 Kings 13:14: *"My father! My father! ... The chariots and horsemen of Israel!"* Feeling all alone, Elisha tears his own cloak in two and then puts on Elijah's cloak instead.[7] He goes back to the River Jordan and strikes his cloak against its waters, shouting in 2:14, *"Where now is the Lord, the God of Elijah?"* When the river parts, just as it did for Elijah, the school's new principal has his reply.

G.K. Chesterton observed that *"Two is not twice one; two is two thousand times one."*[8] Immediately, we see that this is true.

---

[5] Exodus 14:15–22 and Joshua 3:7–17.

[6] See Deuteronomy 21:17.

[7] Elisha needs to tear up his own cloak before he can wear Elijah's, as a symbol of his death and resurrection.

[8] He says this in his novel *The Man Who Was Thursday* (1908). See Leviticus 26:8 and Deuteronomy 32:30.

Elijah's mission carries on without him.[9] The fifty students who witness this miracle are left in no doubt that the same Holy Spirit who empowered Elijah now rests on Elisha. Although Elisha cannot stop them from conducting a fruitless search for their old principal, when they return there is no doubt about who should be their school's new principal now.[10]

A "double portion" of Elijah's anointing does not mean that Elisha had twice as much of the Spirit as Elijah, but it is notable that Elisha goes on to perform twice as many miracles as his former master. The first was the parting of the River Jordan. The second is redeeming Jericho, a cursed city whose foul spring waters were unfit for drinking or for irrigating land. Elisha lifts the curse over Jericho by "healing" its waters so that, even today, it is a fertile oasis city.[11] On his way back to the school class at Bethel, he performs a third miracle to deal with a group of blasphemous teenagers trying to bully him into entertaining them with a supernatural show. *"Go on up, baldy! Go on up baldy!"* is a cry for him to ascend to heaven in a chariot of fire like Elijah.[12] When he turns around to confront their unrepentant hearts cursing them in the name of the Lord, two female bears suddenly run out of the forest and maul forty-two of them. After that, the whole of Israel is forced to acknowledge that the Lord has raised up a new prophet in Israel.[13]

Elisha moves on from the school class at Bethel to the ones at Mount Carmel and Samaria, confident that he has received

---

[9] We are never told why Elijah went up to heaven this way, like Enoch in Genesis 5:22–24, instead of dying like the rest of us. Perhaps it was meant as a prophetic picture of the Messiah's future ascension to heaven.

[10] Since the Holy Spirit appears to "teleport" Philip in Acts 8:39–40, some see 2:16 and 1 Kings 18:12 as a sign he did the same to Elijah, but it may simply reflect rumours sparked by his elusiveness during the drought.

[11] *Salt* was a picture of God's covenant with his people (Numbers 18:19 and 2 Chronicles 13:5). The lowest city in the world below sea level, Jesus would also perform miracles in Jericho (Luke 18:35–19:10).

[12] Author's own translation.

[13] Don't be offended by the violence of this miracle. It was meant as a merciful warning to the whole of Israel. If Elijah had gone and Elisha had come, then time was running out for their jeering nation.

that double portion that he asked for. The school of prophets has a new principal. Elijah is gone but his mission carries on.[14]

---

[14] There is a final footnote to Elijah's ministry in 2 Chronicles 21:12–15, where someone opens a letter that he wrote to King Jehoram before he ascended to heaven. He is gone, yet he continues to prophesy.

Hollow Victory
(2 Kings 3:1–27)

"What!" exclaimed the king of Israel. "Has the Lord called us three kings together only to deliver us into the hands of Moab?"

(2 Kings 3:10)

Visitors to the Louvre museum in Paris can read an ancient record of the battle that takes place in this chapter. It was written by the enemies of Israel 300 years before the prophet wrote 2 Kings. The inscription on the famous *Moabite Stone* reads:

I am Mesha, the King of Moab and the son of the god Chemosh ... Chemosh saved me from all my attackers and made me look on all my enemies with contempt. King Omri of Israel oppressed Moab for many years and Chemosh was angry with his acts of aggression. When his son succeeded him in my day, he too said, "I will oppress Moab", but I triumphed over him and his dynasty! Israel has perished forever! Omri had occupied the land of Madeba and Israel had dwelt there during his reign and half the reign of his son, for forty years. But Chemosh had mercy on it in my time ... I took the vessels of Yahweh and offered them to Chemosh!

Few visitors to the Louvre understand the story behind the story, and why the Lord allowed a pagan idol to chalk up a hollow victory. That's why we need this chapter. The writer explains why God helped Israel to defeat Moab, then helped Moab to defeat Israel.

Joram has succeeded his big brother as king of Israel. At first, it looks as though the Lord's patience towards Ahab's dynasty might actually result in repentance.[1] Joram removes the sacred stone of Baal from his father's temple in Samaria, but then he proves himself a son of Ahab by offering sacrifices to the golden calf at Bethel instead.[2]

Israel has ruled over Moab as a vassal province since the days of Omri, just as Judah has ruled over Edom since the days of David. When Ahab is killed in battle, his puppet ruler Mesha seizes his chance to achieve freedom for his people, quickly driving the Israelite garrisons out of his land.[3] When Joram succeeds his weak older brother Ahaziah, he therefore knows he has to quash the Moabite rebellion fast. He cleverly spots that he can bypass the fortresses on Moab's border with Israel by taking his troops through Judah and across the Desert of Edom to pop up on Moab's undefended southern border. King Jehoshaphat of Judah's response is predictable. He prizes the unity of the twelve tribes of Israel more than faithfulness to the God of Israel. He repeats his foolish pledge a few years earlier to Ahab: *"I am as you are, my people as your people, my horses as your horses."*[4]

Jehoshaphat and his vassal king of Edom soon find out the hard way what happens whenever godly people downplay the truth for the sake of unity. The route from Jerusalem to the southern border of Moab through the Desert of Edom is less than eighty miles, but the writer tells us literally that they *went around in circles*. After seven days they are lost and they have run out of water. Any hope of a surprise attack is also gone. King

---

[1] Ahab and Jehoshaphat's successors were both called Joram/Jehoram. To avoid confusion, regardless of which variant name is used in the text, I will refer to them as *Joram of Israel* and *Jehoram of Judah*.

[2] Jezebel evidently moved the sacred stone back again, because Jehu has to remove it again in 10:26.

[3] 2 Samuel 8:13–14; 1 Kings 22:47 and 2 Kings 1:1.

[4] This time Jehoshaphat really should have known better. The prophet Jehu had rebuked him on his way back from helping Ahab in 2 Chronicles 19:2: *"Should you help the wicked and love those who hate the Lord?"*

Joram cries out in despair that this must be the moment when the Lord will finally judge him, but King Jehoshaphat remembers his faith in the Lord. He asks if any prophet is travelling with the army and is surprised to hear that Elisha is among them.[5]

At first, Elisha refuses to help the sinful King Joram. Rather than being flattered to receive a request from the king, he echoes the words of Elijah by pointing out literally in 13:14 that he *"stands before the Lord"*. Ahab's dynasty has chosen its gods, so let those gods save it now! When Jehoshaphat finally wins him over, Elisha asks for a little music to help him prophesy. As he worships he is filled afresh with the Holy Spirit.[6] We expect a prophecy of judgment, like the one that Ahijah spoke to Jeroboam's wife, but instead Elisha prophesies that the Lord will not only provide water for the three kings and their armies – he will also grant them victory over Moab. They may have strayed a long way from God, but they cannot stray beyond the borders of his immense mercy.

Note the way in which the writer links this fourth miracle of Elisha to the miracle that took place on Mount Carmel. Fire fell from heaven at the moment that the evening sacrifice was being offered in the Temple; now water appears in the desert at the moment when the morning sacrifice is being offered. What is more, the Moabite soldiers are so dazzled by the desert sunrise that they mistake the red reflection on the water for pools of blood. Thinking that the three kings have turned on each other, the Moabite soldiers break ranks and run to the plunder. Their disorganized army is easily destroyed.

All eyes are now on the king of Israel. Will he prove to be as stubborn as his father and his big brother, or will this finally be the moment when Ahab's dynasty repents before the

---

[5] *Pouring water on the hands of Elijah*, in 3:11, means that Joram still thinks of Elisha as Elijah's sidekick.

[6] *The hand of the Lord* is a Hebrew euphemism for the Holy Spirit in 1 Kings 18:46, in Ezra 7:6, 9, 28; 8:18 and 31, in Nehemiah 2:8 and 18, in Ezekiel 1:3 and in Acts 11:21. Worship music is linked elsewhere to the ministry of the Holy Spirit in 1 Samuel 10:5 and 16:23, in 1 Chronicles 25:3 and in Ephesians 5:18–19.

Lord? Sadly, as Elisha predicted in 3:19, King Joram disregards the Lord's command in Deuteronomy 20:19–20 not to show unbridled hatred for his enemies by chopping down their trees, ruining their fields and stopping up their springs.[7] Because he still rejects God's Word despite all that he has done for him, the Lord suddenly switches sides in the battle. Mesha has failed in his attempt to break through to the King of Edom, hoping to negotiate better terms with a fellow vassal ruler. He is so desperate that he sacrifices his own son, the crown prince, as a human sacrifice to his god Chemosh on the city wall. Although Mesha will attribute victory to his demon-god on the *Moabite Stone*, the writer tells us in 3:27 that it was really the result of the Lord's anger towards King Joram: *"The fury against Israel was great; they withdrew and returned to their own land."*

Joram makes it home to Samaria safely, but he has thrown away the fruits of victory. Mesha succeeds in his rebellion. Israel will never rule over Moab again.

But it is also a hollow victory for the Moabites. Mesha's inscription on the *Moabite Stone* proclaims that *"Chemosh saved me ... Chemosh had mercy."* The Lord brushes off the temporary shame of his actions being misunderstood by the world, but it spells disaster for the Moabites. Their kingdom would be destroyed by the Assyrians in 715 BC. Only a tiny remnant would return from exile to witness the arrival of the true King of Israel.[8]

---

[7] King Jehoshaphat of Judah was considerably more repentant. This mighty act of deliverance gave him the faith he needed to defeat a Moabite and Ammonite invasion of Judah a year or two later, in 2 Chronicles 20.

[8] See Isaiah 15:1–16:14, which was prophesied only three years before the destruction of Moab.

Multiply
(2 Kings 4:1–44)

The company of the prophets ... the company of the prophets.

(2 Kings 4:1, 38)

Charles Spurgeon was a giant of a Christian leader. People hailed him as the greatest preacher in Victorian Britain. But he never let his personal successes flatter him that he could revive his nation alone. He founded a college to train up an army of church leaders to serve with him. He warned, *"I tremble for a church whose continuance depends upon the talent and cleverness of one man. If he is removed, the whole thing will collapse: this is a wretched business. May none of us fall into a mean, poverty-stricken dependence on man!"*[1]

Elijah had learned this lesson on Mount Sinai in 1 Kings 19 when he complained to the Lord that *"I am the only one left"* and the Lord opened his eyes to the potential of the *"seven thousand in Israel"*. He had returned from that encounter to commission Elisha as his co-worker and they had founded a "school of prophets" together. We saw in 2 Kings 2 that by the time he ascended to heaven they had school classes in Gilgal, Bethel, Jericho, Mount Carmel and Samaria.[2] But their students clearly still had some way to go. Elisha cried out after Elijah, *"My father! My father! ... The chariots and horsemen of Israel!"*

---

[1] Spurgeon said this at one of his famous Monday-evening prayer meetings at the Metropolitan Tabernacle, published in a collection of his sermons entitled *Only A Prayer Meeting* (2010).

[2] This idea wasn't original to Elijah. Samuel had his own "school of prophets" in 1 Samuel 19:18–20.

When Elijah ended his earthly ministry, he was still operating as a one-man army.

Elisha was determined to complete what his master had started. In 2 Kings 4, the "school of prophets" begins to take centre stage.[3] We start the chapter with a crisis among its students. One of them has died, leaving a debt that his widow cannot afford to repay. His two sons are about to be enslaved to cancel the debt, so the widow pleads with the school's new principal to intervene. There is an obvious similarity to Elijah's ministry when Elisha performs a miracle that multiplies the oil in the widow's jug, but don't miss the differences too. Elijah performed his miracle to help a foreign widow to come to faith in the God of Israel, whereas Elisha performs his miracle to help the school of prophets to see that God has power to multiply Elijah's ministry right across their land.[4]

When Elisha tells the widow to gather all the empty vessels in the neighbourhood and to trust the Lord to multiply the oil in her jug, he is doing more than simply meeting her immediate need. He is teaching the school of prophets to believe that God can multiply their anointing right across the nation. She receives more than she expected, paying off her debt and storing up some savings for the future, but it is less than she might have received. We are told that *"When all the jars were full ... the oil stopped flowing."* That's meant to be a warning. The Lord gives the Holy Spirit without limit (John 3:34), so if his work in us seems limited then the limitations must all be at our end. If we attempt to raise up a mighty army of leaders, we will achieve far more in our own ministries than if we limit his work among us by only gathering a handful of vessels to be filled.[5]

---

[3] The Hebrew text refers to them ten times as *"the sons of the prophets"* (1 Kings 20:35, and 2 Kings 2:3-15; 4:1, 38; 5:22; 6:1 and 9:1). Since they were not literal *sons*, it is best translated *company* or *school*.

[4] The miracle in 1 Kings 17:8-16 took place in Zarephath, in pagan Phoenicia. *"Shut the door"* in 4:4 emphasizes that this miracle was a sign for the school of prophets more than a sign for the world.

[5] The Hebrew word *'āsūk*, translated *jar*, was the normal word used for a *flask of anointing oil*.

Elisha frequently stays at a house in Shunem when travelling between the school classes at Mount Carmel and Samaria. The couple who host him are childless, so he rewards their hospitality by prophesying that they will conceive a child miraculously in their old age. When the boy grows sick and dies, his mother hurries to find the prophet teaching the school class at Mount Carmel. Once again, there are obvious parallels with Elijah's ministry in 1 Kings 17, but don't miss the differences too. Elisha's instinct is to perform this miracle of resurrection through his apprentice Gehazi.[6] It is only after Gehazi touches the corpse with Elisha's staff – a sign of his authority and a prophetic picture of the cross of Jesus – but fails to raise him that Elisha comes in person. Even then he lets Gehazi tell the mother when the boy is raised to life again. Elijah's miracle was performed solo to impart faith to a foreigner, but Elisha's miracle imparts faith that this is something that the Lord can multiply to others.[7]

Elisha demonstrates that miracles come from God's power, not our own.[8] He offers to speak to King Joram on behalf of his hostess, in order to provoke her to ask him to speak to the true King of Israel on her behalf instead. Elisha also teaches us the importance of persistent prayer. He is not satisfied with a warm corpse, and nor must we be. He prays repeatedly until he sees resurrection. Since Jesus has commissioned us to perform miracles, both physical and spiritual, we must persist in prayer too.[9] Elisha also shows us that prayer is no substitute for action.

---

[6] 1 Kings 19:21 and 2 Kings 3:11 indicate that Gehazi was more than just Elisha's servant. He served as his apprentice. We learn a vital lesson in the next chapter as to why Gehazi failed to raise the boy from the dead.

[7] The boy's mother wants Elisha to perform the miracle, saying *"Shalōm!"* to both her husband and Gehazi, meaning either *"It's all right!"* or *"Goodbye!"* Elisha refuses to play the big man. He multiplies his ministry.

[8] Gehazi really could have been used to raise this boy to life using Elisha's staff had his lifestyle matched up to his profession of faith in the Lord. James 5:16–18 insists that Elijah and Elisha were humans just like us.

[9] The fact that we live in an unbelieving generation does not dilute this promise. Elisha's hostess literally accuses him of *lying* in 4:16, but his own faith trumps unbelief in others. So will ours.

He gets face-to-face, mouth-to-mouth, eye-to-eye and hand-to-hand with the dead boy in order to raise him from the dead. Jesus doesn't just command his followers to stay indoors and pray. He also commands us to *"Go!"*[10]

The chapter ends with two more miracles that emphasize the Lord's desire to multiply our ministry to others. The school class at Gilgal is starving in a famine. One desperate student forages for food and brings poisonous plants back to the school canteen. Elisha sprinkles the stew with flour – a picture of Christ the Bread of Life, his body crushed on the cross like grain crushed into flour on a millstone, so that the serpent's venom can be sucked from our veins. Suddenly, the poisonous plants are transformed into healthy food.[11] Elisha then alleviates the famine further by feeding a hundred people with twenty loaves of bread. They can even put the leftovers in a doggy bag for later.

That's where the chapter ends, and it's deliberate. As we will see later, Elisha's school of prophets ultimately failed. It didn't bring revival to the northern kingdom. When Elisha died, people still hailed him as a one-man army in 2 Kings 13:14: *"My father! My father! ... The chariots and horsemen of Israel!"* But his feeding of the hundred closely parallels the way that Jesus later fed a crowd of over 5,000.[12] It points us to the true and better Elisha, who multiplied his ministry to the Twelve and through them multiplied his ministry to the world. He still tells us to expect the Lord to multiply our own ministry: *"The harvest is plentiful but the workers are few. Ask the Lord of the harvest, therefore, to send out workers into his harvest field."*[13]

149

---

[10] Matthew 10:8 and 28:18–20; Acts 9:36–42 and 20:9–12, and 2 Corinthians 1:9.

[11] See Luke 22:19; John 6:35, 48; 12:24, and Revelation 20:2.

[12] Jesus also raised a dead boy to life at Nain, just down the road from Shunem (Luke 7:11–17).

[13] Matthew 9:37–38. Note that Jesus fed the 5,000 *through his disciples* in Mark 6:35–44.

Little Things
(2 Kings 5:1–27)

"If the prophet had told you to do some great thing, would you not have done it? How much more, then, when he tells you, 'Wash and be cleansed'!"

(2 Kings 5:13)

A little thing can make a massive difference. Just ask the tennis legend Boris Becker. After winning his first few matches against Andre Agassi, he lost tournament after tournament to him. It was only many years later, long after the two players had retired, that Agassi revealed why. He had noticed that whenever Becker stuck out his tongue to the left before tossing the ball up for his serve, he always served wide. When he stuck out his tongue in the middle of his mouth, he always served straight. Becker was totally unaware that such a little thing betrayed his game plan to his rival: *"I used to go home and tell my wife – It's like he reads my mind. Little did I know you were just reading my tongue."*[1]

If we want to minister for God like the prophet Elisha, and if we want to multiply that ministry to others, then we need to learn this lesson too. We discover in 2 Kings 5 that little things are never little when it comes to obedience to the Lord.

The young Hebrew slave girl at the start of 2 Kings 5 is so insignificant in the eyes of the world that the writer does not even tell us her name. He tells us all about Naaman, the commander of the Aramean army who is *"a great man"* and *"highly regarded"* for his great deeds on the battlefield. She is merely plunder from one of his raids but she does a little thing that makes a massive difference. Seeing Naaman stripped down to size by the

---

[1] Reported in the Australian newspaper *The Herald Sun* on 18th January 2017.

discovery of leprosy on his skin, she speaks up bravely. She tells her mistress, the great commander's wife, to encourage him to reach out to the God of Israel for healing. If you ever feel too insignificant for the Lord to do great things through you, then this ought to encourage you. The nameless slave girl is a hero. She overcomes her natural resentment towards the man who carried her off into slavery, and her natural fear of proclaiming the God of Israel to a nonbeliever, believing that a little thing can make a massive difference. Sure enough, it does.[2]

Naaman responds to her small act of courage with raw faith.[3] He knows his pagan idols cannot heal him, so he asks the king of Aram to send him across the border to be healed by the God of Israel.[4] We were told in 2 Kings 3:14 that King Joram of Israel is so ungodly that Elisha can hardly bear to look at him, yet even he does something little that makes a massive difference too. When Naaman hands him a letter from the king of Aram requesting healing, he assumes that his northern neighbour is looking for an excuse to mount yet another invasion of his land. He tears his royal robes and cries out in despair, *"Am I God? Can I kill and bring back to life?"* It's not the greatest prayer of repentance in the Old Testament, but it's big enough. The Lord has mercy on him. Joram means *The Lord Is Exalted*, and when Elisha hears that he has humbled himself and exalted the Lord, even ever so slightly, he sends word that the Lord will indeed help him.

Naaman therefore rushes round to Elisha's house with his soldiers.[5] He is bitterly disappointed when Elisha fails to receive

[2] Bitterness and resentment are a form of spiritual self-harm. We are told in 5:1 that *"the Lord had given victory to Aram."* The Sovereign Lord specializes in turning disasters into opportunities. See Genesis 50:20.

[3] Don't miss how remarkable this is. While the Israelites ignore Elisha's preaching, one of their pagan enemies finds salvation in the God of Israel! The name Naaman means *Pleasantness*. See Luke 4:25–27.

[4] The king of Aram assumes that any help to be found in Israel will be found at the king's palace. But Joram is not the true King of Israel. Not all that appears big is big, and not all that appears small is small.

[5] Naaman arrives *"with his horses and chariots"* in 5:9. It is a sign of Israel's weakness that the general of its arch-enemy can travel unchallenged with his men throughout the land.

him in person, simply sending a servant to command him to dip himself seven times in the River Jordan. It sounds like such a little thing that he is offended.[6]

> *"I thought that he would surely come out to me and stand and call on the name of the Lord his God, wave his hand over the spot and cure me of my leprosy. Are not Abana and Pharpar, the rivers of Damascus, better than all the waters of Israel? Couldn't I wash in them and be cleansed?"*

Furiously, he turns his chariot around and heads back home. He hasn't learned the lesson that God taught Elijah through the tiny whisper on Mount Sinai. Naaman expects solutions to look big and impressive. He despises little things.

As a church pastor, I have many conversations with people who think like Naaman. They struggle to accept the first command of Jesus to anyone who wants to follow him. I can quote the words of Peter in Acts 2:38: *"Repent and be baptised, every one of you."* I can quote the words of Jesus himself in Matthew 3:15 and 28:19: *"It is proper for us to do this to fulfil all righteousness ... Go and make disciples of all nations, baptising them."* I can quote all manner of other verses, but the issue isn't that Scripture is unclear. It's that Christian baptism seems like such a little thing to do. People plead that they are nervous or not-quite-ready or that their parents performed a ceremony for them as a nonbelieving baby that exempts them from obedience today. The power of Christian baptism is proved by how hard the Devil works to convince people that it's too small a thing for them to obey.

One of Naaman's servants has caught something of the courage of his master's Hebrew slave girl. He challenges him on his way home. *"If the prophet had told you to do some great*

---

[6] Naaman brings 70 kg of gold, 340 kg of silver and 10 sets of fine clothes, thinking he can buy a miracle from the God of Israel. Elisha crushes his pride, just as the command to be baptized crushes our own pride today.

thing, would you not have done it? How much more, then, when he tells you, 'Wash and be cleansed'!" Like many Christians when they are finally baptized, Naaman is amazed at what his little act of obedience brings.[7] When he comes up from the River Jordan for the seventh time, his skin has been completely healed. Baptism does not save us – faith in the death and resurrection of Jesus does that – but when we identify ourselves with him in his death and resurrection by being buried in the waters of baptism, something changes. It's a little thing, but in God's hands little things are big things.[8]

Naaman understands this. He converts wholeheartedly to the God of Israel: *"there is no God in all the world except in Israel ... Your servant will never again make burnt offerings and sacrifices to any other god but the Lord."* He is so convicted of his sin that he begs God not to judge him for taking part in the pagan ceremonies that come with being a general in the Aramean army. Elisha is delighted that he no longer sees such sins as little things.[9]

Elisha's servant Gehazi, on the other hand, does not understand this at all. He is furious that his master sees such small acts of obedience as a substitute for payment in hard cash. He hurries after Naaman to lie that Elisha needs some payment after all – and he learns the hard way that none of our little acts of disobedience are ever little things to God.

So if we want to be fruitful for God, let's learn what Hudson Taylor, the missionary to China, learned: *"A little thing is a little thing, but faithfulness in a little thing is a great thing."*

---

[7] 1 Corinthians 10:2 likens Christian baptism, not to the Passover, but to the crossing of the Red Sea. It helps us to experience our freedom fully. That's why Paul teaches us to be sanctified in Romans 6:1–7, not by pointing us back to our prayer of conversion, but to the waters of our baptism.

[8] Elisha does not endorse bowing down to idols. He simply majors more on the change that has taken place in Naaman than on the changes yet to come. Naaman scoffed in 5:12 that Aramean rivers are as good as the rivers of Israel, but now he .loads up his mules with soil in recognition that Israel is the Promised Land.

[9] We can tell that Gehazi despises Naaman from the way he refers to him as *"this Aramean"* in 5:20.

Next Generation
(2 Kings 5:19–27)

Elisha asked him, "Where have you been, Gehazi?"
"Your servant didn't go anywhere," Gehazi answered.

(2 Kings 5:25)

Every move of God is just a generation away from extinction. After Joshua led the Israelites to conquer the Promised Land, we are told in Judges 2:10 that *"another generation grew up who knew neither the Lord nor what he had done for Israel"*. There are hints at the end of 2 Kings 5 that history is about to repeat itself in tragedy. We discover that the school of prophets isn't going to bring long-term salvation to the nation of Israel.

Elijah was a first-generation prophet. The Bible compares his ministry to that of John the Baptist, preparing the way for a greater work of God once he was gone.[1] Elisha was a second-generation prophet. His ministry closely parallels that of Jesus, not just because he is anointed with the Holy Spirit at the River Jordan; he cleanses lepers, he multiplies loaves to feed the hungry and he imparts resurrection life to others even as he dies.[2] His ministry also prefigures Jesus because he calls twelve disciples and commissions them to *"Go and make disciples of all nations."* Elisha pours his life into the next generation of leaders.[3]

---

[1] Malachi 4:5; Matthew 3:4; 11:14 and 17:10–13, and Luke 1:17. The comparison isn't perfect, however, since John the Baptist did not perform any of Elijah's miracles (John 10:41).

[2] We are told about this final resurrection miracle in 2 Kings 13:20–21. Elisha means *God Saves*, just as Jesus means *The Lord Saves*. Elisha's father's name Shaphat also points to Jesus, meaning *He Judges*.

[3] Matthew 28:18–20. Elijah ministered from about 870 to about 852 BC. Elisha ministered from about 852 to about 795 BC. Sadly, there was no prophet of the same calibre in the northern kingdom to pick up the reins after 795 BC.

Gehazi is one of those third-generation prophets, and his personal failure predicts the failure of the school of prophets as a whole. Solomon's wisdom had proved to be a false saviour for Israel. So had its Temple buildings and its pursuit of a false unity. The writer of 2 Kings therefore records what happened to Gehazi in order to impress on us that there is only one true Saviour for Israel. These tragic verses are meant to lift our eyes away from Elisha and his school of prophets, and onto Jesus instead.

Gehazi is to Elisha what Elisha was to Elijah. He is an apprentice prophet, serving his master as Elisha did when he *"used to pour water on the hands of Elijah."*[4] It is therefore a big moment in the story when Elisha entrusts his staff to Gehazi in 4:29 and commands him to run on ahead to raise a dead boy to life. It is like the moment when Elijah entrusts his cloak to Elisha in 1 Kings 19:19 and 2 Kings 2:13, testing him to see if he can minister with the same authority as his master. Sadly, although Gehazi's name means *Valley of Vision*, he just can't see what his master has tried to teach him. He has no faith in 4:43 that Elisha can multiply loaves of bread to feed the crowds, nor has he any faith that Elisha's staff gives him authority to raise the dead. He doesn't even pray for the boy to be raised. He simply prods him with the staff half-heartedly before returning to inform Elisha that he was right all along to be sceptical. Gehazi represents a generation that has far less faith than its fathers that God will respond to his people's prayers. Jesus warns us in Matthew 9:29 that God responds: *"According to your faith let it be done to you."*

Gehazi is more interested in money than he is in ministry. He may be blind to the spiritual lessons that Elisha has tried to teach him, but he has no trouble spotting the treasures stowed away in the Aramean chariots. Seventy kilograms of gold would be worth over £2 million today. Three hundred and forty kilograms of silver is five times what King Omri paid for the land on which he built Samaria in 1 Kings 16:24. Gehazi decides to abuse his privileged position in the school of prophets to take

---

[4] 1 Kings 19:21 and 2 Kings 3:11.

advantage of the Aramean general.[5] He runs after Naaman to ask for some of his silver and fine clothing. Gehazi fools himself that, since God has been slow to judge the sins of Israel, he will overlook his own sins. But Gehazi is wrong.

Gehazi learns the lesson of 1 Timothy 5:24–25, that God sometimes judges sin slowly and sometimes instantly. The Lord strikes him down with the same leprosy that he removed from Naaman's body, to warn the school of prophets that it is at a crossroads. Elisha believed God for a double portion of Elijah's ministry, so the next generation must not settle for a watered-down version of Elisha's ministry. They ought to become the breakthrough generation for Israel, but they are in danger of becoming the breakdown generation instead.[6]

This is very relevant for our own day. It can't have escaped your notice that the Church in the Western world is losing the next generation. The average age of churchgoers is getting older, while its former young people run after the treasures of the world. Part of this is the fault of the older generation. For too long Christians have behaved like players in a junior soccer team, where every player surges forward in the hope of becoming the hero that scores the winning goal. We have forgotten that our calling is to serve the next generation, not ourselves. We need to become like the players in a rugby team, passing the ball backwards to those coming up behind us and then lending our weight to them in order to help them run further forward than we ever did ourselves. We need to rediscover the Great Commission, as Paul rephrases it for Timothy: *"The things you have heard me say in the presence of many witnesses entrust to reliable people who will also be*

[5] The Hebrew oath Elisha uses in 5:16 is the same one he used in 3:14 and the same one Elijah used in 1 Kings 17:1 and 18:15. Gehazi never learns to say that he stands before the Lord, but we can say something even better. The Gospel means that we are now seated next to God in the heavens in Jesus (Ephesians 2:6).

[6] Note how patient the Lord is with Gehazi, giving him one last opportunity to confess his sin and to repent in 5:25. It is only after he rejects this offer of restoration that he is finally struck down.

qualified to teach others."[7] Jesus to Paul, Paul to Timothy, Timothy to reliable people, and reliable people to others. That's how the Church advances, when each generation of believers passes the ball behind them and helps the next generation to run.

The writer of 1 and 2 Kings believes that the Jewish exiles in Babylon are about to experience a national revival. The Lord is about to bring them back to the Promised Land, so the older exiles need to start investing their lives in the next generation that will rebuild the nation of Israel. The younger exiles need to respond with greater faith than Gehazi, for the size of their faith will dictate the scale of their revival. If they believe in the Lord's promises and invest their lives in a generation yet to come, then the future of God's people will be very bright before them. If they don't, it is "game over" for Israel.

The same is true for us. Jesus still assures his followers in John 14:12 that *"whoever believes in me will do the works I have been doing, and they will do even greater things than these."* In other words, our churches need not become corrupted by sin, like Gehazi's skin.[8] The best days of our churches ought to lie ahead of us, not behind us. The next generation of believers can be the breakthrough generation, winning converts to God's promise of death and resurrection from every nation of the world.

---

[7] Matthew 28:19 isn't just about making converts. 2 Timothy 2:2 explains that it's about making disciples.

[8] Gehazi ought to love Naaman as a new believer, yet he despises him as *"this Aramean"* (5:20). As a result, like Rahab and Achan in Joshua 6–7, a pagan convert is saved while a Hebrew is cursed and destroyed.

Do You See?
(2 Kings 6:1–7:20)

Elisha prayed, "Open his eyes, Lord, so that he may see." Then the Lord opened the servant's eyes, and he looked and saw the hills full of horses and chariots of fire all round Elisha.

(2 Kings 6:17)

Time is running out for the school of prophets. Unless its students learn to see as clearly as Elijah and Elisha, their revival movement is about to grind to a halt in Israel.[1] The writer therefore gets personal in these two chapters. He asks each of us: "Do you see?"

In 6:1–7, Elisha's students miss the point. They are excited that their school building is so small that they have started a building project on a larger site down by the river. They are like any church leader who gets distracted by quantity instead of focusing on quality. Elisha allows them to start building, but one of the students panics when the head falls off his axe and disappears into the River Jordan. He borrowed it from his neighbour and, since he cannot afford to replace it, he is in danger of being sold into slavery to repay the debt he owes. Elisha sees the bigger picture. He performs a miracle which demonstrates that Israel's hope is to be found in the future death and resurrection of its Messiah. He throws a wooden stick into the river (representing the cross of Jesus) which causes the axe-head to defy the laws of physics by floating to the surface (representing the miraculous

---

[1] The students speak literally in 6:1 about *"the place where we dwell before you."* These two chapters therefore continue to emphasize that Elisha poured his life out to disciple the next generation. So must we.

resurrection of Jesus).[2] The student retrieves the axe-head from the water, but it isn't clear he grasps the bigger picture. The writer asks us: "Do you see?"[3]

In 6:8–12, Elisha demonstrates the power of God to save his people. He receives detailed insight into all of the Aramean battle plans as he prays before the Lord. The king of Aram is furious when he discovers that King Joram of Israel knows his every move. Perhaps he suspects Naaman who, like the axe-head, was baptized in the River Jordan as a prophetic picture of salvation coming through the death and resurrection of the Messiah. He interrogates his army officers until one of them explains the story behind the story, that no scheme of man can ever succeed against the death-and-resurrection power of the Lord.[4] Again the writer asks us: "Do you see?"

In 6:13–20, the writer's imagery becomes increasingly obvious. The Aramean army exposes the weakness of Israel by marching unopposed to Dothan, only eleven miles north of Samaria. Elisha has found a new servant to replace Gehazi but this new apprentice panics when he wakes up to discover that the city is under siege. Elisha prays in 6:17 what he prays for all the prophets at his school: *"Open his eyes, Lord, so that he may see."* Suddenly his servant sees an angel army spread out across the hills around the city, riding in chariots of fire like the one that carried Elijah up to heaven. To underline this lesson, Elisha prays that the Lord will strike the Aramean soldiers blind. He leads them eleven miles south inside the walls of Samaria and then prays for their eyes to be opened.[5] They realize with horror

---

[2] In Acts 5:30 and 10:39, Peter refers to the cross of Jesus as "the thing made of wood". In 1 Peter 3:20-21, he adds that Noah's wooden ark that floated on the waters also represented Christ's death and resurrection.

[3] For a similar prophetic picture of the death and resurrection of Jesus, see Exodus 15:25.

[4] King Ben-Hadad II of Aram stubbornly refuses to repent and turn to the God of Israel, despite the defeat of one general in 1 Kings 20 and the healing of another in 2 Kings 5. He will pay for it with his life in 2 Kings 8.

[5] Elisha isn't lying to the soldiers in 6:19. When they open their eyes, there he is for them in Samaria!

that they are trapped and that the archers on the walls can shoot them like fish in a barrel. Elisha wants us to grasp something of God's power at work all around us. Again the writer asks us: "Do you see?"

In 6:21–23, King Joram of Israel is spiritually blind. He thinks salvation means slaughtering his enemies. Elisha has to teach him that God's promise of death and resurrection extends salvation to the pagan nations too. He tells him to feed the captive Aramean soldiers and then to send them home as a Gospel proclamation to their king.[6]

In 6:24–7:2, King Ben-Hadad of Aram rejects their Gospel message. Instead of repenting, he invades yet again and besieges the capital city of Israel. When Samaria's food supplies run so low that its citizens are reduced to eating donkeys' heads and pigeon droppings, King Joram blames the Lord in 6:27 instead of turning to him in prayer.[7] When he hears that his desperate subjects have even started eating their own children, he decides to execute Elisha instead of enlisting his help.[8] Elisha means *God Saves*, but Joram is so spiritually blind that he misses the offer of salvation under his very own nose. He cries out in despair in 6:33, *"This disaster is from the Lord. Why should I wait for the Lord any longer?"* He is impatient when he ought to be penitent.

The Lord responds with staggering mercy. Although Joram is acting like his murderous father Ahab, the Lord extends a final chance for him to see.[9] He decides to treat his angry words in 6:27 as a prayer like that of King Jehoshaphat in 2 Chronicles 20:12: *"We do not know what to do, but our eyes are on you."* He

---

[6] Dothan is where Joseph's brothers betrayed him in Genesis 37, yet he showed them mercy and fed them in return. King Joram was to do the same, inviting the king of Aram to be saved alongside his general Naaman.

[7] The Hebrew phrase translated *seed pods* in some English Bibles is better translated *dove dung*. It cost over £250 a kilogram, and a donkey's head cost over £500. Things were so desperate in Samaria that we find out in 7:13 that the army had eaten most of its chariot horses.

[8] There is a deliberate contrast here between Joram's weakness and Solomon's wisdom in 1 Kings 3:16–28.

[9] The depth of God's mercy is seen by how slowly he judges King Joram compared to Gehazi.

decides to view the fact that Joram is wearing sackcloth under his clothes as a sign that he is more repentant than at first meets the eye. When he sends an executioner to Elisha's house, the Lord even treats him as if he were a pilgrim in search of salvation. He inspires Elisha to prophesy deliverance for Israel. The Lord will flood Samaria's marketplace with so much food in the next twenty-four hours that all of its food prices will at once revert to normal.[10]

One of Israel's army officers just can't see it, so the Lord makes him a picture of what will happen to the next generation if it fails to follow in the footsteps of Elijah and Elisha. In 7:3–20, the Lord allows the Aramean soldiers besieging the city to hear the sound of the horses and chariots of fire that Elisha's servant saw surrounding Dothan. They panic and flee, believing that it is the sound of the Hittites and Egyptians coming to the aid of their ally. As a result, all of the food in the Aramean camp now belongs to Samaria. The army officer sees it but he never tastes it. He is trampled underfoot by the starving Israelites as they rush out to gather all the food the Lord has given them.

The writer turns to us at the end of these verses and he asks us yet again: "Do you see?" He wants to know if we trust the Lord to work salvation in our own day, or whether we consign such miracles to the days of Elijah and Elisha. He wants to know if our eyes are aware of the angel armies that surround his Church today, or whether such talk makes us doubt and sneer like the army officer of Israel. Make no mistake, our answer to these questions will dictate how much we see of God's power in our own generation and in the generation coming up behind us.

The writer asks us one last time: "Do you see?"

Jesus responds to us in Matthew 9:29: *"According to your faith let it be done to you."*

---

[10] When the king of Aram tried to murder Elisha, the prophet fed his men as an invitation for him to repent. When the king of Israel tries to murder Elisha, the prophet feeds his city as an invitation to repent too.

The Back-Up Plan
(2 Kings 7:3–20)

"What we're doing is not right. This is a day of good news and we are keeping it to ourselves. If we wait until daylight, punishment will overtake us. Let's go at once."

(2 Kings 7:9)

Part of the good news of the Gospel is that its success doesn't actually depend on you and me. It's important that we remember this when the writer of 2 Kings challenges us to be more faithful with the Gospel than Gehazi and the other third-generation prophets who failed Israel. The Gospel isn't meant to be a burden. It is meant to set us free. Mordecai assures us in Esther 4:14 that it cannot fail: *"If you remain silent at this time, relief and deliverance ... will arise from another place, but you and your father's family will perish."*

Even as the third generation of prophets begins to fail Israel, the Lord reveals that he has a back-up plan. It's the same plan that he activated when his Messiah came to first-century Israel and was rejected by the Pharisees, the heirs to a revival movement that had planted synagogues right across Israel. In Israel's hour of need, the Lord reaches down into the gutter and raises up an army of evangelists from its rubbish pile.

The writer leaves Elisha and turns our attention to four Israelites with leprosy outside the city walls. They have been ejected from Samaria for contracting the contagious skin disease that turned Naaman into an outcast and that humbled him to seek salvation from the God of Israel.[1] The Jewish exiles

---

[1] There is also a deliberate link here to Gehazi's leprosy. An unfaithful generation cannot thwart God's plans.

162

in Babylon viewed leprosy as a picture of sin's corruption in our hearts, which is why Jesus commanded lepers, not just to be healed, but to *"Be clean!"*[2] These four men are therefore the most unlikely evangelists in Israel. They are utter nobodies. They are the walking dead.

But they are also desperate. Unlike the Israelites inside Samaria, they have no donkeys' heads or pigeon droppings or chariot horses or babies to turn to as alternative saviours. They have none of the prosperity that prevents so many of us from admitting that we have no hope of salvation but the Lord. They wander to the Aramean camp in the hope of a handout, but instead they find the camp deserted and its treasures all theirs for the taking. This is a prophetic picture of what the apostle Paul describes in Colossians 2:15. Jesus triumphed over the Devil and his demons through his death on the cross, and now he invites his followers to rise up to enjoy the plunder.

The four lepers fill their pockets with Aramean gold and silver, but we have something better. The apostle Paul calls it *"the boundless riches of Christ"* – an Aladdin's cave of God's grace and favour towards us.[3] When the four lepers swap their beggar's clothing for fine Aramean robes, it is meant to remind us that Jesus removes our sin from us and clothes us in *"garments of salvation"* that are *"dazzling white, whiter than anyone in the world could bleach them."*[4] The other objects plundered by the lepers are also meant to make us think of what is ours through Jesus' victory: being granted a part in God's plan, being filled with power to fulfil it through the Holy Spirit, and being adopted as sons and daughters of God who, unlike these lepers, can now make our home inside his holy city.

There is plenty of injustice throughout 1 and 2 Kings. Lepers who ought to be loved are rejected as outcasts. Subjects who ought to be fed by their rulers are forced to eat pigeon

---

[2] Leviticus 13; Matthew 8:2–4 and 10:8; Mark 1:40–44 and Luke 4:27; 5:12–14 and 17:12–19.

[3] Paul celebrates these riches five times in just three chapters, in Ephesians 1:7, 18; 2:7; 3:8 and 16.

[4] Isaiah 1:18 and 61:10; Zechariah 3:3–5; Mark 9:2–3 and Revelation 19:7–8.

droppings while their king still has horses in his stables. Babies who ought to be protected by their mothers are cooked and eaten. But the very worst injustice is described here. The four lepers stop digging holes to hide their treasure from the world and start exclaiming that the greatest injustice in the world is for people to enjoy the good news of God's salvation without sharing it with those who haven't yet heard: *"Then they said to each other, 'What we're doing is not right. This is a day of good news and we are keeping it to ourselves. If we wait until daylight, punishment will overtake us. Let's go at once and report this to the royal palace.'"*

I find this pretty sobering. How many times have I celebrated the riches of God's mercy towards me on a Sunday with my church friends and then kept silent throughout the week about the riches of his mercy towards my non-church friends? Worse than that, how often have I shared the Gospel with my friends who have heard it many times before, while ignoring the vast crowds who have not heard the Gospel even once. The greatest injustice in the world isn't financial poverty, but spiritual poverty. It's that the Church spends 96 per cent of its money on itself, and a further 2 per cent on reaching people who have already been evangelized. How can it be right for some people to hear the Gospel many times when other people have never even heard it once?

At the same time, I find what the four lepers do next very inspiring. It doesn't matter that their message of good news is met initially with cynicism.[5] It only takes a few people to taste and see what the Lord has done for them to cause a stampede of faith in a city. If you consider yourself to be a nobody when it comes to evangelism, untalented and unable to win people to the Lord, then be encouraged. He loves to raise up beggars from the gutter. It is always his glorious back-up plan whenever those

---

[5] King Joram finds it easier to believe in an Aramean trap than in God-given salvation. He came to the end of himself in 6:27, but he refuses to trust in God in 7:12. That's the difference between saving faith and despair.

who are more talented and gifted reject his calling to proclaim the Gospel to the world.

It was this back-up plan that motivated Jesus to choose fishermen and tax collectors to be the first apostles of his Kingdom. When the priests who ran the Temple and the Pharisees who ran the synagogues rejected him, he saved lepers and cripples and demoniacs and pagans, commissioning them as his evangelists instead. It is still the back-up plan he uses to stoke revival movements right across the Church today.

It is the back-up plan that inspired William Booth to found The Salvation Army. When the English middle classes sneered that he would never find enough leaders to fulfil his grand plans to preach the Gospel in every city, he replied: *"We shall get them from the public houses. Men who have felt the fire will be the best men to rescue others, and we shall never fail in getting the right men."* He attributed his success to God's delight in turning vagrants into vicars and prostitutes into preachers. He said it all began with *"the day I got the poor of London on my heart, and a vision of what Jesus Christ could do with the poor"*.[6]

---

[6] Quoted from Charles T. Bateman in *Life of General Booth* (Press, 1912).

School's Out
(2 Kings 8:1–29)

Then the man of God began to weep.

(2 Kings 8:11)

This third section of 1 and 2 Kings has focused on a revival movement which looked for a moment as though it might prove the salvation of Israel. Elijah started well and founded a school of prophets. Elisha built on his predecessor's legacy to turn that school into a force to be reckoned with right across Israel. But in the end, the prophets at the school fail to follow in Elijah and Elisha's footsteps. By the start of 2 Kings 8, school is out and, as revival starts to stall, things unravel pretty fast for God's people.[1]

In 8:1–6, the writer deals with an important question. Does the failure of the school of prophets mean that the Lord was somehow unfaithful to Elijah and Elisha? The writer answers that question by winding the clock back to an event which took place before Naaman was healed of his leprosy and before Gehazi contracted it instead.[2] He returns to the woman who supported Elisha during the heyday of his school by giving him a place to stay whenever he was travelling from one class to another. The writer tells us that Elisha warned her that Israel was about to be judged through a seven-year famine. By the time we read about it in 4:38–44, she is living in the fertile fields of the Philistines.

---

[1] The school of prophets is mentioned nine times in this third section: in 1 Kings 20:35, and in 2 Kings 2:3–15; 4:1, 38; 5:22 and 6:1. It is mentioned one final time in the very first verse of section four, then never again.

[2] Lepers were banned from cities, let alone from the palace. It would be nice to think that Gehazi had repented and been healed, but it is clear from 5:27 that he had not.

In year eight, she returns to discover that her house and land have been stolen by one of her neighbours. Trusting in God's faithfulness, she therefore goes to see the king.

Gehazi is still the servant and apprentice of Elisha. He is a favourite at the royal court since he is happy to entertain King Joram with tales from Elisha's ministry without ever challenging him to repent of his sin.[3] The writer uses this event to show us that the Lord was not unfaithful to Elijah and Elisha's school of prophets – it was the other way around. The woman arrives at the palace just as Gehazi finishes the story of how Elisha raised her son to life. Excited by the story, the king immediately orders one of his officials to do more than she ever dared ask him. Not only will she receive back her house and land, but her neighbour will also have to back-pay her rent for the past seven years! If the Lord is this faithful to a woman who supported the school of prophets, then he was clearly not unfaithful to the school itself. The school was unfaithful to him.

In 8:7–15, the Lord starts to bring the curtain down on his enemies. King Ben-Hadad II of Aram refused to repent when God empowered the weak army of Israel to defeat him twice (1 Kings 20), when God healed his general Naaman (2 Kings 5), and when Elisha captured his soldiers, fed them and sent them back home with a Gospel message of forgiveness for their king (2 Kings 6).[4] He even refused to repent when his army panicked at the sound of angel armies and abandoned camp outside the walls of Samaria (2 Kings 7). Ben-Hadad has repeatedly rejected God's mercy so now he finally reaps God's judgment instead.

It is now 842 BC, so over fifteen years have passed since God commanded Elijah on Mount Sinai to anoint Hazael as the new king of Aram. It is a mark of God's mercy that Elisha only obeys now, having given Ben-Hadad plenty of time to repent. It is also a reminder that the God of Israel is sovereign over events

---

[3] Contrast Gehazi's easy manner with Elisha's reluctance even to look at King Joram in 3:13–14.

[4] Elisha is exceedingly courageous in 8:7. Ben-Hadad had sent troops to capture and kill him in 6:13.

in every nation of the world. Hazael is a common court official but his name means *God Has Seen*.[5] When Ben-Hadad sends him to ask Elisha whether the king will recover from his illness, Elisha says that he will – unless Hazael takes his life before he has time to do so.[6] Emboldened by Elisha's vision of his future, Hazael murders his master and usurps his throne.

In 8:11–15, the Lord finally calls time on Ahab's dynasty too. Although the talk of slaughtered babies and pregnant women is disturbing, we are mostly struck by God's patience and mercy. Fifteen years have passed since 1 Kings 21, when the Lord warned Ahab that his wicked family was about to be destroyed. The Lord promised to do this in the days of Ahab's son, yet he held off during the reign of Ahaziah. It is only now, under Ahaziah's younger brother, that the curtain finally falls on his sinful dynasty. King Joram had been delivered by the Lord through one battlefield miracle against Moab and at least four against Aram. He has heard all about Elisha's miracles from Gehazi, but he has never once repented. The rise of Hazael will result in Joram's injury in battle (8:28–29), then in the slaughter of his dynasty by one of his disgruntled generals (9:24).

In 8:16–24, the Lord begins to judge the southern kingdom of Judah too. Elisha's school of prophets hasn't merely failed to fight the cancer of Ahab's sin in Israel. It has allowed the cancer to spread south over the border to infect David's dynasty too.[7] The writer has said little about the southern kingdom since King Jehoshaphat of Judah pursued false unity with Ahab in 1 Kings 22.[8] Now we discover just how foolish that policy was.

---

[5] An inscription by King Shalmaneser III of Assyria calls Hazael *"the son of a nobody"* – in other words, he was a usurper, not a member of the royal family. He would rule from 842–796 BC.

[6] At first Elisha was despised even by children (2:23–24), but by persisting in his ministry he ends up being hailed as a spiritual father to kings (8:9). Stand firm whenever people mock you. God will vindicate you.

[7] Since Jehoshaphat followed the Lord, Judah maintained control of Edom even when Israel lost control of Moab (1 Kings 22:47 and 2 Kings 1:1). Since Jehoram follows Ahab, Judah now loses control of Edom too.

[8] *"To this day"* (8:22) must be quoting from the court annals of Judah. See also 1 Kings 8:8; 9:20–21 and 12:19.

He married his son Jehoram to Athaliah, the sinful daughter of Ahab and Jezebel. When Jehoram becomes king, she incites him to murder many of his brothers and cousins and to promote idolatry throughout his land. Judah is therefore judged by losing wealthy Edom and the fortress city of Libnah that guards its border with the Philistines.[9]

In 8:25–29, things get even worse. Jehoram's son Ahaziah is heavily influenced by his mother Athaliah and he thoroughly infects the southern kingdom with the sins of Ahab's dynasty. When King Hazael of Aram invades Israel, Ahaziah marches north to fight in support of the army of Israel. He does not even heed the danger when the main battle takes place at Ramoth Gilead, the place where the Arameans defeated Ahab in 1 Kings 22. When Joram of Israel is wounded in the battle, Ahaziah still lacks the good sense to turn around and hurry home to Judah. Instead, he goes to Ahab and Jezebel's old palace at Jezreel to comfort King Joram. He has no idea that it will result in his own death after only one year as king of Judah. He fails to grasp that if Judah mimics the sins of Israel then it will also share in God's judgment against Israel.

School's out. The spiritual revival that started with Elijah and Elisha is well and truly over, and in the wake of its failure one thing is clear. No radical religious leader can ever bring about long-lasting revival. God alone can be the true Saviour of Israel.[10]

---

[9] Some of this detail comes from the more detailed account of the reign of Jehoram in 2 Chronicles 21. He was rebuked by a prophetic letter that Elijah had written for him years earlier. Enemy armies would carry off his treasures and he would die of a hideous bowel disease aged only thirty-nine.

[10] Note how the writer shifts our gaze onto this Saviour in 8:19 by mentioning *the lamp of David's dynasty*. David died over a century before this, yet God remained faithful to Judah in its unfaithfulness to him.

2 Kings 9–17:

Northern Lights

Lights Out
(2 Kings 9:1–37)

"The whole house of Ahab will perish. I will cut off from Ahab every last male in Israel – slave or free."

(2 Kings 9:8)

In the days leading up to the outbreak of World War One, the British foreign secretary Sir Edward Grey sank into pessimism and despair. He lamented that "The lamps are going out all over Europe, we shall not see them lit again in our lifetime."[1]

In this fourth section of 1 and 2 Kings, we are meant to feel the same. The Lord extinguishes any residual hope that the northern kingdom of Israel will survive. The third section ended with a promise to Judah in 8:19 that the Lord would *"maintain a lamp for David and his descendants for ever"*, but there is no such hope for Ahab's dynasty. As we can see from the table below, in the time it took Judah to get through four kings, Israel was already on its ninth king and its fourth dynasty. Now the fourth dynasty falls too. The Lord turns the lights out on Israel so that it has no hope left but its Messiah.

At the start of chapter 9, the lights go out on the school of prophets. From this point on, we hear of it no more. Only two further prophets emerge from the northern kingdom in the Old Testament, and neither Hosea nor Jonah appear to have attended the school. Like Israel's priests, its prophets now go dark. Their lights go out until their nation is destroyed. For all its early promise, the school of prophets proves unable to save Israel.

---

[1] This quote comes from Grey's own memoirs, published in 1925, entitled *Twenty-Five Years: 1892–1916*.

In 9:1–26, the lights go out on King Joram of Israel. Elisha sends a prophet to anoint one of his generals to found a new dynasty for Israel. Jehu is a commoner but, like Hazael, he wastes no time. He announces his intentions to his fellow officers in the army camp at Ramoth Gilead. They lay down an impromptu red carpet, blow their trumpets and declare in 9:13 that *"Jehu is king!"* Then they march behind him forty-five miles to the palace that Ahab built at Jezreel, where his son is still recovering from his injuries in battle.

Joram means *The Lord Is Exalted*, but he has never lived up to his name. Sixteen years have passed since the Lord commanded Elijah to anoint Jehu as the new king of Israel (1 Kings 19). Almost fifteen years have passed since the Lord decreed that he would wipe out Ahab's dynasty during the reign of his son (1 Kings 21). In all that time there is no record of Joram ever repenting, despite seeing more miracles in his short reign than most people see in a lifetime. The wonder isn't that the Lord destroys him now. It's that his mercy held his hand back for so long.

Jehu means *The Lord Is The One*, and he does live up to his name. He takes the prophet seriously when he says in 9:6 that the people of the northern kingdom are as precious to God as those in the south: *"I anoint you king over the Lord's people Israel."* He takes him seriously when he prophesies that the Lord has tasked Jehu with avenging all the righteous blood that has been shed in the name of Jezebel's false gods.[2] He refuses to enter into peace negotiations with the soldiers that Joram sends to intercept him. He orders them to fall in behind him and to help him turn out the lights on Ahab's sinful dynasty. When Joram finally rides out of Jezreel in person, Jehu greets him in 9:22 with a war cry: *"How can there be peace ... as long as all the idolatry and witchcraft of your mother Jezebel*

---

[2] The prophet uses similar language to Elijah in 1 Kings 21:21–24, including likening all of Ahab's male heirs to street dogs – not so much every *"male"* as *"everyone who urinates up against the wall."*

abound?"[3] With a single arrow, the new King Jehu shoots the old King Joram dead.

Jehu was part of Ahab's entourage when Elijah prophesied in 1 Kings 21:19 that the Lord would destroy his dynasty in the vineyard he had stolen from Naboth.[4] When Jehu looks around, he marvels at the sovereignty of God because this is precisely where he has just shot Joram in his chariot. He commands one of his officers to throw the corpse on the ground. Ahab's son will be the compost on Ahab's stolen vegetables today.

In 9:27–29, Jehu turns his attention to King Ahaziah of Judah. He has no intention of extinguishing the northern lights of Ahab's dynasty but of allowing them to continue to burn brightly south of the border.[5] Ahaziah is a grandson of Ahab and Jezebel, so he fires a second arrow to kill this second king.[6] The south is no place for northern lights.[7]

In 9:30–37, Jehu confronts the final arch-enemy, Jezebel. She is old enough to be a great-grandmother but she still puts on make-up and arranges her hair in the hope of seducing the new King Jehu.[8] Her beauty may have ensnared many men in her younger years, but she can tell at once that it will not work this time. Alarmed, she insults Jehu from her upstairs window, accusing him of acting just like Zimri, the army general who killed his king to usurp the throne and establish the third

---

[3] Jehu lists Jezebel's twin crimes literally as *adultery* and *magic*. Revelation 2:20 warns us that the demons that inspired her are still at work today, seducing people into sexual promiscuity and spiritual manipulation.

[4] Jehu's memory is slightly confused, conflating 1 Kings 21:19 with 21:29.

[5] Israel and Judah have become so indistinguishable from one another that their intermarried monarchs even share the same names. There are two J[eh]orams and two Ahaziahs, so Jehu deals with Judah too.

[6] 2 Chronicles 22:9 adds the detail that Jehu's men captured the wounded Ahaziah in Samaria and brought him back for execution at Megiddo. They then allowed the men of Judah to take his body back for burial.

[7] There is no contradiction between the *eleventh* year in 9:29 and *twelfth* year in 8:25. One counts only the complete years, while the other includes the year that King Joram began to reign.

[8] We meet her great-grandson Joash in 11:2, but she remains a seductress (2 Kings 9:22 and Revelation 2:20).

UNITED	David (1010–970 BC)
MONARCHY	Solomon (970–930 BC)

JUDAH	ISRAEL
Rehoboam (930–913 BC)	Jeroboam I (930–909 BC)
Abijah (913–910 BC)	Nadab (909–908 BC)
Asa (910–869 BC)*	Baasha (908–886 BC)
Jehoshaphat	Elah (886–885 BC)
(872–848 BC)*	Zimri (885 BC)
Jehoram (853–841 BC)	Omri (885–874 BC)
Ahaziah (841 BC)	Ahab (874–853 BC)
	Ahaziah (853–852 BC)
* These kings of Judah had overlapping reigns with their sons	Joram (852-841 BC)

dynasty of Israel. The accusation is rather hard to swallow, given that Jezebel's own father-in-law Omri then killed Zimri and usurped the throne himself in order to found Ahab's dynasty!

Jehu isn't listening anyway. He calls out to the servants who are standing behind Jezebel, to throw her down from the window. When they do so, she suffers one of the most gruesome deaths in the Bible. Her blood sprays on the wall as she hits the ground and then smears the chariot horses that crush her bones to pieces under their hooves. While Jehu enjoys his first royal banquet inside the palace, the street dogs feast on what remains of Jezebel, leaving nothing but her skull and feet and hands. Since her window looked out onto Naboth's vineyard, Jehu shouts in triumph that this gruesome fate is the final fulfilment of the curse that Elijah called down on Ahab's dynasty. At last this foul family has been extinguished from Israel. Its northern lights will finally shine no more.

Botched Messiah
(2 Kings 10:1–36)

Yet Jehu was not careful to keep the law of the Lord,
the God of Israel, with all his heart.

(2 Kings 10:31)

Cecilia Gimenez really thought that she was helping when she took her paintbrushes down to her local church to restore a portrait of Jesus that was looking a little worn. The nineteenth-century fresco at Borja, in northern Spain, definitely needed some attention but Cecilia's paintwork was so amateurish that the before-and-after pictures made mocking news headlines all around the world. Google her name and you will easily see why. The church's fresco *Behold the Man* is now better known as *Behold the Monkey*.[1]

I find Jehu a lot like Cecilia Gimenez. It's obvious that the writer wants to use him as a prophetic picture of the Messiah who will one day save Israel, but it's also obvious that Jehu doesn't really know what he is doing. He is the closest that the northern kingdom ever gets to a godly king, but he doesn't come very close at all. Like the fresco on the wall at Borja, he is a botched messiah. He isn't the Saviour Israel is looking for.

On one level, Jehu is like Jesus. He is the only ruler of the northern kingdom who is ever said to be anointed with oil, and the Hebrew for *anointed one* is *messiah*. Other than Jesus, when he rides into Jerusalem on a donkey, Jehu is the only king whose subjects throw down their cloaks in order to form a makeshift red carpet for him. After bringing down God's judgment on sinful Israel and dispatching Jezebel, Jehu feasts on his victory,

---

[1] This story was reported by newspapers all across the world in August 2012.

just like Jesus after he dispatches the prostitute Babylon in Revelation 17:1–19:10.

That's where we have to check that we are not like Cecilia Gimenez ourselves. We live in a generation that has tried to repaint Jesus in its own colours. It tends to downplay his judgment, forgetting the praise he receives in Hebrews 1:9: *"You have loved righteousness **and hated wickedness**; therefore God, your God, has set you above your companions."* Instead of being offended by Jehu's slaughter of Ahab's dynasty, we need to see it as a picture of what Jesus will do to sinful rebels when he comes back from heaven to judge the world. The Lord commands it in 9:7 and commends it in 10:30, which is why the writer tells us repeatedly that this bloodshed was obedience to *"the word of the Lord."*[2] He even uses a Hebrew verb that is usually reserved for the work of priests when he says in 9:33 that Jehu *sprinkled* the blood of Jezebel on the city wall.[3] Unless we grasp that Jesus will one day return from heaven to judge our sinful world, then we are like Cecilia Gimenez, and the false Jesus we are worshipping is a botched messiah.

Jehu is fine with a God of judgment. His problem is that he fails to view him also as a God of grace and mercy. His reckless driving is a sign that he shares King David's love of action but that he lacks David's meticulous devotion to God's Word. In 9:11, his soldiers expect him to dismiss God's prophet as a "maniac". In 9:20, we discover that he is a maniac himself whenever he takes to the reins of his chariot. He invites Jehonadab the Rekabite, one of Israel's most devout spiritual leaders, to take a ride with him: *"Come with me and see my zeal for the Lord."*[4] But it is *zeal*

---

[2] 2 Kings 9:26, 36–37; 10:10 and 17. See the description of Jesus in Isaiah 63:1–6 and Revelation 19:11–21.

[3] The Law of Moses decreed death for Jezebel's idolatry and witchcraft (Deuteronomy 13:1–18 and 18:10–12) and for Ahab's murder (Numbers 35:31–33). Jehu was therefore acting as God's priestly executioner.

[4] The Rekabites were descended from Hobab the Kenite, the Midianite brother-in-law of Moses (Numbers 10:29; Judges 4:11 and 1 Chronicles 2:55). Although technically foreigners, the Lord points out in Jeremiah 35 that Jehonadab and his followers were more devoted to the God of Israel than most of the Israelites.

without knowledge, like that of Cecilia Gimenez.[5] The picture we see here is that of a pretty botched messiah.

In 9:27-29, Jehu goes beyond the mandate that the Lord has given him by murdering King Ahaziah of Judah. He sees him as a grandson of Jezebel and decides that he must therefore die, but in the Lord's eyes Ahaziah is a precious son of David's dynasty. If this feels like a subtle distinction, note how this act of disobedience leads directly to the massacre of David's dynasty by Jezebel's daughter Athaliah and to her supplanting David's dynasty for six terrible years. Hosea 1:4 says that the Lord later destroyed Jehu's own dynasty as a punishment for his botched obedience during this *"massacre at Jezreel"*.

In 10:1-11, Jehu goes beyond his mandate again by forcing some of his leading citizens to murder the seventy surviving sons of Ahab. The Lord had commanded him to do the slaughtering himself, but he reasons in 10:9 that it might be more expedient politically to share the blame around a little.[6] In 10:12-17, Jehu goes beyond his mandate yet again by killing forty-two more members of David's precious royal dynasty.[7]

In 10:18-28, Jehu goes one step further. He decides that a good end justifies sinful means. He pretends he wants to worship Baal even more than Ahab, which is a clever ruse to gather all of the leading idolaters in Israel to the slaughter. When they come to the great temple of Baal in Samaria, he shows how little he truly cares about the Lord by offering sacrifices to Baal with them.[8] He could easily have pounced on them before the

---

[5] Paul warns us in Romans 10:1-2 that many people still suffer from zeal without knowledge today.

[6] The metaphor used in the Hebrew text of 10:10 is *"not a word that the Lord has spoken ... will fall to the ground"* (my own translation). It echoes the one used in 1 Samuel 3:19. If the Jesus we are worshipping is not Judge, we are not worshipping Jesus at all.

[7] Although they describe themselves literally as Ahaziah's brothers, they must be his cousins and nephews, since all his brothers were carried off and killed by the Philistines (2 Chronicles 21:16-17 and 22:1).

[8] Ahab built this temple in 1 Kings 16:32 and Joram tried to destroy its sacred stone in 2 Kings 3:2. With Jezebel dead, the temple becomes a public toilet, a fitting end to the false god that tried to supplant Yahweh.

worship started, but he isn't as zealous for the Lord as he says he is. He is a botched messiah.

In 10:29-36, we discover just how terrible a picture of Jesus he really is. He makes no effort to obey the Law of Moses. He continues to encourage the people of the northern kingdom to worship the golden calves at Bethel and Dan instead of going south to worship at the Temple of the Lord. Although he boasts to Jehonadab that he is passionate about Yahweh, his greatest passion is consolidating his own grip on power. As a result, the Lord judges him for his sin. Jehu loses all of his territory east of the River Jordan. Although his dynasty lasts for eighty-nine years (by far the longest in the northern kingdom) it is eventually annihilated in a bloodbath similar to that of Ahab.[9]

Jehu was the closest that the northern kingdom ever got to a godly ruler. He was its greatest portrait of the Messiah who would one day come to save Israel. The Lord entrusted him with the northern kingdom's greatest opportunity for repentance and revival, but he missed his moment. Like a Spanish fresco, Jehu was a botched messiah.

---

[9] Losing the land of two and a half tribes of Israel must have come as an enormous blow. It also warned Jehu that the rest of the prophecy in 8:12 would also come true. The Lord invited him to repent but he carried on sinning. We know from the *Black Obelisk of Shalmaneser III* that Jehu was also forced to pay tribute to Assyria.

When Athaliah the mother of Ahaziah saw that her son was dead, she proceeded to destroy the whole royal family.

(2 Kings 11:1)

This is the chapter where the Devil almost wins. If that surprises you, coming hot on the heels of his defeat in the north, then be warned. The Devil is always at his most dangerous when we underestimate him. The first three verses of this chapter reveal the Devil's favourite tactic, then the remaining verses teach us how to defeat it.

The Devil had smuggled a Trojan horse into the royal house of Judah. I'm sure you know the famous story. For ten long years, the walls of Troy held out against a besieging Greek army, until Odysseus suddenly had a clever idea. The Greeks would sail away, apparently defeated by the Trojans, leaving behind on the beach a massive wooden horse as an offering to the gods for a safe journey home. When the Trojans woke up to discover that the Greeks were gone, they dragged the massive horse inside their city to take centre stage in their drunken victory celebrations. Only the high priest *Laocoon* was suspicious: "I fear the Greeks, for all the gifts they bear."[1] Sure enough, the hollow horse was filled with Greek soldiers who crept out after nightfall, slaughtering the sleeping Trojans and throwing wide open the gates of the city. What the Greeks failed to do in ten years through force of arms, they achieved in one night through deception.

---

[1] Virgil tells us this story in his epic poem *The Aeneid* (2.49).

The Devil had long failed to destroy Judah through force of arms. Neither the folly of King Rehoboam nor the sins of King Ahijah nor the pride of King Asa had persuaded the Lord to abandon them on the battlefield to the armies that the Devil mustered against them. The Devil therefore resorted to a Trojan horse tactic against King Jehoshaphat, one of the godliest rulers of Judah. He seized upon Jehoshaphat's God-given zeal for greater unity among God's people and pushed it to such an extreme that it morphed into something ungodly. When Jehoshaphat told King Ahab that *"I am as you are, my people as your people, my horses as your horses"*, it sounded very virtuous, but it almost destroyed his dynasty.[2]

King Jehoshaphat probably hoped that if he married his son Jehoram to Athaliah, the daughter of Ahab and Jezebel, their union might lead the northern kingdom back to the Lord. But like many a Christian deciding to date a nonbeliever, he underestimated the Devil's determination to destroy him. Israel wasn't influenced for good. Instead, Athaliah led Judah into idolatry under her husband Jehoram and her son Ahaziah.[3]

Charles Spurgeon spoke out strongly against a call to Christian unity when Victorian preachers modified God's Word to make it sound less offensive.

> *A new religion has been initiated, which is no more Christianity than chalk is cheese; and this religion, being destitute of moral honesty, palms itself off as the old faith with slight improvements ... The atonement is rejected, the inspiration of Scripture is derided, the Holy Spirit is degraded into an influence, the punishment of sin is turned into fiction, and the resurrection into a myth, and yet these enemies of our faith expect us to call them brethren, and maintain a confederacy with them!*[4]

---

[2] 1 Kings 22:4; 2 Kings 3:7, and 2 Chronicles 19:1–2 and 20:35–37.

[3] 2 Kings 8:18, 26–27. It sounds as though Athaliah also married her son Ahaziah into Ahab's dynasty.

[4] Charles Spurgeon wrote this in his *Sword and Trowel* magazine (August 1887).

Spurgeon was criticized for being divisive, but he was convinced that a false call to unity is the Devil's Trojan horse tactic to defeat God's people. Athaliahs look lovely, but they are deadly. Spurgeon insisted that false teaching is far more dangerous than persecution:

> *A chasm is opening between the men who believe their Bibles and the men who are prepared for an advance upon Scripture ... We cannot hold the inspiration of the Word, and yet reject it; we cannot believe in the atonement and deny it; we cannot hold the doctrine of the fall and yet talk of the evolution of spiritual life from human nature; we cannot recognise the punishment of the impenitent and yet indulge the "larger hope". One way or other we must go ... With steadfast faith let us take our places; not in anger, not in the spirit of suspicion or division, but in watchfulness and resolve. Let us not pretend to a fellowship which we do not feel.[5]*

Jehoshaphat just couldn't see the danger in his daughter-in-law. He had no idea how much damage a little compromise could do. But when King Ahaziah's corpse is brought back to the palace in Jerusalem, Athaliah seizes her chance. She has already incited her husband to murder his six brothers. All of their own sons, except for Ahaziah, have already been killed by foreign raiders. Jehu has murdered forty-two of their cousins and nephews.[6] Athaliah therefore fills the power vacuum by quickly commanding the palace guards to murder the remaining royal princes. It doesn't matter that some of them are her own grandchildren. She lusts for power more than progeny. She is the Trojan horse that the Devil has introduced into Judah in order to destroy David's dynasty.[7]

---

[5] He wrote this in *The Sword and Trowel* (September 1887).

[6] 2 Chronicles 21:1–6, 16–17 and 22:1.

[7] The same spirit that inspired Athaliah to destroy her own family also inspired King Herod to destroy the innocent babies of Bethlehem in Matthew 2:16–18. Satan hates the Seed of David.

These verses are pretty sobering about the consequences of our little acts of compromise. The Lord is not exaggerating when he warns us that they lurk at our doorway like little lion cubs and grow up into lions that eventually tear apart our character, our ministry, our churches and our very lives.[8] The Lord speaks with graphic language because he really wants to save us from the Trojan horse of Christian unity at any price.

In the classic children's novel *The Little Prince*, the French writer Antoine de Saint Exupéry describes the prince's constant fight to save his tiny asteroid from being destroyed by the roots of mighty baobab trees. The prince explains that the survival of his asteroid depends on his perpetual vigilance for little seeds of compromise.

> *A baobab is something you will never, never be able to get rid of if you attend to it too late. It spreads over the entire planet. It bores clear through it with its roots. And if the planet is too small, and the baobabs are too many, they split it in pieces ... You must see to it that you pull up all the baobabs regularly, at the very first moment ... Sometimes there is no harm in putting off a piece of work until another day. But when it is a matter of baobabs, that always means catastrophe.[9]*

Ultimately Athaliah fails in this chapter. The Lord will not allow the Devil to thwart his promise to bring forth the Messiah from David's dynasty to be the true Saviour of Israel. But let's not treat God's mercy as a cause for complacency. Athaliah very nearly succeeds. Let's see the story behind the story in these verses and resist a false call to Christian unity that drags a Trojan horse inside the Church to destroy it from within.

---

[8] Genesis 4:7 and James 1:14–16. Note Joseph's determination to drive sin from his doorway in Genesis 39:10.

[9] Antoine de Saint Exupéry in *Le Petit Prince* (1943).

Counter-attack
(2 Kings 11:4–21)

Jehoiada brought out the king's son and put the crown on him ... They anointed him, and the people clapped their hands and shouted, "Long live the king!"

(2 Kings 11:12)

There is a reason why the movie *Darkest Hour* won so many awards. It is very inspiring to watch a person, faced with overwhelming odds, decide to believe that victory is still possible. That's what Winston Churchill does in the movie and it's what a princess from David's dynasty does in the face of Athaliah's slaughter. These verses teach us how to stand up to the Devil and how to go on the counter-attack ourselves.

The writer tells us that *we need to take a stand for truth*. Jehosheba is still reeling from the news that Jehu has killed her brother, Ahaziah.[1] She knows that there is now nobody left in David's dynasty who can stand between the ambitious Athaliah and the throne.[2] Nevertheless, she lives up to her name, which means *The Lord Swears True*. She defies the odds by smuggling her baby nephew Joash into hiding right under the nose of Athaliah at the Temple. If we spot the Trojan horse of sin and compromise in the Church, the writer says the first step of our counter-attack needs to be to stand up firmly against it.

The writer also tells us that *we mustn't think that we are alone*. The Devil always seeks to discourage God's people by

---

[1] Jehosheba was probably not Athaliah's daughter. 2 Chronicles 21:17 says Jehoram had other wives.

[2] 2 Chronicles 22:9 says, *"there was no one in the house of Ahaziah powerful enough to retain the kingdom"*.

making them feel that there is no one else who shares their Christian passion. He loves to trick us into thinking, like Elijah on Mount Sinai, that we are the solitary Christian at our workplace or the only member of our church who is wholeheartedly obedient the Lord. Princess Jehosheba doesn't fall for this trap. She enlists the help of her husband Jehoiada, who is a priest at the Temple, asking him to protect the sole survivor of David's dynasty.[3] She is never mentioned again in the story. She has played her part in God's plan. Now it is her husband's turn to gather a group of conspirators around the young Joash in order to restore him to the throne of Judah.

The writer tells us that *we must be patient.* The priest Jehoiada keeps Joash hidden at the Temple for six long years. During all that time it looks as though the Devil has won and the Lord has been unfaithful to his promise that a man from David's family will rule on David's throne forever.[4] The name Athaliah means *The Lord Restrains*, but it looks to any casual observer as though the Lord has failed to hold back the Trojan horse tactic of the Devil. We need to remember this when the Church seems mired in sin and appears to be losing the next generation. It is all too easy for us to begin doubting the Lord's promises. But the story behind the story in this chapter is that appearances can be deceiving.[5]

The writer tells us that *we must lay hold of the weapons that God has given us.* Jehoiada means *The Lord Knows*, and he grasps that God has already given him everything he needs. David had appointed Carites from Crete to be his royal

---

[3] The writer does not tell us that Jehoiada is her husband. We only find this out in 2 Chronicles 22:11. The first-century historian Josephus argues that Jehoiada was the high priest (*Antiquities of the Jews*, 9.7), although his name is not listed among the high priests in 1 Chronicles 6:3–15.

[4] In fact, nothing could be further from the truth. The Lord granted partial success to the Devil so that Joash would be brought up by his godly Uncle Jehoiada instead of by his idolatrous father Ahaziah.

[5] Note how the writer doesn't use any of his standard formulae to describe the reign of Athaliah. She is the Lady Jane Grey of the southern kingdom – a usurper who is not counted among the true monarchs of Judah.

bodyguards, and those foreigners were still fiercely loyal to David's dynasty.[6] David also filled the Temple storerooms with spears and shields, so Jehoiada has access to enough weapons to equip a mighty army. David also stored the royal crown and the sacred anointing oil at the Temple whenever they were not being used at the palace. When Jehoiada senses that the time is ripe for revolution, after Joash has turned seven, he therefore has all that he needs to proclaim him the new king of Judah.

We need to remember this ourselves, whenever we are tempted to despair that the Church is compromised and overwhelmed with sin. The apostle Paul reminds us that the Christian life is meant to feel like a battle and that the Lord has already given us all the weapons that we need. He reassures us in Ephesians 6:10–20 that the Lord has given us a shield of faith to ward off the Devil's flaming arrows, a belt of truth to help us stand against his lies, and a helmet of salvation and a breastplate of righteousness to guard our head and heart. He has given us marching shoes and the sword of the Spirit to help us go on the counter-attack. Paul encourages us in verse 13 to *"Put on the full armour of God, so that when the day of evil comes, you may be able to stand your ground."* It isn't a case of *if* the day of evil comes, but of *when* it comes. Praise God, he has given us every weapon that we need.

The writer tells us that *we need to trust in the Lord's timing.* Jesus warns us in John 7:1–8 that the Christian life involves a lot of waiting. If Jehoiada had trumpeted too early that one of the king's sons had survived Athaliah's slaughter, no one would have rallied to a baby and Joash would surely have been killed. If he had chosen any normal day after his nephew turned seven, Athaliah might have been powerful enough to put down his rebellion. Jehoiada trusted in the Lord's timing and waited for the Sabbath of a major feast day when *"all the*

---

[6] These Carites are also called *Kerethites* in 1 Samuel 30:14; 2 Samuel 15:18 and 20:23, and 1 Kings 1:38. They were the Greek Sea Peoples who had settled in Crete and in parts of modern Turkey.

people of the land" were in the Temple courtyard.[7] As a result, Athaliah knows at once that she is beaten. Her supporters are terribly outnumbered.

Finally, the writer tells us that *we need to be radical with sin*. If we are faithful in the face of sin and compromise, the Lord will eventually entrust us with an opportunity to reset the spiritual temperature of our nation.[8] Note how firmly Jehoiada deals with Athaliah, finishing off what Jehu started with her mother Jezebel.[9] He ignores her histrionics, as she tears her clothes and shouts, *"Treason! Treason!"*[10] He commands her to be killed outside the palace along with anyone who follows her. Jehoiada tells the people to tear down the temple that she built for Baal in Jerusalem, demolishing its altar and its idols, and slaughtering its priests as they go about their pagan worship.[11] Then he calls the entire southern kingdom to return to the Lord. He leads them in a renewal of their covenant with the Lord, and then leads Joash in a similar renewal of the Lord's covenant with David's dynasty. He will rule over Judah as an earthly regent for its true King. [12]

---

[7] 2 Kings 11:9 and 11:14. It was peak time at Passover, Pentecost or the Feast of Tabernacles. Athaliah could not resist the populist surge that resulted from Jehoiada's sensitivity to God's perfect timing.

[8] Athaliah is so uninterested in the Temple of the Lord that Jehosheba knows she can safely hide Joash there. Athaliah is absent from this festival and only comes running when she hears cries of *"Long live the king!"*

[9] The link is deliberate between Jezebel being trampled under Jehu's horses and Athaliah being killed at the horse gate. So is the link between Jehu and Jehoiada both destroying the temple of Baal in their capital.

[10] Don't be fooled by the Devil's doublespeak. Athaliah is as hypocritical in 11:14 as Jezebel is in 9:31.

[11] The Lord knows what he is doing. Had the Devil not overplayed his hand, this temple of Baal might have been tolerated at the heart of Jerusalem for many years. Because of Athaliah, it was totally destroyed.

[12] The writer tells us literally in 11:19 that Joash *"sat down on the throne of the kings"*. This is not merely the triumph of a boy over his wicked grandmother. It is the renewal of God's covenant with his Messiah. The Lord had commanded new kings of Judah to copy out the Law of Moses as a reminder that they were to rule for the Lord (Deuteronomy 17:18–20). Jehoiada is therefore restoring David's dynasty to its calling.

Do you believe that God could bring about a similar revival in the Church in your own generation? Are you willing to become his agent of revival, like Jehosheba and Jehoiada? Then take a stand for the truth, join with others and lay hold of the spiritual weapons he has given you. If you wait patiently for his perfect timing then you will live to see the moment when the Devil is defeated and when your nation turns back to the Lord.

False Hope
(2 Kings 12:1–21)

Joash king of Judah took ... all the gold found in the treasuries of the temple of the Lord ... and he sent them to Hazael king of Aram, who then withdrew from Jerusalem.

(2 Kings 12:18)

J.R.R. Tolkien warned his readers that *"False hopes are more dangerous than fears."*[1] That was certainly the case for ancient Judah. Instead of trusting in the Lord to be their Saviour after he rescued them from the hands of Athaliah, they soon returned to their old ways and started trusting instead in their Temple to save them.

It can't have escaped your notice how small a part in the story the Temple of the Lord has played since the death of King Solomon. Even at the dedication of his new Temple in Jerusalem, Solomon admitted amid the fanfare that it would take more than a building to save his nation.[2] That's why the first ten chapters of 2 Kings mention the temple of Baal five times and the temple of Rimmon twice, but fail to mention the Temple of the Lord at all. The people of Judah had grown disillusioned with it. God had let their hopes fail in their sanctuary so that he could lift their eyes to place their hope in their Saviour.

False hopes die hard, however. Did you notice the way in which the Temple moved back centre stage in chapter 11? It

189

---

[1] The character Sador says this in *The Children of Húrin* (2007).

[2] Solomon confesses nine times that his Temple can never be God's true dwelling place (1 Kings 8:27, 30, 32, 34, 36, 39, 43, 45 and 49). Like Jeremiah 7:4–15, he focuses our eyes on Jesus as the true and better Temple.

wasn't just a tale of two women – Jehosheba against Athaliah – but a tale of two temples – the sanctuary of Baal against the sanctuary of the Lord. Joash arose as a new King Solomon, anointed with oil by a priest at a contested coronation in the Temple courtyard.[3] Suddenly a Temple that has not featured in the story since 1 Kings 15:18 is mentioned over thirty times in 2 Kings 11–12.[4]

In 12:1–16, hope soars that the Lord's Temple might become the Saviour of God's people. The writer informs us that Joash reigned for forty years, the same length of time as David and Solomon. The priest Jehoiada acts as his regent while he is a child and, when Joash finally comes of age, he chides him for not doing enough to restore the decaying Temple. Joash pays workers to complete the restoration, instead of relying on volunteers, funded by a giving campaign that tops up the census money and the other offerings that already come into the Temple.[5] There is much to encourage us in these verses. They reassure us that God's people will always rise up to restore the Church whenever they are given a clear lead. Church leaders ought to be trustworthy and accountable in the way they spend the money (12:10 and 15), not shying away from paying church workers instead of penny-pinching with volunteers (12:6–16). But amid the encouragement comes a warning. No amount of money or restructuring is a substitute for our Saviour.

In 12:17–21, we are meant to be horrified by the failure of King Joash, of his priests and of his refurbished Temple. The sudden shift in tone is deliberate, because the writer wants to

[3] In 11:14, Joash stands between the two large bronze pillars that hold up the porchway to the Temple. This custom of King Solomon is also repeated by King Josiah in 23:3.

[4] When the priests of Judah failed God's people, the writer shifted his focus to the prophets of Israel. Now that the prophets have failed God's people too, the spotlight shifts back to the priests a second time.

[5] The Jewish Law required every adult male to pay half a shekel of silver each time a census was conducted (Exodus 30:11–16). The twenty-third year of Joash's reign was 812 BC, so the Temple was now almost 150 years old. It had been particularly damaged during the reign of Athaliah (2 Chronicles 24:7).

shock us out of trusting in religious institutions for salvation. We are only told in 2 Chronicles 24:15-27 the full story of what happened. When Jehoiada died, King Joash quickly tired of the Lord's Temple. It couldn't hold his own attention, let alone the attention of the entire southern kingdom. He had never demolished the old Canaanite "high places" throughout Judah, and now he permits his subjects to reinstall the old pagan idols there. When the Lord sends prophets to call him back to Temple worship, Joash refuses to listen. Even when Zechariah (the son of Jehoiada and the childhood friend of Joash) attempts to call him back to God, he has him stoned to death in the Temple courtyard. Here we have the Temple and its priests and a new king from David's dynasty, but things are every bit as bad as in the days of Athaliah.

That's why the Lord does something dramatic to convict the southern kingdom of its false hope in the Temple to save it from its enemies. He allows King Hazael of Aram to invade the land of Judah. Having left behind many of his soldiers to garrison the territory he has captured from Israel east of the River Jordan, his men are outnumbered by the army of Judah, but against all odds he wins. Hazael slaughters the sinful courtiers who turned the heart of King Joash away from the Lord. He captures the fortress city of Gath on the border with Philistia and then lays siege to Jerusalem. King Joash panics. Instead of rushing to the Temple to repent of his sin and to plead with the Lord to deliver Judah as King Solomon hoped that he would in 1 Kings 8:37-40, King Joash rushes to the Temple to strip it of its treasures to buy off the Aramean army.[6] He succeeds, but at a terrible price. He hasn't merely undone his own repairs to the Temple. He has also plundered it of the treasures stored up by his predecessors. The Lord's Temple looks even shabbier now than it did at the start of his reign. It stands as a forlorn sign to the people of Judah that their Temple is a false Saviour.

---

[6] Again the writer gives very little detail about this in order to focus us on the failure of the Temple. We find out this extra detail in 2 Chronicles 24:23-24.

In another of J.R.R. Tolkien's books, he warns his readers that, *"It is wisdom to recognise necessity, when all other courses have been weighed, though as folly it may appear to those who cling to false hope."*[7] The Lord wants the people of Judah to stop looking to their Temple and its priests to save them, because it is only once we set aside our false hopes that we finally start looking to the Messiah.[8] Sadly, the people of Judah just can't see it. The Lord needs to demonstrate clearly that King Joash is not the messiah they are looking for.

Before the Aramean army withdraws, it wounds Joash severely in battle. He loses too much blood to be taken back to Jerusalem, so they lay him in a bed at a house in Beth Millo instead.[9] This is his last chance to repent of his sin and to point his subjects to a true and better Saviour. When he refuses to do so, two of his disgruntled officials avenge the death of Zechariah son of Jehoiada by murdering Joash in his bed.

It is a sad end to a reign that began so well. This kind of intrigue and assassination belongs in the north, not the south. The death of Joash, aged only forty-seven, marks the first time that a king of Judah has been murdered by his own subjects. It also means that every single son and grandson of Jehoshaphat has died a violent death. Judah's pursuit of false unity with Ahab's dynasty has proved to be an unmitigated disaster. So has its false hope in the Temple to save them. Unless they repent of turning the Lord's Temple into a talisman, they will never find deliverance through the true Saviour of Judah.

---

[7] Gandalf the Grey says this to Elrond in *The Fellowship of the Ring* (1954).

[8] Paul explains in Acts 28:20 that only the life, death and resurrection of Jesus is the true *"hope of Israel"*.

[9] We are only told this extra detail in 2 Chronicles 24:25.

The Way Back
(2 Kings 13:1–25)

When the body touched Elisha's bones, the man came to life and stood up on his feet.

(2 Kings 13:21)

When I was a student, I got lost at the top of a French mountain. It was late in the day and the other skiers had gone on ahead of me. The ski lifts had stopped working and I was the last person still out on the slopes. All alone, I realized that I had no idea how to get back to my chalet. I needed to act quickly, because the light was fading fast.

I don't remember how long I struggled around the mountain to find my way back to the chalet. All I remember is that the sun had gone down by the time I fell into a snowdrift and lay exhausted, longing to close my eyes and go to sleep out in the snow. That's when I started praying and was surprised to find a banana in my backpack that gave me enough of a sugar rush to haul my weary body up the brow of the next hill. Looking down, I saw my chalet right in front of me. I had found my way back home.

Being lost on that French mountain was one of the worst moments in my life, so I can hardly begin to imagine what it must have felt like to be one of the Jewish exiles in Babylon. They longed to be set free and sent back to the Promised Land, but there were no indications that the Babylonians would ever reverse their captivity. They had no idea how to find their way back home. That's the story behind the story in 1 and 2 Kings.

It's why the writer insists, in 13:1–3, that *rebellion* is never the way back home. The Jewish exiles might be tempted to blame the Lord in their lowest moments, but resentment towards the Lord is always a spiritual dead end. Jehoahaz had seen his father Jehu's rebellion result in the loss of Israel's territory east of the River Jordan. He ought to have looked across the border to the revival taking place in Judah and repented of his own sin. Instead, he threw himself into the same idolatry as the other kings of Israel before him. The writer says that he provoked the Lord to such anger and that he handed him over to become a puppet ruler for the kings of Aram.[1]

In 13:4–9, the writer also warns the Jewish exiles that *remorse* is never the way back home. In his troubles with the Arameans, King Jehoahaz finally seeks salvation from the Lord. His prayers are answered when a deliverer (probably King Adad-Nirari III of Assyria, who invaded Aram from 806–804 BC) diverts Hazael's attention away from Israel. But remorse is not the same thing as repentance. It is short-lived and superficial. Jehoahaz continues to bow down to the golden calves at Bethel and Dan, and to an image of the goddess Asherah in Samaria.[2] Although his name means *The Lord Possesses*, he acts as if his kingdom is his own. The Lord therefore decimates his army before he dies. Short-lived remorse in Babylon would never bring the Jewish exiles home.

In 13:10–25, the writer warns the Jewish exiles that *religion* is not the way back home. He whizzes very quickly through the reign of King Jehoash of Israel, before backtracking to the moment when he briefly tried religion.[3] Surprised to have defeated the king of Judah in battle, he pays a visit to the prophet Elisha to find out how to do the same to the king of Aram.[4] It is

---

[1] Jehoahaz reigned 814–798 BC and Hazael reigned 842–796 BC. The writer mentions Hazael's son, the future Ben-Hadad III, because he was already the effective ruler of Aram before his ageing father died.

[2] Ahab set up this Asherah pole in 1 Kings 16:33 and it somehow survived the purge of Jehu.

[3] Jehoash was so sinful that he even named his son, King Jeroboam II, after the first king to lead Israel astray.

[4] Joash and Jehoash are Hebrew variants of the same name, both meaning *Given By The Lord*. The writer uses both names interchangeably, but most English Bibles allocate one variant to each king to avoid confusion.

the last time that a king of Israel will ever consult a prophet of the Lord, so this is as religious as the northern kingdom ever gets. The prophet is now aged over eighty and on his deathbed.[5] Jehoash weeps with the same words that Elisha used at the end of Elijah's ministry back in 2:12: *"My father! My father! ... The chariots and horsemen of Israel!"*[6] In a rerun of that moment, when Elijah promised him a double portion of the Spirit if he persisted in his footsteps, Elisha promises that if Jehoash shoots an arrow out of his east window towards the territory his father lost east of the River Jordan, then he will annihilate the Aramean army there.[7] Elisha places his own hands over the king's hands as he takes the shot, to emphasize that this victory will come from the Lord.

So far so good, but now the writer reveals why religion can never be our way back home. Elisha commands Jehoash to hit the ground with his remaining arrows to show his persistence in the prophet's footsteps. When Jehoash hits the ground three times and stops the prophet is furious. Such half-hearted obedience betrays that his profession of faith in the Lord is merely the outward show of religion. He has no genuine heartfelt passion to walk in fellowship with the Lord.[8] That's the problem with religion. It looks impressive on the outside but it has no power to change us on the inside. Jehoash will defeat the Arameans three times – one for each time that he struck the ground with his arrows – but that will only be enough to recapture the towns that the Arameans have captured from the

---

[5] Elisha's bones could raise a man to life but they could not heal his body of *"the illness from which he died"* in 13:14. It is therefore very unhelpful to suggest that, with enough faith, a Christian will always be healed.

[6] Jehoash's cry of faith in Elisha was good, but it must also have saddened the prophet. He had tried so hard to multiply his ministry through the school of prophets, but when he dies he is still a one-man army.

[7] Aphek was just to the east of Lake Galilee and part of the territory captured by Hazael in 10:32–33. An earlier prophet had helped Ahab to win a decisive victory over Aram there in 1 Kings 20:26–30.

[8] This is why persistence in prayer is so important. Prayer is not a slot machine. It is an expression of our passionate desire to partner with God in extending his Kingdom rule throughout the world.

Israelites on the west side of the Jordan. It will not be enough to recapture the territory east of the river. Religion is like driving a Ferrari with the fuel light on. It may look good, but it won't take you very far.

The writer insists that the only way back for the Jewish exiles is *repentance*. They need to die to their old way of living and to ask the Lord to raise their nation back from the dead. This theme of death and resurrection has been the story behind the story since 1 Kings 13, and never more so than now. Elisha dies and is buried. Some Moabite raiders startle a group of gravediggers outside the prophet's tomb. The gravediggers throw the corpse into the tomb so that they can run and hide, but the instant it touches Elisha's bones it is revived. The dead man leaps to his feet and emerges miraculously from the grave.

Now *that's* the way back home, the writer tells the Jewish exiles.[9] It isn't rebellion or remorse or religion. It can be nothing less than death and resurrection. The Jews are not in captivity because the Lord has finished with their nation. He has buried them in a Babylonian grave, near to Abraham's original home, in order to renew their national story. If they embrace the death-and-resurrection pathway of the Gospel, they will find salvation through their Messiah. They will find their way back to the Promised Land.[10]

---

[9] It is also the way back for any church that feels "in exile" and wants to return to God's master plan.

[10] This is why the writer talks about God's *"covenant with Abraham, Isaac and Jacob"* in 13:23. The Lord who had been faithful to the patriarchs over 1,000 years earlier would now be faithful to their exiled children too.

What Might Have Been
(2 Kings 14:1–22)

He did what was right in the eyes of the Lord, but not as his father David had done.

(2 Kings 14:3)

Photography nowadays is a lot about the post-production. There was a time when you simply had to settle for what the camera gave you, but now you can totally transform the feel of a photo by playing with the colours and the contrast.

The writer of 1 and 2 Kings was ahead of his time. As the northern kingdom slides towards destruction, he uses events in the south to form a contrast between what happened to Israel and what might have been. He uses the reign of King Amaziah of Judah to show the blessings that it might have seen if only it had chosen to take the death-and-resurrection road.

In 14:1–6, the writer says King Amaziah was more devoted to the Lord than any of the northern kings. His mother was from Jerusalem – the dynasty of David had learned its lesson about marrying sinful northern girls – and, like his father Joash, he was a regular visitor to the Temple. His sacrifices on its altar expressed his repentance and his faith that the Messiah would one day come and die to raise believers from the dead.[1]

King Amaziah dies to his own desires in order to walk in obedience to the Lord. He executes the court officials who assassinated his father Joash, but he respects the Lord's command in Deuteronomy 24:16 not to execute their children.

---

[1] Amaziah is an imperfect messiah. Unlike King David, who refused to tolerate any idolatry in his kingdom, Amaziah permits his subjects to continue sacrificing to their idols at the "high places" (14:4).

The kings of Israel stopped at nothing to consolidate their grip on power, but King Amaziah demonstrates what their reigns might have been like had they surrendered themselves to God's Law.

In 14:7, he therefore showcases God's blessing on his kingdom. His great-grandfather Jehoram lost control of the wealthy vassal kingdom of Edom in 8:20–22, but now the Lord enables Amaziah to reassert his rule. He re-enacts King David's famous victory over the Edomite army in the Valley of Salt, just south of the Dead Sea, slaughtering 10,000 soldiers on the battlefield and 10,000 more as prisoners of war.[2] He then captures Sela, the impregnable mountain fortress of Edom, which is better known to modern tourists as Petra.[3] He renames it Joktheel, which means both *Subdued By God* and *The Blessedness of God*. Both meanings proclaim to the rulers of the northern kingdom what might have been.

Amid the victory celebrations, King Amaziah of Judah does something very foolish. The writer of 2 Kings does not tell us what he did. He is far too focused on the contrast between the north and south. We are only told what happened in 2 Chronicles 25:14–16. Amid the plunder that Amaziah brought back from Edom were the idols of his defeated foes. He set them up as his own gods and started worshipping them in Jerusalem. When the Lord sent a prophet to point out the stupidity of offering sacrifices to idols that had proved powerless to save their former owners from God's judgment, King Amaziah responded in 25:16 with a haughty threat: *"Have we appointed you an advisor to the king? Stop! Why be struck down?"* Refusing to listen, he is also left to rue what might have been for his reign.

Almost immediately, King Amaziah picks a fight with King Jehoash of Israel. He demands that he extradite some of his mercenaries who have recently raided Judah, but the northern

---

[2] See 1 Chronicles 18:11–13 and the title of Psalm 60.

[3] This extra detail comes from 2 Chronicles 25:11–12. *Sela* and *Petra* both mean *Rock* in Hebrew and in Greek.

king is in no mood to be lectured by his southern rival.[4] He responds rudely, describing the kings of Judah as mere thistles compared to the mighty cedarwood kings of Israel.[5] He follows through on this boast by routing Amaziah's army, dragging the king and many other hostages back to his palace in Samaria. He demolishes 180 metres of the northern city wall of Jerusalem, making it impossible to defend against future Israelite invasion. Having made his rival's capital impossible to defend against Israel, he then plunders the Lord's Temple and royal palace of their treasures.[6] He has no idea that his surprise victory is the Lord's way of reaching out to both him and Amaziah regarding what might have been.[7]

King Jehoash of Israel refuses to face up to his own sin. King Amaziah of Judah is equally stubborn. Even when he tastes the devastating consequences of worshipping the gods of Edom, the king of Judah refuses to throw away his idols and return to what might have been. The Lord gives him over fifteen years in which to change his mind before his judgment finally falls. Some of Amaziah's courtiers are so repulsed by his foreign idols that they conspire to kill him.[8] Although he escapes from Jerusalem to the fortress city of Lachish, thirty-five miles away, even its thick walls cannot protect him from the judgment of the Lord. The assassination of the second king of Judah in a row makes us wonder what might have been for the southern kingdom.

In 14:21–22, the Lord turns up the contrast again. He uses

---

[4] Amaziah reigned 796–767 BC and defeated Edom in about 784 BC. Since Jehoash reigned 798–782 BC, this quarrel must have broken out as a result of the episode described in 2 Chronicles 25:6–13.

[5] This telling of parables denotes a very Hebrew kind of quarrel. See also Judges 9:7–15.

[6] This was the fourth time God had allowed his Temple to be plundered of its treasures (after 1 Kings 14:25–28 and 15:18, and 2 Kings 12:18). Jehoash may have taken hostages in 14:14 because there was so little treasure left in the Temple after it was plundered by Hazael a few years earlier.

[7] The way Jehoash treats God's Temple proves that his outward religion did very little to change his heart.

[8] 2 Chronicles 25:27 says the conspiracy started as soon as he began to worship idols.

Azariah, the son of Amaziah, to demonstrate how much the Lord blesses those who choose to walk the path of repentance.[9] King Azariah starts his reign by recapturing the port city of Elath and rebuilding its lucrative harbour.[10] It all seems so easy when this new king devotes himself wholeheartedly to the Lord that once again we are left to ponder what might have been for all the other kings of Israel and Judah.

So much for Jehoash and Amaziah. So much for the Jewish exiles too. The writer turns to us at the end of these verses and asks us whether we will walk the death-and-resurrection road of repentance ourselves. Let's be spurred on by the words of the Victorian novelist George Eliot: *"It is never too late to be what you might have been."*[11]

---

[9] Azariah began to rule alongside his father in 792 BC, twenty-five years before Amaziah died. This verse is therefore better translated that he was aged sixteen when the people made him king *"under his father Amaziah"*.

[10] This Red Sea harbour is also known by the name of nearby Ezion Geber in 1 Kings 9:26 and 22:48.

[11] Quoted in *The Literary News*, published in New York in 1881.

Have It Your Way
(2 Kings 14:23 – 15:7)

*The Lord had seen how bitterly everyone in Israel,
whether slave or free, was suffering; there was no
one to help them ... he saved them by the hand of
Jeroboam.*

(2 Kings 14:26–27)

There was a rumour going round among the Jewish exiles in Babylon. It was that God had mistreated his people. If only he had been kinder to Israel and Judah, they would have had no reason to rebel against him. They had only turned to foreign idols when the God of Israel ended the prosperity that they had enjoyed under King Solomon. The writer therefore turns to the exiles in these verses and says: "OK, have it your way."

In 14:23–29, he says the northern kingdom actually enjoyed a golden age of renewed prosperity during the reign of King Jeroboam II. There was no reason why the Lord should suddenly have been so gracious to them. Their new king was named after the man who taught their nation to worship golden calves at Bethel and Dan. This second Jeroboam persisted in the same idolatry. Nevertheless, the Lord conducted an experiment through his reign. Would Israel turn back to him if he prospered them?

The writer says that *"The Lord had seen how bitterly everyone in Israel, whether slave or free, was suffering; there was no one to help them."* Those last seven words are vital. The Lord saw that the northern kingdom had run out of false saviours. It was about to be gobbled up by the greedy Aramean empire. That's why *"he saved them by the hand of Jeroboam son of Jehoash."* He decided that the time was ripe to turn their king into a prophetic picture of the Saviour who would one day come to deliver their nation from its sin. If there was any moment when prosperity would bring Israel back to the Lord, then it was now.

King Jeroboam II ruled for forty years, from 793–753 BC. That doesn't just make him the longest-ruling monarch of the northern kingdom. It means that he ruled longer than the next six kings put together. Furthermore, the Lord sent the prophet Jonah to confront him – not with judgment for his sins, like almost every other king of Israel – but with a promise to grant him victory on the battlefield. Not since the days of Solomon had the Lord ever promised to shower such lavish blessings on a king of Israel.

First, Jeroboam reconquered all the territory that Jehu had lost east of the River Jordan. The Aramean empire was gradually being eclipsed by that of the Assyrians, so Jeroboam took advantage of the Assyrian siege of Damascus in 773 BC. Most of the soldiers in the Aramean garrisons east of the Jordan hurried home to defend their capital, so Jeroboam overran them all the way from Lebo Hamath in the far north to the Dead Sea in the far south.[1] This was more than simply a reversal of Jehu's losses in 10:32–33. It meant that Israel now dominated the kingdoms of Ammon and Moab too. The writer says that Jeroboam even marched north and sacked Damascus. Israel had not had an empire like this since the days of Solomon, so it served as a moment of truth. Were the Jewish exiles right? Would God's people serve him faithfully in this new golden age for Israel? Sadly, the answer is an emphatic *no*.

The French novelist Victor Hugo believed that "Adversity makes men, and prosperity makes monsters." It was certainly the case for the northern kingdom. The Lord sent three prophets to Israel during Jeroboam's reign, but the northern tribes were too distracted by the good times to bother listening to the Lord. The writer mentions the prophet Jonah, but Amos and

---

[1] Lebo Hamath marked the northernmost border of the Promised Land in Numbers 34:8 and Joshua 13:5.

Hosea also prophesied to Israel under Jeroboam.[2] They were ignored. Instead of honouring the Lord for their new-found prosperity, the Israelites took it as a sign that they were in his good books and therefore had nothing to fear as a result of their sinful behaviour. In the end, Amos and Hosea gave up on Israel and relocated their ministries to Judah, calling down a curse on Israel's complacent prosperity: *"'The days are coming,' declares the Sovereign Lord, 'when I will send a famine through the land – not a famine of food or a thirst for water, but a famine of hearing the words of the Lord.'"*[3]

In 15:1–7, the writer gives us a second object lesson. King Azariah of Judah ruled for twenty-five years alongside his father and then for twenty-seven more years on his own, making his reign the second longest in the history of Judah.[4] He too presided over a golden age.[5] The writer tells us in 14:22 that he recaptured the Red Sea port of Elath and rebuilt it to harvest the riches of the Orient, just like King Solomon. The writer of 2 Chronicles adds that he also defeated the Philistines, the Arabs and the Ammonites. Even Egypt marvelled at his military strength, and he became a major power broker in the region.[6] If the Jewish exiles were right that their nation would have worshipped the Lord faithfully if he had continued to prosper them, then we would expect King Azariah to be the godliest king of them all.

---

[2] Gath Hepher was in the far north of Israel, near Lake Galilee, which may explain why the prophet disliked the Assyrians so strongly. If their armies marched south, his hometown would be one of the first to fall.

[3] Amos 8:11 in about 760 BC. Amos and Hosea both abandoned Israel by the end of Jeroboam's reign. Ironically, while the Israelites refused to repent, the Assyrian city of Nineveh quickly repented under Jonah.

[4] Azariah means *Helped By The Lord*. He is also known as Uzziah, which means *My Strength Is The Lord*, in order to prevent confusion with the priest named Azariah who confronts him for his sin in 2 Chronicles 26.

[5] He was aged only sixteen when he began to rule alongside his father in 792 BC. He ruled alone after his father's assassination in 767 BC, contracting leprosy in about 750 BC and dying in 740 BC.

[6] We are given much more detail about events during this golden age in 2 Chronicles 26.

But he wasn't. As the American president Abraham Lincoln pointed out, *"Any man can stand adversity – only a great man can stand prosperity."*[7] Instead of letting the good things that the Lord did for him go to his heart, King Azariah let it all go to his head. He defied the Law of Moses by trespassing into the inner sanctuary of the Temple to burn incense on its golden altar. When one of the priests challenged him that this was something that only the Lord's priests were permitted to do, he shouted back proudly that he was the king – and was immediately struck down with leprosy.[8] The priests took one look at his skin and quickly ushered him out of the Lord's sanctuary. The palace guards refused him entry, sending him to live the last ten years of his life in a separate house. He died in quarantine alone.[9] Because King Azariah refused to worship God in the good times, he died amid bad times instead.[10]

So let's not fool ourselves, like the Jewish exiles in Babylon, that the Lord has been unfair to us or that we would serve him better if only he prospered us more. The writer uses these two golden ages in both Israel and Judah to convince us that prosperity is a far bigger threat to our walk with God than adversity. Instead of blaming God for the troubles in our lives, let's thank him for them. C.S. Lewis explains why: *"God whispers to us in our pleasures, speaks in our conscience, but shouts in our pains: it is His megaphone to rouse a deaf world."*[11]

---

[7] Quoted by Horatio Alger in his biography *Abraham Lincoln: The Backwoods Boy* (1883).

[8] Some readers believe that Azariah was given the throne name *Uzziah* to avoid confusion with his high priest of the same name, and that resentment towards this motivated his attempt to usurp priestly power.

[9] We are told this in 2 Chronicles 26:16–21. It is probably why his son Jotham became co-ruler in 750 BC.

[10] He was only buried *near* his ancestors, since leprosy barred him from the royal tombs (2 Chronicles 26:23).

[11] He says this in *The Problem of Pain* (1940).

Dynasty
(2 Kings 15:8–31)

"Shallum son of Jabesh … attacked [Zechariah] in front of the people, assassinated him and succeeded him as king."

(2 Kings 15:10)

You've got to love the classic TV series *Dynasty*. Watching the way the Carringtons and the Colbys slug it out with one another often leaves us open-mouthed and speechless at their cruelty. But those warring families have got nothing on the dynasties that destroyed one another during the final decades of the northern kingdom.

The golden age of King Jeroboam II of Israel lasted forty years. His kingdom outlived him by just thirty-one, but in that time it got through six kings and five dynasties.

In 15:8–12, King Zechariah reigns for only six months before he is assassinated by one of his officials. The Lord fulfils his promise in Hosea 1:4 to wipe out Jehu's dynasty for going beyond his mandate and slaughtering members of David's dynasty at *"the massacre at Jezreel"*. Although tragic, this act of judgment proclaims God's faithfulness to his promises. He had promised Jehu that, despite his sin, the throne of Israel would pass down to his great-great-grandson. That's Zechariah, whose name means *The Lord Remembers*. His brief reign testifies that the Lord is faithful to his Word.[1]

Shallum is a commoner, but he dreams of founding a new royal dynasty by murdering his master. Unfortunately for him, an

---

[1] The promise in 15:12 was originally given to Jehu back in 10:30.

army general named Menahem has similar dreams of his own.[2] In 15:13–16, Shallum's dynasty lasts merely a month before it is toppled and he is killed. Israel refused to worship the Lord in the good times, so now it plunges into some seriously bad times.

In 15:17–22, the army general Menahem strengthens his own grip on power. Marching out from the army garrison at Tirzah, he exacts brutal revenge on any city that refuses to open its gates to him as king.[3] He builds his dynasty on the altars of idols and on the bloodied corpses of pregnant women.[4] The Lord therefore brings a new enemy against him. King Tiglath-Pileser III of Assyria marches south to conquer Israel.[5] Menahem only survives by paying him a staggeringly large amount of money. Thirty-four tons of silver equates to almost six hundred grams for every landowner in the entire kingdom. Its payment ensures that Menahem is the only one of these last six kings to die a natural death, but in the process he cripples Israel's economy.[6]

In 15:23–26, Pekahiah succeeds his father as king. If this chapter feels repetitive, even monotonous, then that's because sin always is. Sin promises us pleasure and fulfilment but in the end it delivers neither. It proves to be yet another false saviour to Israel. Pekahiah's name means *The Lord Sees*, but he acts as though the Lord is blind. He persists in sin and idolatry, so two years into his reign he is assassinated by one of his army

---

[2] Shallum means *Payback* or *Retribution*. Menahem does to him as he did to Zechariah.

[3] Tirzah was the capital of Israel before Samaria (1 Kings 14:17; 15:33; 16:8, 15 and 23–24).

[4] Ironically, Menahem's name means *Comforter* and his father's name means *My Good Fortune*.

[5] Known as Pul to the Hebrews, Tiglath-Pileser reigned 745–727 BC. His own royal annals tell us he exacted this tribute from Israel in 743 BC. Assyria is mentioned almost fifty times between now and the end of 2 Kings.

[6] The tragedy here is that the Lord would have saved Israel had it only repented and turned to him for help. Disobedience is always costly. Hosea 5:13–15 says that this invasion was prompted by Menahem flashing his wealth to the Assyrians in a misguided attempt to secure help from them instead of from the Lord.

generals. Israel's seventh dynasty ends in the same way it began, with a violent military coup.

In 15:27–31, the army general Pekah attempts to shore up his new dynasty, but he lacks the resources to do so. His kingdom has been crippled by the massive tribute which Menahem paid to Assyria.[7] Pekah can't complain about his predecessor's actions, because the writer says he was the real power behind the throne at the time. He pulled the strings during the reigns of Menahem and Pekahiah.[8] When the economy of Israel finally starts to recover, King Tiglath-Pileser III of Assyria invades a second time.[9] There is no money left to buy him off again, so this time he annexes Galilee in the north and most of Israel's territory east of the River Jordan. One of Pekah's subjects is so outraged by this national humiliation that he takes matters into his own hands. Hoshea assassinates Pekah and founds the ninth and final dynasty of Israel.[10]

Hoshea's name means *Salvation*, and he shares it with the prophet whose Old Testament book cries out for the northern kingdom to repent of its sin and to receive the Lord as its only true Saviour.[11] Although the Galilean Captivity of 732 BC is relatively small-scale, it serves as a final warning shot to Israel. It has gone through six kings and five dynasties in the space of thirty-one years, and Hoshea represents the very last of them.

So don't miss the story behind the story in the rapid rise

---

[7] 2 Chronicles 28:1–15 says that Pekah tried to refill his kingdom's coffers by conducting raids on Judah.

[8] Pekah ruled from 740–732 BC, yet the writer says in 15:27 that he ruled for twenty years – in other words, from the moment he helped Menahem usurp the throne in 752 BC.

[9] Remaliah means *Protected By The Lord*, but his son Pekah was never willing to sit under God's protection. Pekah means *Opened Up*, just like the borders he was unable to hold tight against the Assyrians.

[10] Hosea 6:8 warns Pekah that the Lord has not forgotten the brutal manner in which he and his soldiers from Gilead seized the throne. Because Pekah refused to repent, he dies with similar brutality.

[11] English Bibles avoid confusion by referring to the king as *Hoshea* and to the prophet as *Hosea*, but the name is actually the same in Hebrew.

| UNITED | David (1010–970 BC) |
| MONARCHY | Solomon (970–930 BC) |

JUDAH		ISRAEL	
Rehoboam (930–913 BC)		Jeroboam I (930–909 BC)	
Abijah (913–910 BC)		Nadab (909–908 BC)	
Asa (910–869 BC)*		Baasha (908–886 BC)	
Jehoshaphat (872–848 BC)*		Elah (886–885 BC)	
Jehoram (853–841 BC)		Zimri (885 BC)	
Ahaziah (841 BC)		Omri (885–874 BC)	
[Athaliah (841–835 BC)]		Ahab (874–853 BC)	
Joash (835–796 BC)		Ahaziah (853–852 BC)	
Amaziah (796–767 BC)*		Joram (852–841 BC)	
Azariah (792–740 BC)*		Jehu (841–814 BC)	
Jotham (750–732 BC)*		Jehoahaz (814–798 BC)	
Ahaz (735–715 BC)		Jehoash (798–782 BC)*	
		Jeroboam II (793–753 BC)	
		Zechariah (753–752 BC)	
		Shallum (752 BC)	
		Menahem (752–742 BC)	
		Pekahiah (742–740 BC)	
* These kings had overlapping		Pekah (740–732 BC)	
reigns with their sons		Hoshea (732–722 BC)	

and fall of Israel's dynasties. Time is running out for God's people to repent and to seek salvation from the Lord.

The Next Player
(2 Kings 15:32 – 16:20)

Jotham rested with his ancestors and was buried
with them in the City of David, the city of his father.
And Ahaz his son succeeded him as king.

(2 Kings 15:38)

If you've ever played in a rugby team, you will have been taught an important principle. Whenever you pass the ball to another player, you remain responsible for the ball until it leaves that player's hands. A footballer can simply kick the ball upfield and complain about what his teammates do with it, but a rugby player can't. What the next man does with the ball reflects on him. Watch any of the best players and you will notice they are just as passionate to make the next player's move a success as they are their own.

King Jotham of Judah was more of a footballer than a rugby player. He was one of the star strikers of the southern kingdom. He received the ball suddenly, when his father Azariah was struck down with leprosy for trespassing into the Temple sanctuary. It can't have been easy for him to rule for his first ten years from the palace, knowing that his father was living in quarantine at a separate house nearby.[1] Yet he ruled very well. Unlike his father, his grandfather and his great-grandfather before him, he not only started out as a devout believer in the

---

[1] In 15:27, the writer treats the starts of Pekah's reign as 752 BC, since he was the true power behind the throne after Menahem's coup. In 15:32, the writer therefore tells us that Jotham's reign began in 750 BC, ten years before the death of his father. He then ruled solo until about 735 BC, then jointly with his son until 732 BC.

Lord but finished up as one too. Other than the fact that he neglected to demolish the "high places" of Judah, the writer has not a single bad word to say about him.[2] He rebuilt part of the Temple. He married a godly woman.[3] In all his actions he was a true son of David. *"He did what was right in the eyes of the Lord."* For as long as he had the ball, Jotham was one of the greatest players on Judah's team.

Jotham even understood that he needed to take responsibility for how well he passed the ball on to his young son Ahaz. The writer says in 15:30 that he ruled for *twenty* years but then informs us in 15:33 that he ceased to rule as sole king after *sixteen* years. In other words, he had his son crowned co-ruler in 735 BC and spent his final three or four years ruling with him in the background.[4] He orchestrated this overlap of their two reigns so that he could give his son some on-the-job training on how to rule as a regent for God.[5]

But Jotham is a better goal-scorer than a passer of the ball. When he discovers that Ahaz has no desire to worship the Lord, he doesn't have the resolve to overrule him. He allows him to offer sacrifices at the "high places" of Judah. He fails to intervene when his son sacrifices his grandson to Molek, the evil Ammonite god of fire, who made his worshippers prove their devotion to him by burning their children alive on his altar.[6] The writer is horrified at how low the throne of David sinks while Jotham is still alive. The kings of Judah have worshipped foreign idols before, but only when led astray by Ahab's dynasty. This time, King Ahaz has no such excuse. When his godly father

[2] 2 Chronicles 27:2 says it wasn't for lack of trying. The people would not let him demolish the "high places".

[3] Jerusha means *Possessed [By God]*. Her father's name Zadok means *Righteous* and was a common name among the priests at the Lord's Temple.

[4] Isaiah 7:1 reveals that Ahaz acted as the "lead king" in their partnership, since it dates to 734 BC.

[5] Ahaz was aged twenty when Jotham died (16:2) so he was sixteen or seventeen when they started ruling jointly together.

[6] Deuteronomy 12:31 and 18:10–12, and Ezekiel 16:20–21. Although the Hebrew text of 16:3 is a little ambiguous, 2 Chronicles 28:3 confirms that Ahaz burned him in the fire along with several other children.

passes onto him the ball of monarchy, he fumbles it entirely of his own accord.

Since Jotham seems unable to discipline his son, the Lord steps in to do his fatherly duties for him.[7] Ahaz knows that Jotham saw non-stop victories on the battlefield, bringing home a hefty tribute from the Ammonites. The Lord therefore disciplines him through military failure. The coalition armies of King Rezin of Aram and King Pekah of Israel invade the southern kingdom in 734 BC.[8] This gives Jotham a perfect opportunity to teach his sinful son how to repent. We do not know how much he makes of it. All we know is that even after the Lord rescues Jerusalem, Ahaz still keeps on dropping the ball.

Aram and Israel recapture the strategic Red Sea port city of Elath.[9] They kill tens of thousands of Judah's soldiers. They plunder many of Judah's treasures. They carry off thousands of Judah's women and children into slavery. It is now 732 BC, so Jotham is still alive, but Ahaz refuses to listen to his father even when the Edomites and Philistines launch raiding parties on his land. He even refuses to listen to the prophet Isaiah, who brings a Gospel message to the palace: The Lord will thwart Aram and Israel's plan to divide Judah between them. All he needs to do is turn back to the Lord.[10]

Instead of repenting and pleading with the Lord to save him, Ahaz petitions King Tiglath-Pileser of Assyria to become his saviour instead.[11] He strips the royal palace and the Lord's Temple of their remaining gold and silver to buy help from his new ally. Instead of treating the Temple as a place to pray,

---

[7] The Aramean invasion of 734 BC came as a direct result of this sin (2 Chronicles 28:1–6).

[8] The writer records this invasion both at the end of Jotham's reign (15:37) and the start of Ahaz's reign (16:5).

[9] Damascus fell shortly afterwards, so Elath quickly fell into the hands of the Edomites (16:6).

[10] We are given all of this extra detail in 2 Chronicles 28:5–19 and Isaiah 7:1–9.

[11] Note that to woo the king of Assyria, Ahaz removes the Temple *side panels* that sport pictures of the angels God has sent to protect Jerusalem (16:17–18 and 1 Kings 7:28–29). We can only choose one saviour at a time.

he treats it as a convenient place to plunder. At first, his plan seems to work. The Assyrians wipe Aram off the map, executing King Rezin and dragging off his people into captivity.[12] But sin always has a hefty price tag. When Ahaz travels to the ruins of Damascus to confer with the king of Assyria, he spots amid the rubble an altar to one of the Aramean gods.[13] He sends a sketch of it to the Lord's priest in Jerusalem so that he can construct one similar in the Temple.[14] From now on, Ahaz resolves to worship the god of Damascus at the Lord's Temple.[15] Jotham's fine form as king has not carried over to the next player. When he dies, the southern kingdom is more sinful than ever.[16]

Ahaz completely drops the ball. He ends up worshipping a god that has already failed. If the god of Damascus couldn't save Damascus, then it certainly won't save Jerusalem! The best thing we can say about Ahaz is that at least he dies in his mid-thirties. The Lord takes him off the pitch early in order to make way for the next player.

---

[12] The kingdom of Aram ceased to exist with the sack of Damascus in 732 BC, as predicted in Amos 1:3–5. The Assyrian army then moved south to Israel, annexing Galilee and the territory east of the Jordan (15:29).

[13] The Hebrew word *tabnīth*, or *detailed plans*, in 16:10, is the same word used for the plans God gave Moses for the Tabernacle in Exodus 25:9, 40. The command in 16:11 is also a satanic parody of Exodus 40:16.

[14] Here Ahaz represents every church leader who comes back from a conference with faith in his notes about another church's strategy, instead of simply falling to his knees before the Lord.

[15] Ahaz probably fooled himself that he was pleasing the Lord by regularly visiting his Temple. But a modified Gospel is no gospel at all. Corrupted Christian worship is worse than outright rebellion.

[16] At least the priests opposed the sins of Athaliah. Now they are in complete cahoots with their sinful kings.

Behind The Scenes
(2 Kings 17:1–23)

All this took place because the Israelites had sinned against the Lord their God, who had brought them up out of Egypt.

(2 Kings 17:7)

On the face of it, the destruction of the northern kingdom of Israel in 722 BC was a very normal piece of ancient empire building. In 17:1–6, the writer gives us the short version of what happened. He says that Hoshea was the nineteenth and final king of Israel.[1] After murdering his master to usurp the throne, he failed to keep on the right side of the king of Assyria. Having paid him an annual tribute for seven years, he was emboldened by an alliance with Egypt to default on his payments.[2] The new King Shalmaneser V reacted swiftly.[3] He imprisoned Hoshea, invaded his kingdom and surrounded his capital city. Those who survived the long siege and its subsequent slaughter were carried away into captivity.[4] That's the short version of what happened to the northern kingdom. Its destruction was a two-a-penny tale of ancient empire.

213

---

[1] It is not quite clear why the writer calls 732 BC *"the twelfth year of Ahaz"* in 17:1. Jotham may have formally anointed him crown prince nine years before he finally anointed him king of Judah.

[2] The court annals of Tiglath-Pileser say that this tribute, in 732 BC, was 400 kg of gold and 37 tons of silver.

[3] Shalmaneser V (727–722 BC) and Sargon II (722–705 BC) were both sons of Tiglath-Pileser III.

[4] The court annals of Sargon II say that only 27,290 Israelites were taken into captivity. A few of them must have been left behind to work the fields for the Assyrians, but the vast majority were simply slaughtered.

In 17:7–23, however, the writer pulls back the curtain and takes us behind the scenes. He restates the message of 1 and 2 Kings to ensure we understand the story behind the story. *"All this took place because the Israelites had sinned against the Lord their God, who had brought them up out of Egypt from under the power of Pharaoh king of Egypt."*[5] The reasons for the fall of the northern kingdom weren't just military. They were spiritual. Israel had turned to Pharaoh as their saviour, despite the fact that his nation had once enslaved them. Israel's rulers were fools, who viewed God as their enemy and their enemies as friends.

"They worshipped other gods and followed the practices of the nations the Lord had driven out before them, as well as the practices that the kings of Israel had introduced" (verses 7–8). That's another vital factor in the story behind the story. Initially, the people of the northern kingdom felt a little nervous about worshipping Jeroboam's golden calves. It seemed too much like the sin that had almost resulted in the destruction of their nation at the foot of Mount Sinai in Exodus 32. They felt a similar pang of conscience about worshipping the idols of the Canaanites whom Joshua had driven out of the Promised Land before their fathers. At first, in verse 9, *"the Israelites secretly did things against the Lord their God that were not right"*. Soon, however, they lost any such sense of shame and in verses 11–12, we read that: *"At every high place ... they worshipped idols."*[6] They stopped trying to hide the fact that they were acting like *"the nations whom the Lord had driven out before them"*. The story behind the exile of Israel was therefore the same story behind the conquest of the Promised Land. The Lord only tolerates idolatry for so long. For the Canaanites, for the Israelites and for us, the Day of Judgment eventually arrives.

"The Lord warned Israel and Judah through all his prophets ... but they would not listen" (verses 13–14). That's another vital

---

[5] Pharaoh *So* is probably a nickname for Pharaoh Osorkon IV (730–715 BC).

[6] The writer warns us here that sin is never satisfied. Secret sins quickly develop into open rebellion. Our only hope is to deal with sin at its inception, before it can grow up to bite us (Genesis 4:7 and James 1:14–16).

aspect of the story behind the story. These two books are not just listed among the "Former Prophets" because they prophesy to us. It is also because they are full of prophets![7] Each one tries to call God's people back to him, and each one is ignored. They even warn Hoshea not to trust in Egypt as an ally or to renege on his promise to pay tribute to Assyria.[8] Behind the scenes, the true cause of Israel's downfall is the stubborn refusal of its kings to listen to God's Word through his prophets.

"They rejected his decrees and the covenant he had made with their ancestors and the statutes he had warned them to keep. They followed worthless idols and themselves became worthless. They imitated the nations around them" (verse 15). A massive factor in Israel's downfall was its desire to downplay its calling to live as a people distinct from the nations. As soon as the Israelites started worshipping what the rest of the world worships, it was only a matter of time before they started acting like the rest of the world too.[9] None of the kings of Israel took the Law of Moses seriously.[10] Their sinful lifestyle misrepresented the Lord's character to the world, so he destroyed them to preserve the honour of his name.

"They sacrificed their sons and daughters in the fire. They practised divination" (verse 17). I used to feel offended that the Lord commanded Joshua to slaughter the Canaanites, until I studied how those Canaanites actually lived. After reading about the rape, the bestiality, the violence and the child sacrifice, I started marvelling instead that the Lord held back his judgment for so long. The same is true when we look behind the scenes at the downfall of the northern kingdom. Once they became as depraved as the Canaanites that the Lord drove out before them,

---

[7] At least ten prophets are mentioned by name in these two books: Nathan, Shemaiah, Ahijah, Jehu, Elijah, Micaiah, Elisha, Jonah, Isaiah and Huldah.

[8] For example, in Hosea 7:8–16 and 12:1–14.

[9] Note the principle in 17:15 that *we become like what we worship*. See also Hosea 9:10.

[10] The prophets were preachers of God's Law (17:13), not a call to work hard to be righteous but a promise that God makes sinners righteous by faith (17:14). Rejecting it meant they *"did not trust in the Lord their God"*.

justice demanded that he drive them out of the Promised Land too. So don't be offended. Instead be warned. God is still every bit as holy today.[11]

"*Therefore the Lord rejected all the people of Israel; he afflicted them and gave them into the hands of plunderers, until he thrust them from his presence*" (verse 20). We must not complain as if the final destruction of the northern kingdom came out of the blue. God had already disciplined them through the Ammonites, the Moabites, the Edomites, the Philistines, the Arameans, the Egyptians and the Assyrians. Behind the scenes there was plenty of warning.

"*Jeroboam enticed Israel away from following the Lord and caused them to commit a great sin. The Israelites persisted in all the sins of Jeroboam and did not turn away from them*" (verses 21–22). This story is known as 1 and 2 Kings for a reason. It describes the fate of a nation which demanded a king like all the other nations in 1 Samuel 8, and which paid the price of putting such hope in a man-made messiah. The seeds of its destruction were planted the very moment it rejected David's dynasty and started following Jeroboam instead. Don't miss the irony that his last successor is named Hoshea, which means *Salvation*. After nine dynasties, Israel finally discovers that the king it demanded isn't the Messiah we are looking for.[12]

"*So the people of Israel were taken from their homeland into exile in Assyria*" (verse 23). If you are unfamiliar with the geography of the Bible, you might have missed it when the writer told us in 17:6 that many of the Israelites were exiled to the town of Gozan. That was the next city along from Haran, from which Abraham set out in faith for the land of Canaan all the way back in Genesis 12. Behind the scenes of this disaster

---

[11] The writer mentions Judah three times in these verses because its own judgment day was nearing too. The twelve tribes would only be reunified after both kingdoms "died" and were "resurrected" from their land of exile.

[12] Hoshea was also Joshua's other name (Numbers 13:16). One Hoshea led Israel into the Promised Land and now another Hoshea leads Israel out of it. Only the true and better Joshua can rescue Israel now.

is a God so merciful that he takes Israel back to square one in order to reboot its messed-up national story.

So don't read superficially. The destruction of Israel wasn't just a piece of ancient empire building. Look behind the scenes to check you understand the story behind the story.

King of the Nations
(2 Kings 17:24–41)

The king of Assyria brought people from Babylon,
Kuthah, Avva, Hamath and Sepharvaim and settled
them in the towns of Samaria to replace the Israelites.

(2 Kings 17:24)

If you don't have many Jewish friends, you might not understand how painful it was for the exiles in Babylon to read about what happened after the fall of Israel. For them, the tragedy of these chapters wasn't just that the ten northern tribes were deported from the Promised Land. It was that foreigners were settled in it instead.

The Assyrians dispersed the survivors of the northern kingdom throughout their empire to stop them from conspiring together against their new masters. There would be no triumphant return from exile for these Israelites. Although we can tell from Luke 2:36 and Romans 11:1 that a few of them slipped back home from Babylon with the survivors of Judah, the vast majority of them had lost their territory for good. The writer laments in 17:23 that *"they are still there"*. The first-century historian Josephus does the same six centuries later: *"The ten tribes remain the other side of the Euphrates even now."*[1]

They lost the Promised Land because the kings of Assyria settled many of their captives from other nations in it. They could not afford to leave fertile fields unfarmed, so the writer says they brought in workers from Babylon, Kuthah, Avva, Hamath and Sepharvaim instead. The court records of King Sargon II reveal that this is just a sample of the different ethnic

---

[1] Josephus Flavius in his *Antiquities of the Jews* (11.5).

groups forcibly resettled in the Promised Land: *"I deported the Arabs, who live far away in the desert, who know neither overseers nor officials, and who had not yet brought their tribute to any king ... I settled them in Samaria."*[2] Since they lived among the ruins of Samaria, the Jews came to refer to these interlopers as the "Samaritans".

The writer therefore ends this fourth section of 1 and 2 Kings by using the Samaritans as a prophetic picture of God's desire to do more than simply restore the fortunes of his people Israel. False messiahs proved too weak to rescue the ten northern tribes, but the true Messiah will prove strong enough to rescue anyone. The Samaritans in 1 Kings 17 know very little about the God of Israel, but that doesn't mean he cares little about them. He sends lions to attack their settlements until they recognize that they need instruction in how to please the God of Israel. The king of Assyria sends an Israelite priest back to Bethel (yes, Bethel – God really is that gracious!) to transform it into a missionary centre. Unlike the Israelites, the Samaritans actually listen to what God's prophet says. Their response becomes a picture of the Church that the Messiah will establish in every nation. It foreshadows John 4, where a whole townful of Samaritans turn to Jesus and exclaim that *"We have heard for ourselves, and we know that this man really is the Saviour of the world."*

The Jewish exiles in Babylon did not want to hear this. When they returned from exile, they hated their mixed-race new neighbours. They used the name "Samaritan" as an insult and taught their sons that *"the daughters of Samaritans are as [dirty as] menstruating women from the cradle".*[3] Part of the problem was that the Samaritans believed some strange things about the God of Israel – for example, that people ought to worship the Lord on Mount Gerizim instead of on Mount Zion.[4]

---

[2] Later kings of Assyria also did the same. See Ezra 4:1–2, 9–10.

[3] John 8:48 and Niddah 4:1, which is part of the Mishnah in the Jewish Talmud.

[4] John 4:19–24. One reason for this was that Mount Gerizim was in the tribal lands of Ephraim, where the Samaritans lived. The Jewish Talmud refers to it as *"the land of the people of Kuthah".*

In 17:33, the writer agrees that their worship was confused. They *"worshipped the Lord, but they also served their own gods in accordance with the customs of the nations from which they had been brought".* They reinstated the "high places" and even sacrificed their children in the fire to Molek. They were every bit as sinful as the Israelites had been. But that wasn't a reason to hate them. It was a reason to proclaim to them the Good News that God saves people from every nation from their sin.

When Jesus burst onto the scene, he was inspired by Scripture passages such as this one. It is remarkable how often he reaches out in the four gospels towards the descendants of these Samaritans. When he extends forgiveness to a sinful Samaritan woman at the well of Sychar, a whole town of Samaritans repents and hails him as the true Messiah. When he heals a Samaritan leper, he commends him to the Jews as someone who can teach their nation a thing or two about genuine gratitude to God. He even includes a Good Samaritan in one of his most famous parables, who seems to understand more about God's love than a Jewish priest and one of his co-workers at the Temple in Jerusalem.[5]

At first, the disciples fail to grasp what he is saying. They still view the Samaritans as their enemies. When a Samaritan village rejects Jesus, they ask his permission to call down fire from heaven to destroy it, as Elijah did in 2 Kings 1. Jesus refuses. He longs for the day when they will share his Father's passion to reach every nation of the globe.[6]

After his resurrection, Jesus explains to his disciples the story behind the story. He hasn't just come to earth from heaven for the sake of a small patch of land in the Middle East. He has come to build a Kingdom that will gather people from every single nation, tribe and tongue. He commands them to *"Go and make disciples of **all nations**."* In case they don't get what he is saying, he repeats himself even more clearly: *"You will receive*

---

[5] John 4:4–42; Luke 17:11–19 and 10:25–37.

[6] Luke 9:51–56. Peter and John would return to that same area with better fire in Acts 8:14–25.

*power when the Holy Spirit comes on you; and you will be my witnesses in Jerusalem, and in all Judea **and Samaria**, and to the ends of the earth."*[7]

This fourth section of 1 and 2 Kings therefore ends with great hope. It prophesies that God doesn't just have a plan to restore the fortunes of fallen Israel, but to rescue people from every other sinful nation too. The book of Acts says that this plan began to be fulfilled when *"Philip went down to a city in Samaria and proclaimed the Messiah there ... so there was great joy in that city."* As a result, those same disciples who had asked to call fire down from heaven to destroy the Samaritans started *"preaching the gospel in many Samaritan villages"*. After seeing that *"Samaria had accepted the word of God"*, they stopped complaining that the nonbelieving world was nonbelieving.[8] They started sharing with them the Good News about Jesus instead. The proclaimed all over the known world that God has sent his Son to Israel, and that he has crowned him the King of the Nations too.

---

[7] Matthew 28:18–19 and Acts 1:8.

[8] Acts 8:4–8 and 8:14–25.

2 Kings 18–25:

Southern Comfort

Graceland
(2 Kings 18:1–8)

Hezekiah trusted in the Lord, the God of Israel. There was no one like him among all the kings of Judah, either before him or after him.

(2 Kings 18:5)

The fourth section of 1 and 2 Kings felt like a long stay at Heartbreak Hotel. So here's some good news: in the fifth section, the writer takes us back to Graceland.

Now that the northern lights of Israel have been extinguished, the writer takes us back to Judah and offers us some southern comfort instead. Rather than telling us that God's judgment carried on across the border and finished off the last two tribes of Israel, he surprises us with the news that God poured out his lavish grace on the land of Judah instead. Having exposed the northern kings as false saviours, he decided to preach his salvation to the world by raising up a godly ruler who pointed people to his Messiah.

Hezekiah is the son of the idolatrous King Ahaz, but he is nothing like his sinful father. His name means *The Lord Is My Strength*, and he lives up to his name by ridding the land of Judah of any other saviour but the Lord. He destroys the "high places" and demolishes the idols that are worshipped there.[1] Having dealt with false religion, he then deals with corrupted religion. When the Israelites sinned in the desert under Moses and were bitten by a plague of snakes, the Lord told them

---

[1] There were two types of "high place" – those where idols were worshipped and those where the Lord was worshipped instead of at the Temple, contrary to his Law. It seems from 18:22 that Hezekiah destroyed both.

to look at a bronze snake in faith so that their lives could be saved. It was meant as a prophetic picture of the cross of Jesus, but Hezekiah realises that his subjects have turned the bronze snake into a talisman.[2] Crucifixes, communion bread, water baptism and worship services can just as easily be turned into false saviours if we rely on them, instead of looking through them to the Lord. Hezekiah destroys the bronze snake to refocus people's faith back on the Gospel.[3]

Next, Hezekiah reopens the Lord's Temple, which was shut down by his father Ahaz. The writer does not tell us this. He simply gives a top-line summary: *"He did what was right in the eyes of the Lord, just as his father David had done."*[4] We are told the detail in 2 Chronicles 29. Hezekiah removes his father's altar to the god of Damascus, taking it down to the city rubbish tip to be destroyed. He then reconsecrates the Temple and commands the priests to resume offering blood sacrifices on the bronze altar in its courtyard and burning incense on the golden altar in its sanctuary. Hezekiah reappoints the musicians that King David commissioned to lead the people in constant worship to the Lord. He preaches the message of God's grace to everyone. This is the closest the southern kingdom has ever been to genuine spiritual revival.

The people of Judah have done nothing to deserve this mercy. Their previous king sacrificed his children to the false god Molek, and no doubt persuaded many of his subjects to do the same. Nevertheless, the Lord decides to use the southern kingdom to showcase his passion to save sinners. He doesn't just revive the land of Judah in spite of the sins of King Ahaz. He actually revives land of Judah through them. The greatest

---

[2] In John 3:14–15, Jesus explains that the events of Numbers 21:4–9 were a prophetic pointer to him.

[3] Nehushtan sounds like the Hebrew words for both *Bronze* and *Snake*. While it is easy to spot crucifixes, relics and icons as potential talismans, there are plenty of invisible Protestant talismans out there too.

[4] The writer only says this about three other kings of Judah (Asa in 1 Kings 15:11, Jehoshaphat in 1 Kings 22:43 and Josiah in 2 Kings 22:2), and even Asa and Jehoshaphat failed to remove the "high places".

mystery of Hezekiah's reign is how such a godly king could arise from such a wicked father. The answer is simple. Ahaz had sacrificed many of Hezekiah's older brothers, and the crown prince Maaseiah had been killed in battle with his enemies.[5] Hezekiah's accession to the throne was therefore unplanned.[6] He had been overlooked by his sinful father and left to be discipled by his godly mother in the ways of the Lord instead.[7]

The southern kingdom prospered under the godly rule of Hezekiah. *"The Lord was with him; he was successful in whatever he undertook"* (18:7). Not only did he end the one-sided alliance with Assyria which forced his father Ahaz to pay a hefty tribute, but he also defeated the Philistines.[8] The writer makes it clear that he did nothing to earn this constant favour from the Lord. We mustn't imagine for a moment that 1 and 2 Kings preach a gospel of good works – the Sunday school idea that "Jehoram sins so he dies of a hideous bowel disease, while Hezekiah works hard for God so he gets blessed". That's not the real message of 1 and 2 Kings at all. The writer insists that it is all about God blessing people who do not deserve it, simply because they put their faith in him.

*"Hezekiah **trusted in the Lord**, the God of Israel. There was no one like him among all the kings of Judah, either before*

---

[5] 2 Chronicles 28:3–7 says that Ahaz sacrificed his *sons* and that Maaseiah died in battle in about 732 BC.

[6] Hezekiah was crowned king in 715 BC, but we are told in 18:1 that he began his reign 729 BC. This indicates that his father reluctantly recognized him as the new crown prince three years after the death of his brother. The Hebrew text says "sons" which is important in an age of male primogeniture. It cleared the way for a younger brother who was not the expected heir to become the new king of Judah.

[7] Abijah means *The Lord Is My Father* and Zechariah means *The Lord Remembers*.

[8] The court annals of Sennacherib confirm the historicity of 18:8. He boasts that he forced Hezekiah to release Padi of Ekron after Hezekiah imprisoned him in Jerusalem as part of his Philistine campaign.

him or after him."[9] The writer talks about Hezekiah's faith before he talks about his obedience, because salvation always works in that order. It is only after the writer has told us that Hezekiah's trust in the Lord transformed Judah into Graceland that he then goes on to tell us in 18:6, *"He held fast to the Lord and did not stop following him; he kept the commands the Lord had given Moses."* The spiritual revival that swept through Judah under Hezekiah was not a reward for obedience, but a gracious response to his faith in God's Word, which then spilled over into grateful obedience.

So after our long stay at Heartbreak Hotel in section four of 1 and 2 Kings, let's enjoy this visit to Graceland. Let's be encouraged as we read about the best king of Judah so far. Let's see him as a prophetic picture of the glorious Messiah who comes to save his people, not *through* good works, but *for* good works. Let's grasp what the apostle Paul teaches us in Ephesians 2:8–10:

> *For it is by grace you have been saved, through faith –*
> *and this is not from yourselves, it is the gift of God – not*
> *by works, so that no one can boast. For we are God's*
> *handiwork, created in Christ Jesus to do good works,*
> *which God prepared in advance for us to do.*

---

[9] 18:5. Note that the writer still refers to the Lord as the God of Israel, not as the God of Judah. Under Hezekiah, God's grace spilled out to the survivors of Israel as well as to the southern tribes (2 Chronicles 30:5–11).

Daily Battle
(2 Kings 18:9–37)

"Have I come to attack and destroy this place without word from the Lord? The Lord himself told me to march against this country and destroy it."

(2 Kings 18:25)

The street on which I live in London was bombed by the Nazis during World War Two. Some of the house numbers are still missing as a reminder of the many former dwellings that were destroyed. The owners of my house must have thought many things while the bombs were falling, but I don't imagine they were too surprised that they faced a daily battle. They understood that their street was part of a nation that was at war.

As Christians, however, we do tend to get surprised when bombs start raining down on our lives. Perhaps we have listened to too many preachers who promise us that following Jesus ought to be an easy ride. We don't tend to speak much about the Devil or about his anger that we no longer live like the people of this sinful world. The writer therefore uses these verses to remind us that following the Messiah means being caught up in a daily battle. He warns us seven times to expect an altercation with the Devil.

First, the writer warns us that *the Devil is our enemy*. We shouldn't be surprised by this, any more than King Hezekiah ought to have been surprised when the king of Assyria marched his armies south into Judah after finishing off the northern kingdom.[1] The Devil hates Jesus with a passion and, since

---

[1] The writer refers ambiguously to *"the king of Assyria"* in 18:11 because Shalmaneser V (727–722 BC) began the campaign against Israel and Sargon II (722–705 BC) completed it.

he can't touch Jesus, it's only to be expected that he focuses on hurting those that Jesus loves instead. He might ignore a compromiser like King Ahaz, but the moment King Hezekiah nails his colours to the mast by stopping paying tribute to the king of Assyria, conflict is inevitable. The writer warns us that it's the same whenever we renounce sin. We ought to expect a daily battle.

Second, the writer warns us that *the Devil lies*. [2]That's pretty obvious, since his name comes from the Greek word for *Deceiver*, but Hezekiah shows how easy it is for us to forget it. When King Sennacherib of Assyria invades the southern kingdom in 701 BC, Hezekiah fools himself that he can buy peace by paying the tribute that he owes him.[3] He foolishly goes to the Temple for plunder instead of going to the Temple for prayer. Sennacherib takes the money – a ton of gold and ten tons of silver – but having promised to withdraw his armies, he then decides to stick around to conquer Jerusalem after all. Hezekiah's misjudgment warns us never to believe the smooth promises of the Enemy.[4]

Third, the writer warns us to *expect setbacks in the battle*. He says that the Assyrian army conquered all of the southern kingdom but the capital. The court annals of Sennacherib confirm this, boasting that he carried off over 200,000 captives, reducing Hezekiah to *"a prisoner in Jerusalem his royal residence, like a bird in a cage"*. Some of Hezekiah's troubles are self-inflicted, since he ignored God's warning through the prophet Isaiah not to trust in an alliance with Egypt, and since he made

[2] 2 Kings 18:17–20:19 is so similar to Isaiah 36:1–39:8 that it would appear the writer copied much of it from Isaiah. He adds some extra detail, but the repetition largely emphasizes how vital these seven warnings are.

[3] Rather confusingly, the writer dates events in 18:1 and 9 from Hezekiah's recognition as crown prince, but events in 18:13 from his actual coronation as king. We know this because Sennacherib ruled 705–681 BC.

[4] In a moment of weakness, Hezekiah undoes his earlier restoration work by plundering the Temple for a sixth time (after 1 Kings 14:25–28 and 15:18, and 2 Kings 12:18; 14:14 and 16:7–8). He confesses literally to Sennacherib in 18:4 – "*I have sinned*" – but it was actually by negotiating that he sinned against the Lord.

himself a target by boasting of his wealth to foreign envoys.[5] But some of his troubles are simply part and parcel of following the Lord. If they crucified our Master then we are foolish to expect an easy ride ourselves. Suffering and setbacks are all part of God's plan.[6]

Fourth, the writer warns us to *expect the Devil's lies to be convincing*. He has been deceiving people since the dawn of time, so it shouldn't surprise us that he is good at his job.[7] The truth is that Pharaoh really *is* a lousy ally, that Hezekiah really *has* demolished the "high places" devoted to the Lord, and that Judah really *hasn't* got much cavalry left inside the city. The writer wants to teach us to look behind the lies. The Lord had warned Hezekiah not to trust in Pharaoh.[8] He had commanded him to destroy those "high places" and he definitely *hadn't* told Sennacherib that he wanted to use Assyria to destroy the southern kingdom. Don't let the Devil twist the facts in your mind.[9]

Fifth, the writer warns us to *expect the Devil to fight low down and dirty*. When King Hezekiah's officials refuse to be swayed by his threats, the Assyrian envoy starts shouting his lies to the crowds of people looking down from the city walls. When church leaders resist the Devil's attacks, they therefore shouldn't be surprised that he seeks to pick off weaker church members by infiltrating the congregation with gossip and fear. Note the envoy's satanic parody of what the Lord had truly pledged to Judah if it held onto its Promised Land. The Devil has no land

---

[5] Isaiah 20:1–6; 30:1–5 and 31:1–3. We'll see later that 2 Kings 20:12–19 takes place before 2 Kings 18:13–19:37.

[6] Matthew 10:21–25; John 16:33; Acts 14:22 and 2 Timothy 3:12.

[7] The Devil tries to weaken our inner resolve so that we surrender without a fight. He will even try to make us doubt whether our godly passion is in fact sinful intolerance. But remember 1 John 4:4.

[8] Egypt betrayed King Hoshea in 17:4. History also tells us that Pharaoh betrayed an earlier coalition of nations against Assyria, in 711 BC, by handing the king of Ashdod over to Assyria to save his own skin.

[9] 2 Kings 18:25 echoes 1 Kings 13:18. Instead of trusting other people's revelation, seek your own.

flowing with milk and honey. The fact that he fights so dirty proves that he is desperate. He knows that he is a defeated foe.[10]

Sixth, the writer warns us to *expect the Devil to overstretch himself and fail.* One of the most glorious moments in the envoy's speech is when he describes Sennacherib in 18:19 as *"the great king, the king of Assyria".* When Sennacherib tries to steal one of the Lord's titles, it's pretty obvious that he is heading for a fall. Another glorious moment is when he reasons that, since the king of Assyria has already defeated the gods of Mesopotamia, Aram and Israel, he is bound to defeat Yahweh too.[11] *"How then can the Lord deliver Jerusalem from my hand?"* It's as if we know from that moment that the Lord is going to have to beat him. The Devil always overreaches himself when he blasphemes the honour of God's name.

Seventh, the writer warns us to *fight against the Devil in prayer.* Hezekiah's officials must have been very tempted to correct the envoy's muddled thinking, but they say nothing. They set a great example for the people who are watching from the wall.[12] They tear their clothes in repentance and take the problem straight to their messiah. So must we.

So let's not be surprised that the Christian life often feels like a battle. Let's wise up to the Devil's hatred, to his lies, to his logic and to his dirty tactics. Let's expect setbacks but let's also expect the Devil to overstretch himself and fail. Let's see the battle for what it is. This isn't a battle between Assyria and Judah, but between the Devil and the Lord.

---

[10] Revelation 12:12. Compare 18:31–32 with Leviticus 20:24; 1 Kings 4:25; Micah 4:4 and Zechariah 3:10. The envoy fails to mention that the land he is describing is in fact a land of captivity and slavery!

[11] The envoy sounds as convincing as a teacher of comparative religions, but he fails to grasp the story behind the story. God had judged the Israelites for worshipping idols. The fall of Samaria proved his power.

[12] One of Eve's mistakes in Genesis 3 was to start reasoning with the Devil. Don't argue – pray.

The Real King of Judah
(2 Kings 19:1–37)

Hezekiah prayed to the Lord: "Lord, the God of Israel, enthroned between the cherubim, you alone are God over all the kingdoms of the earth."

(2 Kings 19:15)

A few years ago, I organized a day of paintballing with my friends. We dressed up in army fatigues. We rubbed army camouflage on our faces. We gave each other army call signs and rehearsed our military manoeuvres while we loaded up our paintball guns. Then the marshal blew the whistle for our battle to begin with the other team. Within sixty seconds they had surrounded us. Sixty seconds more, and they had pummelled each of us with their paintball bullets several times. In a daze, I went over to the captain of the other team and shook his hand. He explained that he and his friends were all off-duty Royal Marines. We were only playing at being soldiers but they were the real deal.

Like his predecessors, Hezekiah has been playing at being the real king of Judah. In the good times it was easy, like when my friends and I applied our army camouflage and boasted to one another before the start of our first paintball game. But the moment King Sennacherib of Assyria besieges Jerusalem, Hezekiah is forced to confess he is a fraud.[1] He rushes to the Temple to bow down before the real King of Judah.[2]

---

[1] Hezekiah uses a vivid Hebrew metaphor in 19:3 to say effectively, "All of my outward show of strength for the past few months has been exposed as a lie by this sudden moment of truth."

[2] When Solomon dedicated the Temple in 1 Kings 8, he always envisaged that kings would run there to pray to the Lord in their hour of need. Yet Hezekiah is the first king to do so.

Hezekiah tears his clothes and puts on sackcloth as an expression of repentance and of his desperate need for God to help him.[3] He tells his officials to do the same, then he sends them to ask Isaiah, the prophet of the Lord, to assist him in his panicked prayers. Isaiah is encouraging, but then a letter arrives from King Sennacherib.[4] Like the envoy's speech, it is full of threats towards Hezekiah and of boasting against the Lord.

Hezekiah reads the letter and then he looks around the Temple courtyard. He remembers that it was in this very place that Isaiah saw *"the Lord, high and exalted, seated on a throne."*[5] He remembers how David addresses the real King of Judah in Psalm 5:2: *"Hear my cry for help, my King and my God, for to you I pray."* Spreading out the letter from King Sennacherib before the Lord, he therefore declares that its contents are the Lord's problem and not his. The Lord alone is the real Messiah that Judah is looking for.

We do not truly understand Hezekiah's prayer in 19:14–19 unless we grasp this. It is a speech of abdication. He is stepping off the throne and calling on the Lord to be the real King of Judah. He worships the Lord as the one who is *"enthroned between the cherubim"*, reigning from his Temple in Jerusalem as the earthly extension of his heavenly throne. He worships the Lord as the great Creator of the heavens and the earth – as *"the living God"*, who can never be compared with pagan idols. They are man-made images; he is the Maker of men. He stands apart in a league of his own. He is the one against whom Sennacherib has really boasted, and if Jerusalem falls like a pagan city then the world will assume he is just as weak as the Sepharvite sun-god Adrammelek or the Israelite fertility-goddess Asherah. That can never be. Hezekiah therefore ends his prayer with an impassioned plea to the real King of Judah: *"Lord our God,*

---

[3] Less than a century earlier, the Lord had saved a sinful king of Assyria who repented this way in Jonah 3:6.

[4] Isaiah's reply counters *"Thus says the king of Assyria"* (18:31) with *"Thus says the Lord"* (19:6).

[5] Isaiah 6:1. Isaiah means *Salvation of the Lord* and he now enters the story as the greatest prophet of Judah.

deliver us from his hand, so that all the kingdoms of the earth may know that you alone, Lord, are God."[6]

This is the moment that the Lord has been waiting for. Never before in 1 and 2 Kings has any ruler acknowledged so clearly that the Lord is the real King of Judah. King Azariah sauntered into the Temple to offer incense because he trusted his own instincts more than what the Law of Moses said. King Ahaz rearranged the Temple furniture to bring his own pagan altar centre stage and to turn the Lord's altar into a sideshow. Now, at last, a better ruler of the southern kingdom has come to the Temple to confess that the Lord is the real King of Judah. In doing so, his humble faith unleashes one of the most astonishing reversals in the whole of military history.

In 19:5-7, Isaiah spoke initial words of comfort, but in 19:20-34 he sends a second letter for Hezekiah to spread out in the Temple alongside Sennacherib's.[7] Isaiah's letter promises that the real King of Judah will deliver his capital city that very night. The Lord describes Jerusalem tenderly as his *"Daughter Jerusalem"*. He still regards her as his *"Virgin Daughter Zion"*, despite her spiritual adultery with foreign idols. Since he is the real King of Judah, he has taken the king of Assyria's boasting personally (19:22). Sennacherib is nothing more than the boastful mouthpiece of the Devil (19:23-24), who has forgotten that Assyria's victories have all come as a gift from the Lord (19:25-26). Because of Sennacherib's pride, the Lord will send him home in shame, like a beast of burden (19:27-28). Isaiah even gives Hezekiah a sign to prove it, although it's interesting that the sign will not be visible until long after the siege has been lifted. This suggests that the deliverance of Jerusalem under Hezekiah will become a sign of something bigger – how the real Messiah will save the New Jerusalem in days to come (19:29-34).[8]

---

[6] Hezekiah prays in 19:17, *"It is true, Lord."* Faith doesn't deny facts. It simply believes that heavenly facts trump earthly facts every time.

[7] Isaiah's prophecy in 19:20–34 is the longest in the whole of 1 and 2 Kings, largely lifted from Isaiah 37:21–35.

[8] For similar "signs" that are only visible after the fact, see Exodus 3:12 and John 7:17.

The chapter therefore ends with an unprecedented miracle. For perspective, bear in mind that 80,000 people were killed when the atomic bomb was dropped on Hiroshima in 1945. The writer says that one single angel killed more people in one night than were killed by the two bombs dropped on Hiroshima and Nagasaki combined. This is actually the largest number of people that have ever been killed in battle on a single day in history, and it was accomplished through one solitary angel! No wonder the Lord recounts this story for us three times in three different places in the Bible. He strikes down 185,000 Assyrian soldiers in one night to fulfil the promise that he made in Isaiah 31:8: *"Assyria will fall by no human sword; a sword, not of mortals, will devour them."* It is a miracle which proclaims loud and clear that the Lord Almighty is the real King of Judah.

God is very gracious to Sennacherib. He doesn't strike him down with his soldiers. He lets him flee back to his palace in Nineveh to spend the next twenty years pondering the meaning of this night-time slaughter. Sadly, instead of repenting and turning to the God of Israel, he simply orders his craftsmen to create a series of enormous reliefs for his palace that major on his victory at Lachish and that downplay his defeat at Jerusalem.[9] In 681 BC, after two whole decades in which to change his mind, he is assassinated by his own sons as he worships at the temple of the Assyrian fertility-god Nisrok. Sennacherib learned the hard way he should never have picked a fight with the real King of Judah.

---

[9] Those giant reliefs are now on display in the British Museum in London.

Half-Time Substitution
(2 Kings 20:1–21)

"The time will surely come when everything in your palace, and all that your predecessors have stored up until this day, will be carried off to Babylon."

(2 Kings 20:17)

Hezekiah had defied the odds to defeat the Assyrian Empire at the gates of Jerusalem. He had scored a mighty victory for the southern kingdom. Nevertheless, the original readers of 1 and 2 Kings knew that Jerusalem was still destroyed little more than a century later. They had still become exiles in Babylon, and they wanted to know why.

That's why the writer records the two events in this chapter slightly out of order in the story. We know this because Marduk-Baladan, who is mentioned in 20:12, was deposed as king of Babylon in 702 BC. This means that the envoys who visited Hezekiah in this chapter came as part of the diplomatic to-and-fro that took place *before* King Sennacherib besieged Jerusalem in 701 BC. The writer records these two events out of order in the story because they show us where King Hezekiah went wrong and why his kingdom went into exile after all. They are all about the idea of half-time substitution.

In 20:1–11, the writer tells us about something that took place at the midway mark of Hezekiah's reign. Having begun with a great spiritual revival in 715 BC, there is evidence in the book of Isaiah that by 703 BC the revival was on the wane. The Lord was confronting the southern kingdom once again about its *"idols overlaid with silver"* and its *"images covered with gold"*. He was urging them once again to *"reject the idols of silver and gold your sinful hands have made."*[1] Hezekiah needed to take a time out to reflect on what he needed to do differently to foster fresh revival in the second half of his reign.

The Lord used a serious sickness to force him into the locker room. One day in 703 BC, Hezekiah began to feel unwell. He noticed that a strange boil on his skin was spreading fast. Remembering his great-grandfather Azariah's leprosy, he consulted the prophet Isaiah for some advice on what to do. The reply in 20:1 stopped him in his tracks: *"This is what the Lord says: put your house in order, because you are going to die; you will not recover."*

Hezekiah was devastated. He was only in his thirteenth year as king. His life couldn't be over – he had so many things still left to do. He went into an inner room of the palace, turned his face to the wall so that none of his courtiers could see him and wept bitterly.[2] He prayed and pleaded with the Lord not to make this illness the final whistle on his reign. He pleaded for it to be a half-time break instead. After all, he wasn't even forty.[3]

The Lord answered Hezekiah's prayer at once. Isaiah hadn't even left the palace by the time God prompted him to turn around and go back with better news for the king.[4] His illness wouldn't be the final whistle, but a chance to make a half-time substitution. He would live another fifteen years – time enough to send the king of Assyria packing from the gates of Jerusalem and to work out how to pass the ball of kingship on to his son. The healing wouldn't be instant. Isaiah dictates a remedy to the royal doctors which will aid a slow recovery, giving Hezekiah enough time in the locker room to ponder his

---

[1] Isaiah 30:22 and 31:7.

[2] 2 Kings 20:4 says Hezekiah rushed so quickly to prayer that Isaiah was still on his way home when God told him to turn around and go back to correct what he had said.

[3] 2 Kings 18:1–2 says he was aged twenty-five when he became king in 715 BC.

[4] The fact that the Lord has ordained everything in our lives (Psalm 139:16 and Ephesians 1:11) shouldn't turn us into fatalists. It should stir us into active cooperation with the Sovereign Lord in prayer.

second-half plans.[5] The Lord performs a miracle to interrupt the course of the sun in the sky in order to emphasize how big a moment this is in the history of Judah.[6] A lot is riding on what Hezekiah decides to do with the extra fifteen years he has been given.

Some readers argue that Hezekiah was wrong to pray for fifteen more years because of what he goes on to do with them in 20:12–19. That's because they haven't spotted the detail in 20:6, that this miracle took place *before* he defeated Sennacherib. It's a good job that he didn't leave that to his son Manasseh! No, the real tragedy of this chapter is that Hezekiah fails to grasp that God has given him these extra fifteen years in order to plan for the day of substitution. He reflects in Isaiah 38:17 that *"Surely it was for **my** benefit that I suffered such anguish."* His eyes are on himself instead of on his son.[7] He isn't thinking about how he can shore up his legacy by discipling Manasseh in the ways of the Lord.[8]

No sooner is Hezekiah back on his feet than he is visited by a group of foreign envoys. A man named Marduk-Baladan has declared himself king of the city of Babylon and he is looking for allies in his fight for independence from the Assyrian Empire.[9] Hezekiah feels flattered, especially when the envoys tell him that news about his miraculous healing has made it all the way to their city. He decides to give them a tour of his treasure rooms. When Isaiah hears about it, he is furious. It doesn't matter that these envoys come *"from a distant land"* (verse 14). The Lord

---

[5] Isaiah 38:9–20 records Hezekiah's long, reflective testimony about this healing.

[6] The Hebrew text of 20:9–11 could refer to the notches on a sundial rather than the steps on a staircase.

[7] We are told in 20:20 and 2 Chronicles 32:30 that he got distracted in these extra years building an underground tunnel to bring water into the city from the spring of Gihon in case the Assyrians returned.

[8] Part of the tragedy here is that, in his healing testimony, Hezekiah proclaims the paramount importance of parents instructing their children in the faithfulness of God, the very thing he fails to do (Isaiah 38:19).

[9] Marduk-Baladan failed in both of his attempts to achieve this (721–710 and 703–702 BC).

is about to make a half-time substitution of his own, even if Hezekiah is slow to do the same. Over the course of the next century, Assyria will collapse and be replaced by a new arch-villain: the city of Babylon. Isaiah informs Hezekiah that these same Babylonians will invade his land, plunder his treasure rooms, castrate his children and carry off many of his subjects into captivity.[10]

This is the moment of truth for Hezekiah. The Lord has made a half-time substitution, taking off Assyria and bringing on Babylon, so it remains to be seen if Hezekiah will respond by making a half-time substitution of his own. Will he repent of his short-sightedness in showing off to his nation's future enemies? Will he recognize that the Lord has given him these extra fifteen years of life so that he can invest the second half of his reign in teaching his son Manasseh how to rule as a godly king? Sadly, the answer is no. In response to Isaiah's prophecy about the fall of Judah, he gives a feeble reply that is short-sighted, self-centred and woefully complacent. The man who prayed so hard for the deliverance of Jerusalem from the Assyrians in his own day simply shrugs his shoulders (verse 19): *"The word of the Lord you have spoken is good. Will there not be peace and security in my lifetime?"* The man who wept bitterly at the thought of his own premature demise does not shed a tear over the future destruction of Jerusalem.

As we will see in the next chapter, Manasseh would go on to become the worst king of Judah. Hezekiah completely misses his half-time opportunity to bring him onto the field well. His own reign was a great success, but success without a successor equals failure.

---

[10] Initially, the news about these palace treasures would provoke Sennacherib to invade and seize them (18:13–16). The larger fulfilment of Isaiah's prophecy would then come years later, in 2 Kings 24:10–15.

Forgetfulness
(2 Kings 21:1–26)

This is what the Lord, the God of Israel, says: "I am going to bring such disaster on Jerusalem and Judah that the ears of everyone who hears of it will tingle."

(2 Kings 21:12)

In 1932, a British newspaper published a famous political cartoon. Three years after the great Wall Street Crash, the Americans were pulling money out of Europe fast, which the cartoonist feared would eventually trigger a second world war. He drew a picture of a lifeboat that was sinking at one end. The Americans were high in the water, looking down on the Europeans who were frantically attempting to bail the water out of their end of the boat with buckets. One of the Americans remarked to his friends: *"Phew! That's a nasty leak. Thank goodness it's not at our end of the boat."*[1]

That's how Hezekiah had felt about teaching his son Manasseh how to reign after he was gone on behalf of the true King of Judah.[2] To his credit, he at least had Manasseh crowned joint king in 697 BC as a way of giving him a few years of on-the-job apprenticeship. It's pretty clear, however, that Hezekiah remained the main ruler right up until his death in 686 BC.[3] By

---

[1] The *Evening Standard*, 24th March 1932. The cartoonist was David Low.

[2] In 20:5, the Lord calls Hezekiah the *nāgīd* of his people. The word means *prince* or *captain* or *governor*. It serves as a great reminder that the kings of Judah were only ever regents for the real King of Judah.

[3] Manasseh ruled for fifty-five years and died in 642 BC, so he was still young enough for his father to shape him. His mother's name Hephzibah means *"my delight is in her"*, a name God gave to Jerusalem in Isaiah 62:4.

the time his son finally got his hands on the tiller, his father was no longer around to stop his boat from sinking.

Manasseh means *Forgetfulness*, and he lived up to his name. He remembered nothing of his father's example of how to rule the southern kingdom successfully for the Lord. He rebuilt the "high places". He replaced the altars and the images of false gods that Hezekiah had demolished. He not only worshipped Baal and Asherah, but adopted the morals of the Canaanites who had worshipped them in the days of Joshua too. He imitated Ahab's dynasty by performing sorcery through the power of demon-gods.[4] He even sacrificed his own sons as burnt offerings to Molek. Hezekiah's short-sighted contempt for his own legacy therefore led directly to the murder of his grandchildren.[5]

Terrible though this was, the writer is even more horrified by the way Manasseh defiled the Temple of the Lord. He describes in great detail how the new king of Judah erected pagan altars inside the Temple where the Lord had promised to put his Name – that is, the place from which he pledged to rule as the earthly footstool of his heavenly throne.[6] Having forgotten his father's example, Manasseh promptly forgot the Law too. He led his subjects so far astray from the instructions that the Lord gave Moses at Mount Sinai that the people of Judah became even more depraved than the Canaanites the Lord had

---

[4] The "host of heaven" in 21:3–5 means more than simply sacrificing to the sun, moon and stars. It means sacrificing to the demons which inhabit the heavenly realms (1 Kings 22:19). This marked a new low for Judah. None of its previous kings had been sorcerers. Manasseh had become the prince regent of Satan.

[5] 2 Chronicles 33:6 explains that Manasseh actually sacrificed several of his *sons*. What's important here is that he didn't just kill his baby boys and girls. He killed his heirs and would-be successors. Jeremiah 7:30–32 and 19:1–6 say that he started a trend in Judah and that many of his subjects sacrificed their own children too.

[6] 1 Kings 8:29 and 9:3. Before we rush to judge Manasseh, we need to reflect on what false teaching and practices we may have brought into the Church ourselves. See 1 Corinthians 10:6.

driven out through Joshua.[7] Hezekiah had been a fool not to pay more attention to the flaws in his son's character. He had been complacent, like the men in the cartoon, thinking only of his own end of the boat. Now it was sinking fast.

The Lord sent prophets to warn Manasseh that he was setting the southern kingdom on a path towards its destruction. They make their words shocking to try to elicit a reaction from his stony heart. They warn that he and his subjects are more sinful than the Canaanites that the Lord annihilated in the book of Joshua.[8] They warn that his family is about to suffer the same judgment as Ahab's dynasty. They warn that his capital city of Jerusalem is about to be sacked like Samaria. Yet Manasseh forgets their words as quickly as he hears them. In the end, he wants to hear no more. He launches a campaign of persecution against God's prophets that turns Jerusalem into an abattoir. He has the prophet Isaiah sawn in half – a fitting picture of his contempt for the Word of the Lord.[9]

Manasseh is by far the worst king of Judah. Several times the writer goes on to pinpoint his reign as the moment when it became certain that the southern kingdom would go into exile too.[10] But if his reign marks the "death" of Judah, it also marks its "resurrection" too. One of the big themes of 1 and 2 Kings has been that God's people need to recognize they have no saviour but the Lord. It's not a case of "we have sinned and we need to get our act together or we will die", but rather a case of "we have sinned and we know the wages of that sin is death – but might God send a Saviour who can raise us from the dead?"[11]

---

[7] The Hebrew verb *tā'āh* in 21:9 was normally used to describe a man *seducing* a married woman. Godly Hezekiah and sinful Manasseh both demonstrate just how much influence a leader has over his people.

[8] Amorites is a generic term for all of those nations (Genesis 15:16 and Joshua 24:15).

[9] Manasseh's violence has earned him the nickname "the Nero of Judah". The fate of Isaiah comes from a longstanding Jewish oral tradition.

[10] 2 Kings 21:12–15; 23:26–27 and 24:3–4, and Jeremiah 15:4.

[11] Genesis 2:17; Romans 6:23 and Hebrews 9:27–28. The writer prophesies about dying and being raised to life with the Messiah in 1 Kings 13:31 and 17:17–24, and in 2 Kings 4:18–37; 5:10–15; 6:1–7 and 13:20–21.

Praise God, the answer is yes. The writer encourages us in 21:17 to read up on the life of Manasseh elsewhere, and we discover something amazing when we do. We are told in 2 Chronicles 33:10–20 that Manasseh was captured in battle by the Assyrians and taken back to the city of Babylon. *"In his distress he sought the favour of the Lord his God and humbled himself greatly before the God of his ancestors. And when he prayed to him, the Lord was moved by his entreaty and listened to his plea; so he brought him back to Jerusalem and to his kingdom. Then Manasseh knew that the Lord is God."* That's simply stunning news. If the grace of God can reach even an old sinner like Manasseh, then there is hope for anybody who puts their trust in the death and resurrection of his Messiah.

In 21:19–26, the writer laments that Manasseh's repentance came too late to influence his son. Amon's name means *Master Builder*, but his reign was exceedingly destructive. He reversed any traces of his father's belated repentance, pursuing all of the same sins that dominated the bulk of his father's reign. After only two years, he was assassinated by his own courtiers.[12] If that sounds a lot like the final kings of Israel, then it's intentional. The writer wants us to realize with horror that Judah's boat is sinking equally fast.

---

[12] Like Manasseh in 21:18, Amon is buried in a royal garden rather than in the royal tombs. Having sacrificed princes from David's dynasty to Molek, they had both forfeited any right to be buried with him.

Jewish Idol
(2 Kings 22:1–20)

*Hilkiah the high priest said to Shaphan the secretary,
"I have found the Book of the Law in the temple of
the Lord."*

(2 Kings 22:8)

Nobody could ever accuse Simon Cowell of hiding his true opinions on the TV show *American Idol*. He is merciless in the way he tears contestants apart. He has a simple response for those who accuse him of excessive harshness: *"Harshness to me is giving somebody false hopes and not following through. That's harsh. Telling some guy or some girl who's got zero talent that they have zero talent actually is a kindness."*

The Jewish exiles in Babylon had never been subjected to the kindness of Simon Cowell. As a result, they still believed they could be saved through the great Jewish idol. They were convinced that, if only they obeyed the Law of Moses thoroughly, the Lord would be obliged to bring them back to the Promised Land.[1] That's why the writer uses the reign of Josiah to demonstrate that obedience to the Law can never save anyone.[2]

Josiah became king of Judah at the tender age of eight. That was a mercy, since the premature death of Amon meant he learned little of his father's sinful ways. Josiah means *Given A Foundation By The Lord* and, sure enough, the priests and

---

[1] They quoted verses such as Deuteronomy 17:18–20 and Joshua 1:8. But they had forgotten verses such as Leviticus 18:5 and Deuteronomy 27:26. See Romans 3:19–21 and 10:5; Galatians 3:10–13 and James 2:9–11.

[2] Note the way that the writer deliberately uses stock phrases from the Law in these verses. In 22:2, for example, *"not turning aside to the right or to the left"* deliberately echoes Deuteronomy 5:32–33 and 28:14.

prophets stepped into his dead father's shoes and taught him how to rule as regent for the real King of Judah.[3] In 632 BC, aged sixteen, Josiah experienced a genuine conversion to the Lord. Four years later, he started to purge the land of Judah of his father's idols.[4] In 622 BC, he launched a project to repair the dilapidated Temple of the Lord.

That's when it happened. That's when the high priest Hilkiah discovered an old copy of the Law of Moses while clearing out some rubbish from the Temple.[5] We can tell how little people studied the Law during the reigns of Manasseh and Amon from the way that Hilkiah seems surprised to have got his hands on a copy, and from the way that Josiah is horrified to discover what it actually says. He tears his royal clothes as a mark of his repentance, just as Hezekiah did back in 19:1. By the time his secretary has finished reading the Law, Josiah has reached a sobering conclusion in 22:13: *"Great is the Lord's anger that burns against us because those who have gone before us have not obeyed the words of this book; they have not acted in accordance with all that is written there concerning us."*

This was meant to get the Jewish exiles in Babylon nodding their heads. By this point in 1 and 2 Kings, they recognized that their nation had gone into exile for ignoring the Law of Moses. The Law is so absent throughout these pages that when the king's secretary is handed a copy he looks at it blankly in 22:10 and tells Josiah that *"Hilkiah the priest has given me a book."* That's a pretty good indication of how little the Torah was studied and obeyed in this period of Jewish history. The sudden rediscovery of the Law was not so much like a person finding their missing set of car keys as like a person being reminded that they even have a car!

---

[3] The prophet Zephaniah was part of the royal family of Judah (Zephaniah 1:1), so it appears the young Josiah was deeply influenced by his call to choose between God's judgment and God's salvation.

[4] We are given this additional information in 2 Chronicles 34:3–7.

[5] Hilkiah means *My Portion Is The Lord*. He has not been a good high priest up until this moment, showing little initiative to repair the Temple, and allowing priests and prostitutes to defile it (23:4–7; Zephaniah 3:4).

Disobedience to God's Law had led to the exile, but the writer wants to teach his readers that obedience to the Law will not reverse it.[6] He is as kind as Simon Cowell to the Jewish exiles in his frank assessment of their Jewish idol. No king of Judah ever sought salvation through the Law as diligently as Josiah in these verses. He studies it, he tears his clothes over it, he prays about it and he asks the prophetess Huldah to teach him more about it.[7] If anybody could have saved the southern kingdom through obedience to the Law, then it was Josiah. However, note what Huldah tells him in 22:16. The Law brings judgment on sinners; it isn't their saviour. The best Huldah can promise is that the Lord will hold off the destruction of Judah until after Josiah has died.[8]

The New Testament expands on the prophetic message of this chapter. It insists that the Law of Moses did not fail the Jewish nation. God never intended them to treat it as their Saviour. It was only ever meant to do for them what it succeeds in doing for King Josiah here – it was meant to convict them of their sin and of their utter hopelessness unless God sends them a Saviour. Israel and Judah forfeited the Promised Land through their *disobedience* to the Law, but they couldn't get it back through renewed *obedience*. The Law is like a doctor who knows how to point out cancer but who lacks any medicine to remove the cancer that he sees.[9]

At the start of 1 Kings, we hoped that *wisdom* might save Israel, but then its wisest king went off the rails. Next we hoped *the Temple* might save Israel, but it is largely ignored except

---

[6] Breaking the Law results in judgment (21:8), but obedience to the Law can no more atone for our sin than stopping at traffic lights atones for every other traffic violation. Good works can never earn us righteousness.

[7] Huldah is the only female prophet named in 1 and 2 Kings. Her name means *Weasel* – an inauspicious name for a great woman of God. Jeremiah and Zephaniah were in Jerusalem, yet the high priest goes to her.

[8] Huldah tells Josiah: because you listened to God's Word, God will listen to your prayer. See Isaiah 66:2.

[9] Joshua 1:7–8; Habakkuk 1:4; Romans 3:19–20, and Galatians 2:21; 3:19–24 and 5:4.

when rulers are in a tight spot and need to go salvaging for gold. Next we hoped that a godly *king* might save Israel, but even the best of them dropped the ball. When we hoped instead that *unity* might save Israel, Jehoshaphat's alliance with the north actually made matters worse. The final Jewish idol was the idea that *obedience to the Law of Moses* might save Israel. Huldah's words are meant to shatter that hope too. Nothing within Israel can save Israel.

A friend of mine recently filled up his petrol car with diesel. Fortunately he realized what he had done before he started the engine. He could have shut his eyes and tried to drive away, but he wouldn't have got very far. He knew he had to call an expert to empty his fuel tank so that he could fill it up with the right fuel. That's what the writer is trying to do for us here when he speaks about obedience to the Law.

He is teaching us that obedience to God's commands can't save anyone. We just don't have it in us to obey the Law of God perfectly. We need more than reformation; we need resurrection. We don't just need the Law of God; we need the living Word of God inside us to convict us of our sin and to fill us with his Spirit to empower us to obey the Lord in a manner that the Law of Moses never could.

The nineteenth-century evangelist D.L. Moody urges us to heed the prophetic warning in this chapter:

> *The Law was given not to save men, but to measure them ... It was never meant for men to save themselves by. Ask Paul why it was given. Here is his answer: "That every mouth may be stopped, and all the world may become guilty before God" (Romans 3:19) ... This, then, is why God gives us the Law – to show us ourselves in our true colours.*[10]

---

[10] D.L. Moody in his *Twelve Select Sermons* (1881).

Inside Out
(2 Kings 23:1–30)

Then all the people pledged themselves to the covenant.

(2 Kings 23:3)

In the TV series *Prison Break*, Lincoln Burrows is sent to a maximum security prison for a crime he didn't commit. His brother Michael is convinced that Lincoln is innocent, but he has no time to prove it before his execution. He has to break his brother out of prison, and he knows that he can't do that from the outside. He has to break *in* so that he can break his brother *out*. He tattoos detailed schematics of the prison onto his body, then commits armed robbery in order to be incarcerated with Lincoln. Knowing that he can only save his brother from the inside out, Michael pays whatever price it costs to get inside.

Hold that thought. You're going to need it if you want to understand what the writer tries to convey to us in this chapter. The second half of Josiah's reign contains the second half of the writer's warning that obedience to the Jewish religion has never saved anyone. Religion is all about *outside in*, but God's salvation is all about *inside out*.

On the surface, things look pretty positive in this chapter. Next to that of Hezekiah, this is the greatest spiritual revival that ever swept through the land of Judah.[1] King Josiah summons the whole of his kingdom to the Temple and then reads the entire

---

[1] Hezekiah and Josiah are the only two kings of Judah that are given unqualified approval for their loyalty to the Lord (2 Kings 18:3 and 22:2).

Law of Moses to them.² He helps them to renew their covenant to obey all of the Lord's commands. *"Then all the people pledged themselves to the covenant"* (23:3).

This renewal of the covenant brings about some great changes, at least superficially.³ Josiah purges the Temple of all the idols that were put there by Manasseh and Amon. He destroys all the "high places", demolishing their altars and their images, then scattering the rubble on the graves of dead idolaters as a sign that Judah wants no god but the Lord in this new generation.⁴ Josiah desecrates the shrine of Molek in the valley outside Jerusalem so that parents can no longer sacrifice their children there.⁵ He drives out the male prostitutes so that they can no longer sell anal sex to visitors to the Lord's Temple. He even goes to Bethel to fulfil the prophecy spoken against King Jeroboam in 1 Kings 13:1–6 that a descendant of David named Josiah would burn the bones of its priests on their own pagan altars.⁶

It all looks pretty positive, especially when King Josiah commands his subjects to celebrate the Passover.⁷ *"Neither in*

---

² People who are changed by God's Word cannot help sharing God's Word with others. Josiah reads the Law while standing next to one of the two huge bronze pillars which held up the porch of the Temple. The high priest Jehoiada also followed this custom when he led Judah in a renewal of the covenant in 11:14–17.

³ Having purified the southern kingdom ("*Geba to Beersheba*" in 23:8), Josiah also travels north to purify the lands of the former northern kingdom. But even this "reunification" of the twelve tribes can't save Israel.

⁴ Many of Judah's problems started in 1 Kings 11:7 when Solomon built temples to foreign idols on the Hill of Corruption (almost certainly the Mount of Olives). Now at last, 350 years later, Josiah demolishes them.

⁵ Topheth means *Fire Pit* and it was part of the Valley of Ben Hinnom (Isaiah 30:33), which is transliterated from Hebrew into Greek as *Gehenna*. It became the rubbish dump of Jerusalem, its flames burning night and day, so Jesus uses it as one of his main words for *Hell* (see Matthew 5:22–30 and Mark 9:43–47).

⁶ Josiah takes the ashes of Judah's idols to Bethel in 23:4 because he sees it as the root of all Judah's idolatry. There is no mention of the golden calf of Bethel in this chapter, so did the Assyrians steal it in 722 BC?

⁷ 2 Chronicles 35:1–19 describes this Passover in great detail. Josiah sacrificed over 33,000 animals.

the days of the judges who led Israel nor in the days of the kings of Israel and the kings of Judah had any such Passover been observed" (23:22). After Josiah exiles all of the occultists from the land, the writer summarizes his achievements under one big headline: Josiah thoroughly obeyed the Law.

> *This he did to fulfil the requirements of the law written in the book that Hilkiah the priest had discovered in the temple of the Lord. Neither before nor after Josiah was there a king like him who turned to the Lord as he did – with all his heart and with all his soul and with all his strength, in accordance with all the Law of Moses.*[8]

Have you got that? Josiah completely obeyed the Law. Now get ready for the sucker punch. The writer says in the very next verse (23:26) that *"Nevertheless, the Lord did not turn away from the heat of his fierce anger, which burned against Judah because of all that Manasseh had done."* Judah's new-found obedience to the Law didn't save them. It didn't even save Josiah. He dies in battle with Pharaoh Necho of Egypt in 609 BC, aged only thirty-nine.[9]

The writer wants us to be shocked by this. He wants us to ask ourselves what on earth went wrong. He wants to challenge the view that we can ever square things with God by becoming a bit more diligent in our Bible reading, a bit more intense in our obedience, a bit more committed in our church attendance and a bit louder in our worship songs. He wants us to grasp that

---

[8] 23:24–25. Note the deliberate echo of what Jesus refers to as the Greatest Commandment (Deuteronomy 6:5 and Matthew 22:35–38). The writer holds Josiah up as the perfect Law-keeper, yet the Law fails to save him.

[9] This was caused by Josiah's pride (2 Chronicles 35:20–24), but it was actually God's merciful way of sparing him from seeing the destruction of Jerusalem (22:19–20 and Isaiah 57:1–2). Pharaoh Necho was trying to help the Assyrians to resist the rise of Babylon, so Josiah was foolish to get involved. The Greek transliteration of the Hebrew for Hill of Megiddo is *Armageddon*, so Revelation 16:16 treats this event as a prophetic picture.

nobody has ever been saved through outside-in religion.[10] King Josiah's revival failed to save the southern kingdom because it wasn't inside out.

In some of the most shocking verses in the Old Testament, the prophet Jeremiah reveals what really happened during King Josiah's revival. He says that, although it all looked good on the outside, it didn't transform people on the inside. In Jeremiah 3:10, the Lord dismisses the revival as *sheqer* – the Hebrew word for *a lie* or *pretence*. In Jeremiah 3:11, he says that Judah is actually more guilty than Israel, because at least the northern kingdom never promised to follow him. Far from saving them, the Lord says that the renewal of the covenant at the Temple brought them even more under his judgment. Promises of obedience in the future cannot atone for disobedience in the past. It takes more than loud religious protestations on the outside to change us on the inside.

So back to Lincoln Burrows in *Prison Break*. There isn't any hope for our salvation while we cling to the hope that increasing our religious activity might make things right between us and God. We need somebody like Lincoln's brother Michael, who is willing to pay the price to step inside the prison with us and to break us out. That's what Jesus did when he became one of us and filled his followers with the Holy Spirit to transform them from the inside out by God's Almighty power. That's the story behind the story throughout 1 and 2 Kings. It is a prophetic exhortation to renounce our false saviours – even ones that seem as noble as the Law – in order to receive the only true Saviour.

The eighteenth-century revivalist George Whitefield told the crowds who flocked to hear him that this alone is our hope of salvation:

> *When a poor soul is somewhat awakened ... then the poor creature, being born under a covenant of works,*

---

[10] The writer focuses on the Jewish Law, but he might just as easily be talking about our acts of Christian obedience. Jesus warns in John 5:39–40 that they are equally powerless to save us.

flies directly to a covenant of works again. And as Adam and Eve hid themselves among the trees of the garden, and sewed fig leaves together to cover their nakedness, so the poor sinner, when awakened, flies to his duties and to his performances, to hide himself from God, and goes to patch up a righteousness of his own. Says he, "I will be mighty good now – I will reform – I will do all I can; and then certainly Jesus Christ will have mercy on me." But ... our best duties are as so many splendid sins.[11]

---

[11] Whitefield said this in a sermon on Jeremiah 6:14 entitled "The Method of Grace".

Avalanche
(2 Kings 23:31 – 24:20)

*The Lord sent Babylonian, Aramean, Moabite and
Ammonite raiders ... in accordance with the word of
the Lord proclaimed by his servants the prophets.*

(2 Kings 24:2)

In September 1962, the American scientists David Bernays and
Charles Sawyer took a holiday to Peru. Both keen climbers, they
had decided to explore some of the lesser-known peaks of the
Andes together. What they discovered brought them running
back down the mountains in a hurry. A vast chunk of ice, the size
of 500 Olympic swimming pools, was about to plummet down
the slopes of the Huascarán mountain and obliterate the town
of Yungay in the valley below.

When Bernays and Sawyer ran a story in the local *Espreso*
newspaper to warn of the impending disaster, the Peruvian
government threw the two scientists in jail. After two weeks,
they were reprimanded for endangering the local tourist
industry, then released on the condition that they left the
country and spoke no more of what they had seen. Their silence
was costly. On 31st May 1970, their vast chunk of ice finally fell,
provoking the deadliest avalanche in history. Eighty million
cubic metres of debris hurtled down the mountain at over 300
miles per hour, killing the 20,000 people who lived in Yungay.
Those deaths could have been avoided had the government
simply listened to the warning voices eight years earlier.

The kings of Judah had been treating the Lord's prophets
like David Bernays and Charles Sawyer for far too long. They
had dismissed their warnings of God's impending judgment as

the scaremongering of troublemakers. The Lord therefore gave them twenty-three years after the death of King Josiah to listen. Meanwhile he filled the reigns of the final four kings of Judah, in the table below, with deadly avalanche warnings.

JUDAH	Rehoboam (930–913 BC)	Jotham (750–732 BC)*
	Abijah (913–910 BC)	Ahaz (735–715 BC)
	Asa (910–869 BC)*	Hezekiah (715–686 BC)*
	Jehoshaphat (872–848 BC)*	Manasseh (697–642 BC)
	Jehoram (853–841 BC)	Amon (642–640 BC)
	Ahaziah (841 BC)	Josiah (640–609 BC)
	[Athaliah (841–835 BC)]	Jehoahaz (609 BC)
	Joash (835–796 BC)	Jehoiakim (609–598 BC)
	Amaziah (796–767 BC)*	Jehoiachin (598–597 BC)
	Azariah (792–740 BC)*	Zedekiah (597–586 BC)

* These kings had overlapping reigns with their sons

In 23:31–35, we are told that the reign of Jehoahaz lasted only three months. He was the fourth son of Josiah, and his throne name expressed his surprise that God had chosen him to reign. Jehoahaz means *The Lord Has Taken Hold Of Me*, but when he refused to lay hold of the Lord, his reign became an avalanche warning instead.[1] Pharaoh Necho took him captive at Riblah, on the Orontes River, the very place where the royal family of Judah would be slaughtered by the Babylonians in 586 BC. His death in captivity acted as a dress rehearsal for what would happen if the Lord's warnings continued to be ignored.

In 23:36–24:7, we are told that his elder brother succeeded him as king. Pharaoh Necho hoped that Jehoiakim would prove more malleable than his little brother, and so it proved. He sent much of the southern kingdom's wealth to Egypt.[2] Sadly, however, he was not as obedient to the Lord as

---

[1] Jehoahaz was originally named *Shallum* (Jeremiah 22:10–12). His older brothers are listed in 1 Chronicles 3:15. The Jeremiah mentioned in 23:31 is *not* the famous prophet, who was pretty scathing towards Jehoahaz.

[2] We are told in 23:33–35 that he was forced to send 34 kg of gold and 3.5 tons of silver to Egypt.

he was to a foreign pharaoh. Necho had a genuine encounter with God in 2 Chronicles 35:21–22 that inspired him to change the new king's name from Eliakim, which means *God Raises Up*, to Jehoiakim, which means *The Lord Raises Up*. It was meant to remind him that he was accountable to the Lord, but instead he was as forgetful as Manasseh. He continued to ignore the avalanche warnings.[3]

The balance of power was changing in the region. King Nebuchadnezzar of Babylon trounced Pharaoh Necho at the Battle of Carchemish in 605 BC.[4] Jehoiakim promptly switched sides, failing to listen when the prophets urged him to heed the story behind the story.[5] Even when his land was raided by the Babylonians, the Arameans, the Moabites and the Ammonites, he still refused to listen. When Judah was reduced to a puppet kingdom of Babylon, he still refused to repent and turn back to the Lord. We are told elsewhere in the Old Testament that he burned Jeremiah's prophecies, murdered the prophet Uriah and reintroduced idols into the Temple.[6] Therefore Nebuchadnezzar plundered the Temple and took 7,000 Jewish men into captivity in 605 BC.[7] The Lord's avalanche warnings were getting louder.[8]

---

[3] The statement in 24:3–4 that *"the Lord was not willing to forgive"* offers us a dire warning. The royal family of Judah was now utterly ingrained with the sins of King Manasseh, rather than the godliness of King David.

[4] This battle also marked the end of the Assyrian Empire, after its capital Nineveh was destroyed in 612 BC.

[5] Jeremiah 22:13–19 predicts Jehoiakim's fate if he refuses to listen to God's avalanche warnings. 2 Kings 24:2–3 therefore attributes all of these disasters to *"the word of the Lord proclaimed by his servants the prophets"*.

[6] Jeremiah 26:20–23 and 36:1–32, and Ezekiel 8:5–17. Habakkuk also prophesied to him in 605 BC.

[7] We are told about this in 2 Chronicles 36:6–7 and Daniel 1:1–5. We get the number 7,000 from 2 Kings 24:14 minus Jeremiah 52:28. Jehoiakim himself was among the exiles but was permitted to return if he paid tribute.

[8] The writer does not say that Jehoiakim was assassinated, but it is suspicious that he died aged only thirty-six and there is no mention of his burial with his fathers. Jeremiah 22:18–19 and 36:30 confirm that he died brutally and that his body was left to rot unburied.

In 24:8–17, we are told that the new King Jehoiachin reigned a mere three months.[9] That's how long it took for the Babylonian army to arrive at the walls of Jerusalem to enforce the tribute payments that his father had stopped paying in 24:1.[10] Yet again Nebuchadnezzar plundered the Temple of the Lord. Yet again he took Jewish captives into exile, including King Jehoiachin himself, his royal officials, his army officers and his best soldiers and craftsmen.[11] We are told in 24:13 that all this happened *"As the Lord had declared"* through his prophets, because still the kings of Judah refused to listen.[12]

In 24:18–20, we are told that Jehoiachin's uncle Zedekiah, the last king of Judah, began his reign. Although his kingdom was evidently on the brink of destruction, he still stubbornly refused to repent and serve the Lord. The seventeenth-century English theologian Stephen Charnock therefore urges us to see the story behind the story in these tragic verses. We need to respond to God's avalanche warnings ourselves:

> *Presume not upon God's patience. The exercise of it is not eternal ... You know not how soon His anger may turn His patience aside, and step before it. It may be His sword is drawn out of the scabbard, His arrows may be settled in His bow, and perhaps there is but a little time before you*

---

[9] Jehoiachin means *The Lord Establishes*, but Jeremiah 13:18 suggests that his mother Nehushta was the real power behind his throne. Her name means *Brazen* or *Snake*. The Babylonian royal annals tell us that Jerusalem surrendered to Nebuchadnezzar on 16th March 597 BC.

[10] A minor Egyptian victory against the Babylonians had emboldened Jehoiakim to switch sides yet again. In doing so, he ignored the Lord's prophetic warning in Jeremiah 27:9–11.

[11] 605 BC saw 7,000 Jewish men exiled to Babylon along with their wives and children. Among them was the prophet Daniel. 597 BC saw 3,023 Jewish men exiled to Babylon along with their wives and children (Jeremiah 52:28). Among them was the prophet Ezekiel. Don't miss God's grace in giving Jerusalem two deafening avalanche warnings in 605 and 597 BC before its final destruction in 586 BC.

[12] *"As the Lord had declared"* in 24:13 refers to Isaiah's prophecy in 2 Kings 20:12–18.

may feel the edge of the one or the point of the other, and then there will be no more time for patience in God to us, or petition from us to Him.[13]

---

[13] Stephen Charnock in his *Discourses upon the Existence and Attributes of God* (1682).

The End Of The Road
(2 Kings 25:1–30)

So Judah went into captivity, away from her land.

(2 Kings 25:21)

None of the Jewish exiles in Babylon could forget what had happened to Jerusalem on 18th July 586 BC. That was the day on which the avalanche of God's judgment finally struck the southern kingdom. It was when Judah finally reached the end of the road.

Josiah had trembled and repented at the Word of the Lord, but his son Jehoiakim had cut it up and burned it instead.[1] His son Jehoahaz and his grandson Jehoiachin had also ignored God's Word to their nation. When King Nebuchadnezzar of Babylon installed Josiah's third son as the new king of Judah, he was therefore doing him a favour when he changed his name to Zedekiah, which means *The Lord Is Righteous*.[2] He didn't know it, but he was issuing God's final warning to the southern kingdom. Unless it remembered that the Lord is righteous and repented of its sins, it was "game over" for Judah.

Sadly, King Zedekiah ignored the Lord's final avalanche warning. He reneged on the oath of allegiance he had made to Nebuchadnezzar in God's name.[3] He filled the Lord's Temple with idols, fooled himself that an alliance with Egypt could save

---

[1] Contrast 2 Kings 22:10–20 with Jeremiah 36:20–26. Zedekiah and Jehoahaz were full brothers, while Jehoiakim was their half-brother.

[2] Mattaniah means *Gift Of The Lord*, but the kings of Babylon changed the names of their defeated foes as a means of asserting their supremacy (Daniel 1:7).

[3] 2 Chronicles 36:13 and Ezekiel 17:15–19 say that breaking this oath wasn't just foolish – it was sinful.

him and imprisoned the prophet Jeremiah for warning him that Pharaoh would prove a false friend.[4] He was so ungodly that he did not even notice when the presence of the Lord upped and left the Temple on 17th September 592 BC.[5] He didn't even repent when King Nebuchadnezzar invaded Judah on 15th January 588 BC, besieging Jerusalem for thirty months until it finally fell on 18th July 586 BC. The rebellious dynasty of David had at long last reached the end of the road.

The destruction of Jerusalem marked such a major milestone in the history of the Jewish nation that 2 Kings 25 is repeated almost word-for-word in Jeremiah 52. Judah's *wisdom* proves to be a false saviour when Zedekiah's politicking with Pharaoh Hophra engenders recklessness, not rescue. The Egyptian king isn't even mentioned in these verses.[6] Judah's *military strength* fails to save it when, instead of keeping out the Babylonians, the mighty walls of Jerusalem merely keep out food supplies. When they are breached, the army that is defending them seems almost relieved, since it enables them to abandon the city and run away. With great irony, the writer describes them literally in 25:4 as *"men of battle"*. Judah's soldiers prove to be false saviours when the rubber hits the road.[7]

Judah is let down by *David's dynasty*. Zedekiah's sin provokes this invasion but he abandons Jerusalem to its fate in order to save his own skin. His flight is intercepted and he is captured along with his children.[8] They are put to death in front of him, and then his eyes are gouged out so their bloodied

---

[4] 2 Chronicles 36:11–16, and Jeremiah 32:1–5 and 37:1–21.

[5] We are told that this happened in Ezekiel 8:1; 9:3; 10:4–5, 18–19; 11:22–23.

[6] Better known as Pharaoh Apries (589–570 BC), he marched out to help Judah but quickly retreated to save his own skin. He was eventually murdered by his own subjects (Jeremiah 37:5–10 and 44:30).

[7] The writer says something similar in 24:14–16, calling them literally *"the mighty men of valour ... the mighty ones of the land ... the mighty heroes, men of battle"*. What people call us matters less than what we actually are!

[8] God had specifically warned Zedekiah not to try to flee from the Babylonians because he would be captured (Jeremiah 34:1–3). His disobedience directly contributed to his downfall.

corpses are the last thing that he sees.[9] After he is led away in chains to Babylon, the writer no longer dates events by the reigns of the kings of Judah.[10] In 25:8, for the first time, he dates them by the kings of Babylon.

Judah is let down by its *Temple*. Instead of saving the southern kingdom from destruction, it provides a motive to press home for the plunder.[11] It is torched to the ground and the victorious Babylonians grind its ruins to dust along with the rest of the city. The writer gives us an inventory of its ornaments in order to emphasize how much the Temple failed to be a saviour to the southern kingdom.[12] It couldn't even save its priests and doorkeepers from being slaughtered alongside the royal family at Riblah, let alone the thousands of citizens of Jerusalem who were hacked down in its streets.[13]

Worst of all, it appears on the surface as though Judah has been let down by *the Lord*. Nebuchadnezzar means *May The God Nebo Protect My Son*, echoed by the name of his general Nebuzaradan, which means *The God Nebo Has a Son*. The destruction of Jerusalem therefore looked like the victory of Nebo, the Babylonian god of wisdom, over the God of Israel.[14]

---

[9] The Lord had issued an avalanche warning by allowing a dress rehearsal of this to take place in 23:33.

[10] Abraham had begun the Hebrew story by setting out in faith from Ur, in Chaldea. Now the Hebrew story comes full circle when this unfaithful generation is forcibly returned to Babylon, also in Chaldea.

[11] This is the ninth and final time the Temple was plundered, after 1 Kings 14:25–28 and 15:18; 2 Kings 12:18; 14:14; 16:7–8; 18:15–16 and 24:13, and 2 Chronicles 36:7. The Temple only lasted 372 years, from 958–586 BC.

[12] The Hebrew for *"pure gold and silver"* in 25:15 is literally *"gold gold"* and *"silver silver"*. This helps us to understand what the Lord intends to convey by revealing himself in Isaiah 6:3 as *"holy holy holy"*.

[13] Very few people were taken into captivity in the exile of 586 BC – only the 832 Jewish men who had listened to the Lord and already surrendered to the Babylonians (Jeremiah 21:9–10 and 52:29). Other than a few poor peasants who were left to farm the land, anybody found in Jerusalem was now slaughtered.

[14] Nebo hadn't actually won. We are told in Daniel 5 that Babylon fell on the very night that King Belshazzar attempted to toast his pagan gods with cups stolen from the Temple in Jerusalem.

This was the day when all hope in the Jewish religion appeared to have reached the end of the road.

Even when Nebuchadnezzar appoints a governor to oversee the few survivors left in Judah, there is more disappointment left to come. His name is Gedaliah, which means *The Lord Is Great*, and he lived up to his name by saving the prophet Jeremiah from execution under King Jehoiakim. He does so again now by encouraging the survivors to accept that the destruction of their nation is an act of God's judgment.[15] Before he can lead them to repent of their sin, however, a renegade prince from David's dynasty assassinates him. The few Jewish survivors left in the land of Judah flee to Egypt for fear of reprisals from Babylon.[16] Judah is dead and buried as a nation. The southern kingdom of Judah has well and truly reached the end of the road.[17]

But what's this? The story doesn't end with the destruction of Jerusalem. In his final four verses, the writer describes an event which took place on 22nd March 561 BC and which points us to the story behind the story.[18] Remember Jehoiachin, who reigned for only three months before being taken into exile in Babylon? Thirty-seven years later, he is set free by Nebuchadnezzar's son and appointed one of his top courtiers.[19] Now aged fifty-five, the Lord turns him into a symbol of his promise to restore David's

---

[15] Jeremiah 40:9–10. Gedaliah was the son of one of Jeremiah's friends (Jeremiah 26:24) and was appointed governor in August 586 BC. He was assassinated a few weeks later in October, during the seventh month of the Jewish calendar.

[16] Ishmael hoped to make himself king, but his selfish ambition caused yet more disaster for the people of Judah. Self-promotion in the Church always does (Proverbs 3:34; James 4:6 and 1 Peter 5:5).

[17] In 1932, archaeologists excavating Gedaliah's base at Mizpah found an onyx seal with the inscription: *"Belonging to Jaazaniah the servant of the king"*. We can trust the historicity of detail such as 2 Kings 25:23.

[18] By God's grace, in 25:27 events start being dated again with regard to Judah's exile, not to Babylon's kings.

[19] Marduk was one of the main gods of Babylon. Amel-Marduk meant *Labourer of Marduk*, but those who disapproved of him gave him the nickname *Awel-Marduk*, meaning *Fool Of Marduk*, instead.

dynasty in order to save his nation.[20] The writer reassures the exiles that their nation hasn't reached the end of the road at all. In Jehoiachin, they can see a promise of resurrection.

We only find out fully how this is possible in Matthew 1:11, which reveals that Jesus of Nazareth is the direct descendant and heir of King Jehoiachin. As all of Israel's false saviours reach the end of the road, Jehoiachin becomes a prophetic picture of a better Son of David who is coming into view. The glorious story behind the story, in the midst of Judah's great disaster, is that God has not forgotten his people.[21] Israel's true Saviour is visible in the distance down towards the end of the road.

---

[20] Jehoiachin means *The Lord Establishes*, and there is no other reason why he should have been promoted in this way. The Babylonians castrated and blinded their defeated kings (20:18 and 25:7). They didn't wine and dine them! Perhaps he had repented during his thirty-seven years in prison, helped by visits from Ezekiel and Daniel.

[21] Although the high priest Seraiah was executed in 25:18–21, God would re-establish his grandson Joshua as the new high priest of Israel when the Jews returned from exile. See 1 Chronicles 6:14–15 and Haggai 1:1.

Conclusion: The Story Behind The Story

In the thirty-seventh year of the exile of Jehoiachin king of Judah, in the year Awel-Marduk became king of Babylon, he released Jehoiachin king of Judah from prison.

(2 Kings 25:27)

During the football World Cup in 2002, a chain of stores across London displayed posters of the England captain David Beckham. His arms outstretched against the cross on the English flag behind him, the caption underneath declared: *"Beckham, our saviour".*

False saviours are attractive, but they are false all the same. David Beckham failed to find the net in two lacklustre draws against Sweden and Nigeria. Having failed to win their group, the England team were forced to play Brazil in a trickier-than-expected quarter-final. When David Beckham again failed to score, his team crashed out of the competition. The England players found themselves on the next plane back home.

The message of 1 and 2 Kings is that the Lord will not allow people to trust in their false saviours undisturbed. When we look to the wrong things to save us, God expresses his kindness towards us by allowing those false saviours to topple and fall. He makes them fail us in order to lift up our eyes to receive Jesus as the only true Saviour of the world.

In 1 Kings 1–11, when the Israelites looked to Solomon's *wisdom* to save them, the Lord demonstrated that they needed more than a wise guy to act as their deliverer. Solomon chose his wives and gods so badly that the Hebrew word for wisdom is never used again in 1 and 2 Kings after his reign. The Lord topples wisdom as an idol in order to lift Israel's eyes to the Messiah who would describe himself as *"one greater than Solomon"*.[1]

The Israelites are stubborn. They respond by grasping for a different false saviour. They fool themselves that their *Temple* can save them, but its magnificence proves powerless to protect the kings of Judah from their own sin and idolatry. Although Solomon declares in 1 Kings 8 that the blood sacrifices offered on the altar of the Temple have power to undo the curse of sin, it is remarkable how infrequently the kings ever come to the Temple to offer them. When faced with trouble, even those kings who seem most committed to the Temple come into its precincts to plunder rather than to pray. That's why the final chapter of 2 Kings records the systematic destruction of the Temple. Israel can't be saved through a wise king, but only through the true King who is Wisdom. Israel can't be saved through a man-made Temple, but only through the one who is the true and living Temple.[2]

The Israelites are slow learners. They reach out for a third and fourth false saviour. The northern kingdom hopes that Elijah and Elisha's *school of prophets* will revive their nation, but despite its early promise it runs out of steam in the third generation. The southern kingdom hopes that *renewed unity* will revive their nation, but finds that any unity that is not built on sincere devotion to the Lord yields only bitter disaster.[3] We cannot be saved through unity with one another, but only through unity with Christ.

After the fall of the northern kingdom, the kings of Judah hope to find salvation in their *obedience to the Jewish Law*. King Josiah quickly discovers with horror that, although the Law

---

[1] Matthew 12:42 and Luke 11:31. See also 1 Corinthians 1:24, 30; 2:16, and Colossians 2:2–3.

[2] This is how Jesus understood the message of 1 and 2 Kings. See what he says in John 2:13–22.

[3] King Jehoshaphat of Judah was the prime culprit here (1 Kings 22:4 and 2 Kings 3:7), but King Josiah also found that heading north and attempting to reunify the land wasn't enough to save Israel (2 Kings 23:15–26).

promises success and salvation to those who obey it, it can't empower him to follow it, let alone to lead his nation to follow it with him.[4] The penalty for sin in Genesis 2:17 isn't being put on probation. It's being put to death. The nation of Judah doesn't need New Year's resolutions. It needs nothing less than death and resurrection.

This call to believe in the Gospel of a crucified and risen Messiah runs throughout 1 and 2 Kings. The strange events in 1 Kings 13 warn us that salvation will only come to the divided tribes of Israel through their "dying" and being "buried" together in a land of exile. Elijah's miracle in 1 Kings 17 reassures us that the exile is his doing, because the Lord knows how to raise the dead. In 1 Kings 18, he whispers resurrection promises to anyone who stops to listen to what he says. In 2 Kings, this message rings out even louder. We see prophecies about death and resurrection in the healing of polluted waters (2:19–22), in the raising of a dead boy to life (4:32–35), and in the baptism that a pagan general receives in the River Jordan (5:1–15). It doesn't matter how dead a situation, the death and resurrection of the coming Messiah can still bring it back from the grave (6:1–7 and 13:20–21). That's the story behind the story throughout 1 and 2 Kings. This is a forty-seven-chapter-long prophecy about our need for God's Messiah to come and be our only true Saviour. It points to the birth, the life, the death, the resurrection, the victory and the eternal reign of King Jesus our Lord.[5]

These two books were successful. They helped the Jewish exiles to find their way back to the Promised Land through their faith in God's death-and-resurrection pathway. In 516 BC, seventy years after the destruction of Jerusalem, they were sent back home by the Persians. They rebuilt the Temple but quickly discovered that building it was easier than becoming the Temple of God themselves. They read the Law of Moses out

---

[4] Deuteronomy 17:18–20 and Joshua 1:8. No sooner are we told that Josiah embraces the Law more than any of his predecessors (2 Kings 23:25) than we are also told that God is still angry with Judah (2 Kings 23:26).

[5] Jesus was fully aware of this. He claimed that these books were *"written about me"* (Luke 24:25–27 and 44).

loud to one another but discovered that reading it was easier than writing the Law on their hearts so that they walked in daily obedience to it.[6] Diagnosing the problem of sin is always easier than rescuing ourselves from sin's power. Like the people of Israel and Judah, we need the true Messiah to rescue us, the one who promises death and resurrection to all who put their trust in him: *"Repent, for the kingdom of heaven has come near."*[7]

So as we end 1 and 2 Kings, let's not treat them as mere history books. They were written by a prophet to point us to the true Messiah. They tell us that if we want to know God and to enjoy the life he has for us, then it isn't a case of "get your act together or you will die", but a case of "die to yourself and let the Holy Spirit raise you with Christ". Put this way, it's pretty obvious why the message of 1 and 2 Kings is known as the Good News.

For churches that need reviving and for nations that need saving, this is the story behind the story. There is a true and better King of Judah, a true and better Son of David. All other saviours are imposters. So put down this book and worship Jesus Christ as King, then go out and call the world to worship him with you. Tell them that the world has only one true King and Saviour. Tell them that's the story behind the story.

---

[6] Ezekiel 36:26–27 and 37:27; 1 Corinthians 3:16–17 and 6:19; 2 Corinthians 3:3 and 6:16; Ephesians 2:21–22 and 1 Peter 2:5.

[7] Matthew 4:17. Jesus calls us to proclaim this same message today, declaring to the world that the true King of Israel has come. See Matthew 10:7 and Acts 1:3; 8:12; 14:22; 19:8; 20:2; 28:23 and 28:31.

STRAIGHT TO THE HEART SERIES

TITLES AVAILABLE: OLD TESTAMENT

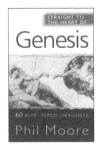

ISBN 978 0 85721 001 2

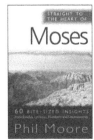

ISBN 978 0 85721 056 2

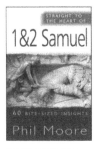

ISBN 978 0 85721 252 8

ISBN 978 0 85721 428 7

ISBN 978 0 85721 426 3

ISBN 978 0 85721 754 7

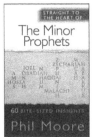

ISBN 978 0 85721 837 7

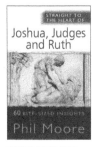

ISBN 978 0 85721 894 0

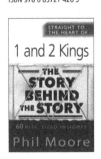

ISBN 978 0 85721 940 4

STRAIGHT TO THE HEART SERIES

TITLES AVAILABLE: NEW TESTAMENT

ISBN 978 1 85424 988 3

ISBN 978 0 85721 642 7

ISBN 978 0 85721 799 8

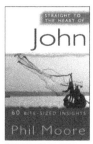

ISBN 978 0 85721 253 5

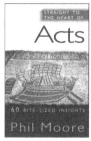

ISBN 978 1 85424 989 0

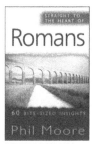

ISBN 978 0 85721 057 9

ISBN 978 0 85721 002 9

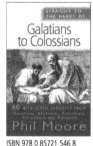

ISBN 978 0 85721 546 8

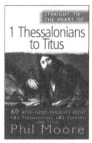

ISBN 978 0 85721 548 2

ISBN 978 0 85721 668 7

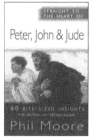

ISBN 978 0 85721 756 1

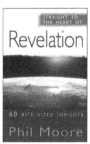

ISBN 978 1 85424 990 6

OTHER TITLES FROM PHIL MOORE:

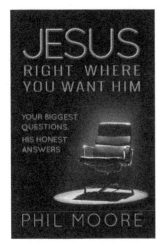

ISBN 978 0 85721 677 9

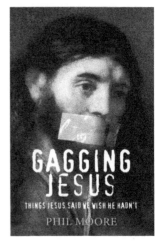

ISBN 978 0 85721 453 9

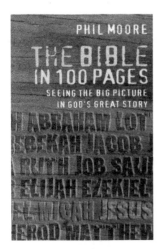

ISBN 978 0 85721 551 2

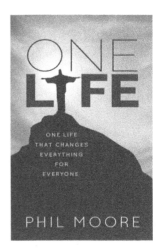

ISBN 978 0 85721 801 8